Traditional Chinese Culture

Edited by Zhang Qizhi

Foreign Languages Press

First Edition 2004
Fourth Printing 2008

Edited by Zhang Qizhi
Written by Zhang Qizhi Gong Jie Liu Baocai
   Meng Zhaoyan Wang Zhong Shen Cheng
   He Qinggu Cheng Guoqing Zhao Congcang
   Huang Shuguang Fang Guanghua Liu Yujie
   Liu Wan
Translated by Li Xingjian

Home Page:
  http://www.flp.com.cn
E-mail Addresses:
  Info@flp.com.cn
  sales@flp.com.cn

ISBN 978-7-119-02033-4
©Foreign Languages Press, Beijing, China, 2004
Published by Foreign Languages Press
24 Baiwanzhuang Road, Beijing 100037, China
Distributed by China International Book Trading Corporation
35 Chegongzhuang Xilu, Beijing 100044, China

Printed in the People's Republic of China

Contents

Introduction

As a product of human thought, the word "culture" encompasses a great deal. A system of thought and theory is known as ideological culture, which is the theoretical base underlying various modes of culture. In ancient China, ideological culture usually involved Confucianism (advocating the rule of rites, with the accent on the traditional feudal order of importance and seniority in human relationships); Taoism (upholding nature, tranquillity, non-action, or letting things take their own course, and opposing struggle); Legalism (encouraging the rule of law and opposing the rule of rites); and Buddhism. In addition, traditional Chinese cultures also include historical and cultural relics, such as pottery and porcelain, bronze, jade, silver, gold, and lacquer, bronze mirrors, and antique coins and currency; and art forms such as calligraphy and painting. Also included are ancient architecture, mausoleums, and ancient costumes and fittings. Apart from these, traditional culture embraces social systems as well as ancient books and publications on literature, history, medicines and life-nourishing approaches, agronomy, and astronomical chronicles. The Chinese nation, with its industriousness and wisdom, has created a long and everlasting history and a rich and colorful civilization.

Is there any generality underlying the various forms of traditional Chinese culture? Or what is their common and fundamental ethos? In our opinion, it may involve such aspects as follows:

The ethos of humanism. Ancient Chinese humanism came into being side by side with the evolution of Chinese history. In the

1

periods of emperors Yandi and Huangdi, dating back about 5,000 years, the idea of humanity was embryonic. Later, it developed and finally established the form of a system with a complete theory through the Xia (about the 21st to the early 17th century BC), Shang (about the early 17th to 11th century BC), and Zhou (about 11th century to 256 BC) dynasties until the end of the Spring and Autumn Period (770-476 BC). This accomplishment must be credited to Confucius (551-479 BC), a great thinker and educator of the late Spring and Autumn Period and founder of Confucianism. He inherited the ethos of humanism passed down from the Shang and Zhou dynasties and further developed it with his creative theory. After his death, new developments and creations were made to enrich and improve the ethos of humanism not only in Confucianism, but also in other schools of thought and various academic disciplines.

The ethos of humanism has the following characteristics: It stresses moral self-cultivation and learning in order that one might become a man of virtue, with lofty ideals. In ancient China, ritual form and the rule of law were emphasized, striving for a harmonious coexistence between people of various social classes and status. To maintain social stability, particular attention was paid to the basic unit of society — the family, working out a variety of ethical codes and rules that family members should observe. It was believed that only by achieving harmony within the family, could stability and equilibrium in society be achieved. The ancient ethos of humanism was also expressed in the model of an ideal future society, in an attempt to build a world as one community, in which the talent of each member could be brought into full play. This kind of ethos of humanism has promoted a series of virtues for the Chinese nation: enterprise, persistence and firmness, deference to and support of elders, help for the childless elderly and the disabled, managing a household on the principles of industriousness and frugality and building the country through thrift and hard work. These virtues are precious intellectual wealth and the essence of the ancient Chinese ethos of humanism.

History is complicated. The ancient Chinese ethos of humanism was sometimes distorted in the course of development. In some aspects, it was misunderstood and abused by those with biased or extreme views. Due to over-emphasis on the family's role in society, for instance, the function and the social value of kinship among family members attained the most important position in social life. Also due to over-emphasis on the role of moral cultivation, social and legal systems were neglected. Morality was often personified as an omnipotent and omniscient "sage" or "god." As a result, the contributions made by the whole of society in social progress and development were neglected and diminished.

In this book, the introduction to traditional Chinese culture focuses primarily on the fine aspects of the culture that have been passed down. Some aspects appear incongruous with modern life and in these cases analysis and practical explanations are given. The ethos of humanism, demonstrated by ideological culture, also permeated various aspects of traditional Chinese culture. Descriptions of this will be given in the following chapters of this book.

The ethos of naturalism. In ancient China, different aspects of the relationship between nature and man were studied and explored by thinkers of various schools. Its appearance was by no means accidental, because in ancient China, the creation of a material culture, a system culture, as well as an ideological culture was based on the material foundation of agriculture. The scientific astronomical chronicle was invented very early in China as a result of agricultural demands. Theories on the relationship between nature and man sprang from the same source. The strongest demonstration of this was Taoism.

The Taoist classic *The Book of Lao Zi* regards "that which with no name" as the origin of heaven and earth, and "that which with a name" as the noumenon of everything in the world. ("Name" is merely a concept. Lao Zi, the founder of Taoism, believed that before the formation of heaven and earth there was only the "nameless" and that the "named" was only produced by man after heaven and earth and everything in the world had come into being.) They are used as nouns with a broad and extended range of meanings. All the scientific creations and inventions made by successive generations, when categorized on the philosophical plane, could not transcend the limit of extension of the meanings of "being" and "non-being." Lao Zi also proposed to recognize nature in a practical way, without any modification of human subjective imagination, because heaven, earth and the universe all came from the "Tao" or the "Way" (that is, the origin or noumenon of the universe and everything in the world) and Tao is naturalistic. This is the starting point of the ethos of naturalism in traditional Chinese culture.

The Book of Zhuang Zi, another Taoist classic, emphasizes that nature should be revered, loved and protected. This includes protection of the natural ecological balance. It by no means, however, requires people to do nothing in face of nature, but to recognize it by way of discovering and understanding its structure and properties. So long as nature is not harmed, people can use it to support their existence. The story of how to dismember an ox carcass as skillfully as a butcher described in *The Book of Zhuang Zi* is a typical demonstration of the doctrine.

This ethos of naturalism was the motive force of the development of ancient China's science and technology, and great achievements were made in astronomical chronicles, agriculture, and traditional Chinese medical science. The relationship between man and nature was not limited to the means of existence. It extended to art works with a sense of aesthetics inspired by natural phenomenon, enriching people's lives. This can be seen especially in calligraphy, painting, literature, cuisine, gardening and architecture. The relationship between man and nature can be harmonious or disharmonious. Natural calamities inflicted sufferings on humanity and our ancestors were often horror-stricken by nature's roar. They could not scientifically explain the disasters caused by natural phenomena and supposed that man could not fight against the enormous power of nature ("heaven") and must be reconciled to it. Nature was personified and attributed with consciousness as a God of nature to be worshipped. This contradicts the rational spirit of "nature." Two schools of doctrines arose, therefore, concerning the "unity of the universe and man." One dealt with the coordinated relationship between man and nature, concerning man's recognition, protection and usage of nature, while the other deified nature and resigned itself to psychological and spiritual submission. The two schools of thought were separate but related.

The ethos of the "odd and even principle." The ancients observed that a hill has a sunny side and shaded side. They also observed the directions of the blowing wind and began to forecast changes in the weather. From these observations, they induced the two principles or categories of Yin and Yang which became an integral part of philosophy and other cultural disciplines. They also induced the concept of odd and even numbers from calculations while applying the idea of Yin and Yang to explain natural phenomena and human affairs. While exploring the mysteries of nature or seeking answers to various questions, the properties and changes of things were often observed through the figure "five," as in the "five elements" (metal, wood, water, fire and earth), "five sounds" (the notes of the ancient pentatonic scale), "five colors" (blue, red, yellow, white and black, as known as the cardinal five colors), and "five flavors" (sweet, sour, bitter, hot and salty). Laws of nature and changes in human life were also perceived from a standpoint which, they believed, could explain the inter-promoting relations between a contradictory pair of opposites. In ancient China, natural sciences such as Chinese medical science, were permeated with this odd and even principle. Before the Tang Dynasty (618-907), physiological and therapeutic theories were greatly affected by the "five elements" theory. After the Tang, Chinese medicine was gradually but markedly influenced by the "eight trigrams" of *The Book of Changes.*

The separation and combination of the odd and even principle were characteristic of the way of thinking in ancient China, through which many lively and colorful ideas were produced and developed. Accordingly many ideas of relativity were established such as inter-promotion and inter-restraint, restriction of destruction and support to construction, safety and danger, dynamic and static, left and right, up and down, complete and incomplete, noble and ignoble, superior and inferior, sense and sensibility, and

5

knowledge and practice.

The "doctrine of the mean" (that is, taking an impartial attitude of compromise in human affairs and relations) advocated by Confucius and Lao Zi's doctrine of "curbing destruction while supporting construction" is an example of theories on the alternation of the odd and even principle. In Confucius' view, the "mean" is a whole (or one body, and "one" is an odd number), exclusive of anything "more"(over) or "less" (under) than it. That is to say, "one" is derived from the exclusion of the "two" extremities in a situation. The doctrine of the mean is a dialectical way of thinking induced from the alternation of odd and even numbers, which is commonly used in various ancient Chinese classics. This way of thinking was successfully applied to military affairs, the national economy and people's livelihood.

The doctrine of "one is divided into two" conceived by the Confucians of the Song Dynasty (960-1279), is another example of the combination of the odd and even principle. When people observe the "one," or a unity, they should perceive the "two" in itself, or the integrated two parts of itself. And ultimately they sum up to the "one." Only then can a genuine and realistic understanding of something be attained.

The combination of odd and even permeates many other forms of Chinese culture as well as philosophy. Ancient architecture and the layout of ancient state capitals all embody the odd and even principle. The term "symmetry makes a unity" means that "odd" numbers are derived from "even" numbers.

Ancient architecture consists of a symmetry that must be incorporated to create a harmonious unity of a group of constructions.

The shaping beauty of ancient Chinese artifacts, in a sense, embodies the ethos of the odd and even principle. These articles, being molded in shapes to suggest a feeling of steadiness and dignity and taking into consideration of the relativity between the positions of the object and the viewer, are usually exquisite products of a combination of the odd and even principle.

The ethos of "communication" or "absorption and assimilation." Traditional Chinese culture is a common achievement made by the whole Chinese people of various ethnic groups, in addition to assimilating the fine achievement of foreign cultures. The fine traditions of Chinese culture, far from being self-satisfied and conservative, have been enriched through mastering and assimilating the merits of various other systems of culture. This is the ethos of "communication" or "absorption and assimilation."

As early as in the Warring States Period (475-221 BC), Chinese culture was developing without regional limitation, with exchanges of cultures between various feudal states in central China becoming more and more frequent. For example, Xun Zi, though a follower of the teachings of Confucius, extracted knowledge from various other schools of thought. He also criticized sharply aspects of all schools of thought including Confucianism itself. At the end of the period, *Lu's Spring and Autumn Annals* which had attempted to make a summary of those contradictory schools of thought, was also characteristic of this ethos, and at the time it was known as Eclectics.

Foreign cultures were also absorbed and assimilated. When Buddhism was first introduced into China, a good deal of it was explained using traditional Chinese concepts or metaphysical Taoist terms. As more translations of Buddhist scriptures became available, diverse schools of Buddhism were founded, many of which having marked Chinese characteristics and differing from the Buddhism of India. The Indian Buddhist scriptures were revised and blended with traditional Chinese cultural thought, producing a positive influence on various aspects of ancient Chinese culture.

During the Qing Dynasty (1644-1911), particularly in the late part of the period, many farsighted Chinese strove to learn from Western culture, especially Western science and technology.

By "communication," we also mean exchange and interaction between various schools of thought. By the time of the Western Han (206 BC to 24 AD), the doctrines of Confucianism and Legalism had been blended, Confucianism and Taoism supplemented each other, and some of the teachings of Buddhism were beginning to be absorbed.

The foregoing ethos is like a string underlying and going through various other aspects of the traditional culture.

We have just given a brief account of four aspects of the fundamental ethos of traditional Chinese culture, and more explicit demonstrations will be given in the following chapters of this book.

Now, about the value of traditional culture in modern times.

Traditional culture is a product of history but it also has value in modern times. Confucianism was founded 2,500 years ago and has been developed through the ages, but the original Confucian classics such as *The Analects of Confucius*, *The Book of Mencius*, and *The Book of Xun Zi* are still widely read. By "reviewing what one has learned and knowing the new," people can be enlightened in new ways about the meanings of life through reading these and Taoist classics such as *The Book of Lao Zi* and *The Book of Zhuang Zi*. Some of the ancient works are true masterpieces, handed down from generation to generation, never failing to appeal to their readers. Practically speaking, so long as mankind continues to exist, the flames of wisdom emanating from such works can never be extinguished, always lighting up the past, present and future of mankind.

The history of mankind has developed from the deep past to the present day and will continue to develop into the future. Its development is a whole and continuous process, as is the development of the ideological and cultural history.

For example, the theories of *The Yellow Emperor's Classic of Internal Medicine* (the first medical classic in China) are still valuable today, though they were formulated about 2,000 years ago. In a sense, some of its theories will always be valuable. Although people today live in much better conditions than did their ancestors 2,000 years ago, and have different ideas and concepts, human physiological structure remains the same.

Another example can be seen in the ideas of *The Book of Lao Zi* relating to a small state with a sparse population. These were products of past history under specific conditions and as history has developed, they have gradually lost their relevance. But the book's descriptions about the evolution of nature, the relations between nature and man and many other important issues, are very close to some aspects of the laws of nature. These theories and doctrines are still valuable today.

The value of these classics can be understood in two different senses: superficial and deep. The superficial value is their popularity, being understood and used by many ordinary people. For instance, the maxims of Confucius and Lao Zi are regarded as good advice and are frequently referred to. It is common to quote Confucius, saying "When a friend coming from afar, isn't that after all a pleasure?" and Lao Zi, saying "A journey of a thousand miles begins with the first step." But their value is by no means limited to this superficial sense. From an ideological and cultural viewpoint, past theories and doctrines have a deeper value for modern times. To discover this value requires a thorough and scientific study of them, reaching deep into their essence. In the case of *The Book of Lao Zi*, we must ask: What influence have his doctrines exerted on science in ancient Chinese and the world? What will modern scientists learn when they explore the mystery of nature? How should his views and observations about the structure of the universe be evaluated? These issues cannot be solved simply by quoting a few teachings and sayings from his book. They require arduous and painstaking thought and study on this important scientific subject. This is a subject which has been profitably studied by scholars around the world.

In the process of exploring such traditional values, one should not merely discuss ideology. Ancient artifacts, calligraphy, painting, costume, cuisine, and architecture should not be neglected. They all embody a certain historical and aesthetic value, which is almost eternal. For instance, the beauty of the calligraphy of Wang Xizhi (321-379), extremely popular in the Tang Dynasty, is still admired and enjoyed. There are countless examples such as this. Such tangible products of traditional Chinese culture embody much more value than that of the products of ideology. From these tangible products, people can clearly perceive a certain respect of the truth of history.

To study the value of traditional Chinese culture for the present requires researchers to have a historical point of view. But it does not mean that today's scientific creations are merely copies of past thought and culture. Carrying on the fine aspects of traditional culture without making innovations will only end up in a dead end.

As we advance to explore the past along a pathway, the creations of our ancestors will light up the torch of wisdom for us.

Chapter 1

The Dawn of Chinese Culture

Section 1 The Achievements of the Chinese Ancestors

The history of the later stage of primitive Chinese society was replete with legends passed down orally over the course of about three thousand years until they were set down in written form during the Western Zhou Dynasty (c.11th century-771 BC). The period related in these legends is known as the legendary age of ancient history, or the late stage of clan society. In archeology, it corresponds to the late Neolithic Age. At that time, personal belongings or effects and division of the rich and the poor had already appeared and drastic changes in the social system and social ideology had taken place.

Yandi and Huangdi (Yellow Emperor) were the first cultural forefathers of the Chinese nation during the legendary age. Both were leaders of tribes in China's western Loess Plateau. The era of Huangdi dates back 5,000 years and that of Yandi another 500 years earlier.

Yandi is most significantly known for the development of primitive farming. He is also known as Shen Nong.

Primitive farming appeared during the early Neolithic Age. However, agriculture occupied not the dominant position in economic life at that time, and hunting and fishing remained the primary sources of food. As time went by, the population grew, but the source of wild animals and birds for food progressively dwindled. Hunting and fishing were no longer sufficient, and more food had to be produced for people to survive.

Yandi invented the earliest farming tool called *si*, similar in shape to a spade, to till the land instead of using one's hands, thus improving efficiency of production. He also cultivated millet, the earliest agricultural grain, which is drought-resistant, provides a high yield and can be stored for long periods. He is also credited with the invention of pottery, which is closely related to agricultural production. He created the "day market," in which regular gatherings took place for the exchange of products. These inventions and creations improved people's lives and he was loved and supported by the people.

Another of Yandi's achievements was in the development of medicine. Yandi sought out herbal medicines to treat diseases and to promote longevity, tasting and trying hundreds of herbal roots and materials. He was said to have been "afflicted by seventy kinds of poisonous plants in a day" and "narrowly escaped death a hundred times in a day" while tasting and trying so many herbs. Despite this, he never wavered in his experiments. He discovered a multitude of herbal medicines for the curing of diseases and the alleviation of suffering. To honor the founder of Chinese medicine, the posterity call his medicinal classic *Shen Nong's Materia Medica*.

Yandi also invented the five-stringed *qin* and composed music for dances. At the end of a year he led people to sing and dance, giving thanks to heaven and earth for their benevolence and wishing for a good harvest in the coming year.

There were so many inventions made by Huangdi's tribe, so many that they could be found almost in every aspect of social life. The most important of these inventions were written characters, clothes and headwear as well as various social systems.

According to legend, the inventor of Chinese characters was either Chang Jie or Ju Song. Both were subjects of Huangdi who acted as his historians. It is said that headwear was invented by Huangdi himself and clothes by his subject Hu Cao. The invention of clothes and headwear was not only to protect their wearers from cold, but also had a bearing on civilized cultivation and the institution of a personal effects system. Huangdi also established rules on official positions and administration, marking the beginning of China's administrative system. These inventions of the tribe of Huangdi, helping develop material civilization into a moral and systematic civilization, greatly promoted the development of society at that time.

These two tribes in the Loess Plateau gradually moved eastwards, entering central China (around the middle and lower reaches of the Yellow River). Here, they encountered the tribe of Jiu Li, provoking an armed conflict between them. The migrants of the two tribes united in military alliance and defeated the tribe of Jiu Li, killing their leader. Later, the two groups of migrants fought against each other, resulting in the defeat of the tribe of Yandi. This group now broke up and left central China, moving to other areas. Having won the conflict, the tribe of Huangdi now dominated the area. During the fight between the new migrants and the tribe of Jiu Li, the tribes in the east of China supported the migrants. These struggles, which occurred frequently in the age of legends, resulted in the blending of competing tribes, which developed to become the principal part of the Chinese nation.

The migration and movement of the forefathers of various tribes, a very long process, led to frequent contacts between different clans and tribes and to the development of cultures.

As the tribes of Yandi and Huangdi migrated east, they left a number of cultural relics with unique characteristics, which indicate the cultural exchanges that took place between the migrants and the local tribes on their route. Meanwhile, as these migrants were moving eastwards, tribes living in the lower reaches of the Yellow River were also moving westwards. The western migrants brought advanced farming skills to the eastern areas, while some of the ways and customs of the lower reaches were spread to the middle reaches of the river in the west.

Both winners and losers in battle had to continue to till the land and live on in China, creating together the ancient Chinese civilization. Chinese history has been created by all the peoples of the Chinese nation, and the tribes of Yandi and Huangdi are the first cultural ancestors of the whole nation.

The 5000-year-long Chinese culture originated from the age of Yandi and Huangdi. It is no exaggeration to say that Chinese culture has a remote source and a long stream of development.

Traditional Chinese culture stresses the unity and harmony of nature and man. Since ancient times, this has been one of the implications of the concept of the "unity of universe and man." This concept differs from the religious idea "unity of universe and man," in that it does not deify the forces of nature as gods for people to worship. Instead, it urges people to positively recognize, make use of and protect nature. This idea was budding even in the age of Yandi and Huangdi. The farming skills invented by Yandi were a comprehensive product of this cognition, and included rudimentary knowledge of plants, soil, climate and astronomy. All this helped the ancestors escape from the state of barbarism and ignorance.

The humanism of Chinese culture also originated from the age of Yandi and Huangdi. In early literature, what we read is a history of human beings. Yandi and Huangdi themselves appeared in history as humans who had their own parents and children. They were not gods. They owed their achievements and success simply to their enterprising spirit.

Section 2 Farm Produce of the South and North

Long before farming and animal husbandry came into being, human beings had lived and thrived for a million years. During that long period, people supported themselves on fruits, herbal roots, hunting and fishing. With the application of farming and animal husbandry, people began to cultivate natural food through their own labor, and started to lead a productive life.

Compared to that of elsewhere in the world, the history of China's productive economy in some respects is identical to that in other parts of the world, while in others it bears its own characteristics. China's productive economy appeared as early as the Neolithic Age, identical to other parts of the world. The reaches of the Yellow River and the Yangtze were the birthplace of China's primitive agricultural production. In the reaches of the Yellow River, many cultural relics of the early Neolithic Age have been found, on the site of which many farm tools were also excavated. These testify that primitive farming had appeared in the reaches 7,000 years ago. On the lower reaches of the Yangtze River, farm tools and various grains have also been excavated, showing that primitive agricultural production had also reached a certain level 7,000 years ago in the area. Another similarity to other parts of the world was the fact that the first animal husbandry began in China by domesticating wild animals which would otherwise be hunted, and the first agricultural production began by fostering wild plants.

Farm production and animal husbandry, however, had different functions in the history of different societies. Some first developed animal husbandry, with crop production then being developed to provide feed to the animals. Others first invented farming skills while animal husbandry followed as a sideline production, always attached to the former. Along the Yellow River and the Yangtze, farm production was dominant in economic life and animal husbandry occupied a less important position. Crop production constituted the principal part of China's productive economy during the Neolithic Age, having a significant influence on China's social and cultural development.

The development of primitive agricultural production occured in different stages. Initially, slash-and-burn cultivation was necessary to claim land for growing crops. At first, it was possible to reap good harvests, but after several years of cultivation, the soil would become arid, resulting in declining yields. This forced people to develop new land for cultivation. Later, it was discovered that after several years, the abandoned land could be used to plant crops again with harvests that were as good as before. From this they came to understand the land they had claimed could be used alternately for cultivation. As a result, primitive farm production made much headway during the time of Yandi and Huangdi.

Such great development in agricultural production could be attributed to natural conditions. Soil, sources of water, and fish are natural resources which can be used as a means of subsistence by mankind, while waterfalls, navigated waterways, forests and mineral reserves are a natural wealth which mankind can use as means of labor. During the primary stage of social development of mankind, people could make little or no use of such natural wealth because of the low level of the productive forces. At that time, wherever resources which could be used as a means of subsistence were abundant, that place would be readily and quickly developed. Situated on the East Asian continent, China boasts a vast and rich land and abundant sources of water, which provide adequate and favorable natural conditions for its farm production. As a result, China was one of the world's most ancient birthplaces of agricultural production.

Prehistoric farming culture in China had its own features which differed from that in prehistoric Western Asia, Northern Africa and India. Since it originated from two centers around the Yellow River and the middle and lower reaches of the Yangtze River, this culture could be further differentiated by their respective geographical, rich and colourful features, to form two main systems of farm culture. This has been demonstrated clearly in the variety of grains, the strains of domesticated animals, farming tools, and the manner of settlement.

Millet and rice were the main varieties of cereal crops of this farming culture. At that time, China had no wheat, sorghum or maize, which were introduced into China at a later time.

The northern area centered around the reaches of the Yellow River mainly produced millet, or *Setaria italica*, hence the farming of the area may be called farming of millet crops. As it has become the principal variety of crops in the north, in some areas, millet is also sometimes simply called grain or cereal, which was originally cultivated and developed from a kind of wild plant, suitable to grow in arid yellow soil. Millet has been discovered at 27 prehistoric sites. The earliest of these may date back more than

7,000 years, and most may date back 4,000 to 6,000 years. Nineteen of these 27 sites are located in the Yellow River valley.

Cultivation of millet in Africa and Europe began around 4,000 years ago. Millet discovered in excavations in other Asian countries such as India, Japan and Korea, shows that it was first grown by local people at a time later than that of other places.

The southern area, centered on the middle and lower reaches of the Yangtze River, mainly produced rice, or *Oryza sativa*. As rice is the primary variety of grown crops in the area, it is usually called cereal or grain in some places of the area. Rice was cultivated and developed from a kind of wild rice plant, suitable for growing in the south where the climate is warm and humid and has ample sources of water. Rice produced in the prehistoric stage has been discovered so far from 45 unearthed sites. Analysis suggests that the earliest site from which relics of rice were found may be as far back as 7,000 years, and most of these sites may date back 4,000 to 6,000 years. Of the 45 excavated sites, 27 are distributed in the middle and lower reaches of the Yangtze River. All these discoveries show that, in China, the growing of rice originated from the Yangtze River valley, and the primitive tribes in southeastern China had been the inventors and disseminators of rice-growing. The middle and lower reaches of the Yangtze River were the earliest region of growing rice in the world. In the past, some scholars abroad believed that rice growing had originated in India, and been introduced into China from there. In fact, rice growing in India appeared much later than in China. The earliest discovery of rice in India dates back about 3,700 years ago. The earliest Sanskrit record of rice was around 3,000 years ago, or several thousand years later than in China.

Unearthed prehistoric farm tools in China also showed the thriving of its primitive agricultural production about 5,000 years ago.

During that time, the main farm tools included cultivating tools like the ancient plough, spade, and hoe, harvesting tools such as ancient cutter and sickle, and processing tools as mill stones and clubs. The tools first appeared early in the Neolithic period about 7,000 years ago. They were modified and improved over time, and a number of new farm tools that had never been seen before appeared in the Yellow River valley and the middle and lower reaches of the Yangtze River about 5,000 years ago. Farm tools at that time were made of various materials including stone, clamshells, pottery and wood. Most, however, were made of stone. Tools for processing grains, like the pestle and mortar, were mostly made of wood. Wooden tools were liable to decay and so have seldom been found.

Domestic animal breeding, a sideline of prehistoric agricultural production, had made much headway by the end of the Neolithic Age. Pigs, dogs, chickens, cows and sheep were widely raised by households at the time. Pigs, dogs and chickens had been domesticated as early as the early stage of the Neolithic Age. Pigs and dogs became the primary stock at that time, with pigs making up the majority of animals being raised. Remains of pigs have been found at a great many sites, showing a booming development of pig rearing at the time, and indicating that animal husbandry had become subordinate to crop production, which had developed to such a considerable high level that could afford sufficient feed for raised animals.

Settlements were closely related with farming. Relative stability of settlement was a precondition for farm production and, in turn, the development of farm production promoted the formation of large group settlement. Group settlement, therefore, serves as an important witness to the development of farm production. Rich sources of water for subsistence, patches of land suitable for tilling, and easy access to communications were indispensable to the settlement of tribal groups.

All the sites of the relics of Neolithic group settlement found so far were by rivers or around lakes and natural springs, where there was yellow soil and moist fertile land for growing crops. Many relics have been found around modern cities or villages. This demonstrates that the location of a group settlement at that time was purposely selected by inhabitants to meet their needs for living, production and communications.

There were two patterns of settlement: one was set up on a terrace at the water's edge, another was on a high place above its surroundings. And the scale of group settlement had developed through a small — large — small process. Before the Yangshao Culture period (a Neolithic culture in the middle and lower reaches of the Yellow River, dating back 5,000 to 7,000 years), settled communities were small, generally covering 10,000 to 20,000 square meters. During the Yangshao Culture period, large group settlement communities appeared. The largest of these covered several million square meters, though they were generally between 10,000 and 60,000 square meters. During the period of Longshan Culture (a late Neolithic culture in the middle and lower reaches of the Yellow River, dating back 4,000 to 4,900 years), the number of small group settlement communities covering areas less than 10,000 square meters increased. The number of inhabitants varied according to the size of communities. Before the Yangshao Culture period, a settlement community with a population of 80 to 200 was very common. During the Yangshao Culture period, the size of population was between 80 and 600 inhabitants. The largest community has been estimated to have had a possible population of 60,000. During the Longshan Culture period, about one-third of the communities had a population of less than 100, the rest having between 80 and 500. This shows an increase in migration during the late Neolithic Age.

Most communities were divided into a dwelling area, a pottery kiln area and a graveyard. In the dwelling areas, there were houses and kiln pits. The layout of many small houses was usually centered round a large house or a square. Around community borders, ditches and high walls were usually built up for defense.

Agriculture was the economic base of ancient civilization. All such civilizations in the world were based on agriculture, whether in the civilized regions of western, central and eastern Asia as well or in the ancient civilized region of Mexico. But the ancient farming skills in China, which have developed without a break over several thousands of years, are unique in the world. Agriculture was important in China at a very early stage. It is especially worth noting that the Western Zhou and Qin dynasties (221-206 B.C.) that established the mode of traditional Chinese culture for the next two or three thousand years inherited and developed the farming skills of the times of Yandi and Huangdi. During the Western Zhou, farm tools remained the same as they had been before, being made of stone, wood, bone or clam, and occasionally of bronze. Apart from the principal tools such as the *lei* (fork) and *si* (spade), many other varieties appeared including the *bo*, in the shape of a modern hoe, and *zhi*, like a sickle. In addition to millet, rice and broomcorn millet, many other crops were also grown, including wheat, beans and sorghum. A rotation system was introduced in which a field would be abandoned after having been cultivated for three years. Techniques of artificial irrigation, weeding and growing seedlings were also developed. During the Warring States Period (475-221 BC), farming developed rapidly in the State of Qin. At this time, like other states in central China, Qin began to use farm tools made of iron and build irrigation works, bringing about an unprecedented advance in agricultural production. It was based on this that Western Zhou civilization, which advocated harmony between the various strata in society, and Qin civilization, which stressed national unification, appeared. These two types of civilization became two major pillars of traditional Chinese culture. The agricultural economy underlying the cultures of the Zhou and Qin dynasties may date from at least the times of Yandi and Huangdi, justifying the claim that the dawn of civilization in China may date back to the time of these two legendary rulers.

Section 3 A World of Pottery and Jade

The production of pottery and jade works during the prehistoric stage occurred and developed side by side with prehistoric farming. At the same time as primitive farming came about during the early Neolithic Age, early pottery and objects made of jade also appeared. In the late Neolithic Age when primitive farming was flourishing, the production of pottery and jade also had entered its prime stage of development. To meet the needs of the farming economy and with the conditions provided by the economy, pottery and jade production developed and great artistic achievements were made, becoming the pioneer of model art works in China.

Historically, pottery ware and jade articles differ from each other in that pottery was primarily made for use in daily life while jade articles were mostly used in ritual ceremonies. As to the regional distribution of these products, most painted pottery ware was produced along the upper and middle reaches of the Yellow River, and jade articles mostly produced in northeast China and the lower reaches of the Yangtze River, though both of them have been found among unearthed relics of the late Neolithic Age in various cultural regions. This difference is simply due to different resources. In the middle and upper reaches of the Yellow River, there is an enormous supply of yellow soil for producing pottery ware while deposits of jade are generally to be found in East China and the southeastern coastal areas. During the Neolithic Age, the "jade" was in fact any kind of stone that looked more beautiful than others. The phrase "millet in the north and rice in the south" is sometimes used when talking of the regional distribution of prehistoric farming. In a sense, we can also use the term "pottery in the west and jade in the east" for this period.

Here, we will not discuss the materials and skills used in the making of pottery and jade products. Rather, we wish to use them as a carrier of cultural information, through which we can observe the social life, primitive religion and primitive aesthetics during the late Neolithic Age and explain how they played their part in the ancient history of Chinese culture.

The shape of different kinds of pottery was mainly chosen for practical reasons. For instance, one kind of bottle with a sharp bottom was made in the shape of the kernel of a date. The whole thing was slim and long with both ends tapering off. This was for ease of taking water from a shallow stream. A type of flask with a long neck and a small mouth was made with a potbelly in the midsection. This configuration was designed for containing water and to enable it to be carried easily. Ancient stemmed cups were designed like goblets of the present day for holding. Such shapes were dictated by practical needs. Many of other designs were imitations of animals or plants, reflecting the life of that time. For example, the shape of one kind of bottle was copied from that of a bottle gourd, while another was copied from the shape of a section of knotted bamboo. A kind of earthenware, called *gui*, was designed in the shape of a dog ready to leap on something. Several other pieces of animal-shaped articles, produced with the head raised, mouth open and ears erect, standing firmly on its four feet, were vivid and lively models of dogs. This reflected the economic life of that time. Moreover, a historical background of pottery ware can also be seen from their shapes. Before the invention of pottery, fruit shells, bamboo-splint woven articles, cane and rope-woven products had been used as articles for daily life, all of which had a round bottom. Pottery ware imitated this, also having a round bottom, sometimes having three legs attached. Some were specially decorated with rope or bamboo woven patterns, mirroring the historical relationship between the shaping of pottery and articles produced earlier.

Compared with the shaping, the content of social life, reflected in the decorations of painted pottery ware, was richer and more varied. Fish, birds, deer and frogs were important decorations on some pottery ware. Other earthenware was decorated with vivid depictions of frogs, salamanders and house lizards. Other decorations included seeds, sunflowers, leaves, trees and strings of beans. All these decorations present lively and varied scenes of nature. Some had highly developed pattern designs, such as beautiful and colorful hook-type leaves, passionate whirlpools, thunder, lotus, shells and dual hook-like curves; no one knows their original patterns, and so no consensus has been reached about their significance. Some believe that they were derived from realistic imitations of biological patterns, but others disagree. However, they were artistic products derived and extracted from natural phenomena. Imitating natural images at first, then infusing them with human feelings, people produced these wonderful works of art with skillful craftsmanship excelling over nature.

It is most interesting to find figurines designed on earthenware. Three examples will be given as follows: One is a painted pottery basin, an unearthed relic in Qinghai Province, on the inside layer of which, three groups of dancers were drawn. In each group, five young girls wearing short plaits dance hand in hand, presenting a joyful atmosphere. With its outstanding theme, lively picture, and simple and bold sketch, this work is not only one of the most valuable piece of painted pottery ware, but also a masterpiece of the earliest pictures of figures in China. Another one is a painted pot, an excavation also discovered in Qinghai. The shaping of its mouth is the head of a man, with an air of gravity and solemnity. Decorated with a lotus and shell pattern on the neck, and with a potbelly and two ears in the lower part and some semi-circular patterns, it looks like a tough warrior when looked at from the front, with a very strong artistic effect. The last one is a painted pottery bottle, unearthed in Gansu Province. It was shaped as a pretty maiden's head on the section from its mouth to the neck, with trimmed and neat short hair and a quiet and elegant look. Its slender body is painted with black-colored and curve-lined triangles in a chain in three rounds. As a whole, it looks like a maiden in a beautiful dress. In the last two works, painting is combined with sculpture, giving a full third dimension.

As a man-made product, pottery ware or jade articles must necessarily reflect the subjective ideology of human beings while reflecting the objective world. Primitive religion was the principal ideological form during the Neolithic Age. That was sure to be reflected in the pottery ware and jade articles.

The rich and colorful decorations, however, were not used carelessly to describe various natural phenomena. In a certain area, some decorations would be used repeatedly on a number of painted pottery ware. And they would be developed into many kinds of the same pattern. In such patterns, taking the image of an animal for instance, if it had been used in the whole course of development of a certain culture, the image, in most cases, could be regarded in relation to totemistic art. Earthenware of the Yangshao

Culture of the middle reaches of the Yellow River was decorated with fish and birds. Images of fish were mostly used in the area west of Mount Huashan while birds were used as the chief design in the area east of the mountain. Around the periphery of the mountain, a combination of images of fish and birds were used. This suggests that fish were the totem of the Yangshao Culture clan society west of the mountain, while birds were the totem of the clan society to the east. Of course, the use of birds as a totem was not limited to the middle reaches of the Yellow River. But so far, we could have only dealt with the problem in this limitation in terms of the designs of Yangshao Culture.

The appearance of the totemistic system during the prehistoric stage can be confirmed by a large quantity of literature. It was a representation of primitive religion, functioning as a symbol to unite all the members of a clan society and was worshipped by the whole society. Thus, it is not surprising that it appeared on pottery of that time.

A painted earthen urn was unearthed in Henan Province which was decorated with a large painting of a stork and a fish together with a stone axe. This rare, large painting of animals includes a white stork with a pair of wide-opened eyes, a big stiffened fish in its mouth, together with a well-decorated stone axe, full of mysterious fascination. Judged on the basis of time, region, and cultural background, the stork and fish were clearly the totems of two different clan communities. The stone axe symbolized their patriarchal ancestors. This painting was doubtlessly made in memory of the feats of their forefathers, reflecting their worship of ancestors.

According to ancient literature, the use of totems in relation to the ancestors of a clan was very common. For example, fish were used in relation to the ancestors of a clan named Zhou. It was recorded that Houji (a god of agriculture, the founder of the Zhou clan in ancient China, who was skilled in the cultivation of a variety of grain crops) was cared for by a bird after he was born. When he died, he became half man and half fish. The mother of Daye, the ancestor of a clan called Qin, gave birth to him after swallowing the egg of a black bird. In all these records, birds and fish were symbols of divine ancestors. It seems certain that the stork and fish painted on the urn found in Henan were used to represent ancestor worship.

Since jade products were primarily used as ritual vessels, they are clear reflections of the primitive religious ideology of their time.

During the Neolithic Age, the most common jade articles used for ceremonial purposes were the Bi, Cong, and Huang. The Bi is a round, flat piece of jade with a small hole in the center. When the hole is larger, it is given a different name and is called Huan, and when the hole is larger still, it is called Yuan. The Bi were variously made as single pieces or in pairs or in chains of three pieces. Cong were long hollow pieces of jade with rectangular sides, like a hollow cylinder sheathed by rectangular columns. They are classified into two categories. The single-section Cong is made with a height shorter than its width in measurement. So it may be used as a bracelet. The multi-section Cong is made with a height taller than its width to become a rectangular pier. Huang is a semi-annular jade pendant, called "a half-piece of Bi."

As to their use, it is said "the blue Bi is used in ritual for paying homage to Heaven," "the yellow Cong is used in ritual for paying homage to Earth," and "the black Huang is used in ritual for paying homage to the North." Each must have played a particular function in religious ceremonies. That a great deal of them were produced is the most telling witness to the popularity of religion at that time.

Jade articles were produced without paintings. But decorations were carved on them to match their shapes harmoniously. Jade decorations were more standardized than pottery paintings, and their style was more mysterious. Bi found from the prehistoric period are plain and without any decoration, but Cong and Huang are carved with animal faces. A Cong excavated among relics of Liangzhu Culture (a culture of the Neolithic Age in China, dating back to about 2,200 to 3,300 BC. In 1936, it was first discovered in Liangzhu Town of Yuhang in Zhejiang Province) on the lower reaches of the Yangtze River is the best example. One found among relics in Yuhang may be called "the king of Cong." It has a bow-like crown on top, and under the crown there is a reversed ladder-type man's face with a pair of double-circular eyes, a flat nose, a wide mouth and a row of neatly engraved teeth. Around the brim of the crown are many swirling cloud patterns and at its top are spread feathers. The man's upper arms stretch out straight, while the forearms turn inward. A pair of animal's eyes is set in the center of his chest. The ridges of the animal's eyebrows and its nose were made in low relief together with straight and whirling lines. From its wide-open bloody mouth protrude four ferocious teeth. The man's feet are crossed under the animal's face. At first glance, the design appears to be a forbidding animal's face with an unlively man's face on its forehead. But on closer inspection, one can find that the ears of the animal may be taken as the arms of the man and his feet as the beard of the animal. As a whole, it may be taken as either a figure of man or a pattern of an animal's head. This man-animal combination may also be seen as a god of war with a shield in hand or a jade craftsman, holding a piece of jade, providing a design of man-god combination. Similar, but less elaborate, designs may also be found on other pieces of jade from the relics of Liangzhu Culture.

Many valuable works of art have been discovered from the earthenware and jade articles produced in the ages of Yandi and Huangdi. These works of art had the budding characteristics of China's modeling art, representing the trend of development of Chinese art traditions. For instance, the tradition of freehand brushwork in Chinese modeling art began to appear in pottery and jade art works. The model of many pottery and jade articles was not simply a copy of natural phenomena, since it also stressed the relationships between man and other things or between one thing and another. Through modeling, the expressed theme was not things themselves, but man's ideas about nature, his imagination, feelings and ideals.

While the decorations of Cong and Bi embodied man's ideology, the images of birds, animals, fish and grass painted on earthenware also reflected man's ideas. The most famous example is the Banpo human-mask motif and fish design in which two lively fishes were painted on both sides of a man's mouth. Such an image is not seen in daily life, but it was completely in conformity with the people's ideas at that time. In the final analysis, it fully accorded with the reality of the social life at that time. After 5,000 years, people still marvel at such a design that is comprehensible even today. Since motif is the first thing in the design, man's ideas and emotions are injected into the images of all kinds of things of the world, such as birds, fish, animals and plants, as well as sailing clouds and running water. The communication between man's ideas and feelings and natural phenomena and their evolution presented many designs full of wit and fantasy.

Pottery articles produced around the Yellow River and the Yangtze were designed with straight and level lines, suggesting a feeling of neatness and gravity and still-life. China's painted earthenwares are mostly designed with curves, arcs, and round points, giving a feeling of movement. The uninterrupted lines of whirl patterns, painted on the upper part of a water pot unearthed in the upper reaches of the Yellow River, for instance, can be viewed as pelting waves from the front, but overlooked as surging waves. The bird-design on a pot unearthed in the middle reaches of the Yellow River features a series of variations. The pattern of the bird's three feet and two raised wings in the front develop into round points and curved triangles. The side pattern of the open-mouthed and tail-raised bird turns into a round point and three curved lines. It gives a very strong feeling of the smooth and graceful flight of a bird. The continuation and repetition of the patterns give a full presentation of the rhymes and styles of movement as if a duet is being performed. As to such abstract designs as clouds, thunder and double hooks, the implications and styles of movement still remain, though the origin of the patterns is still at issue.

The high aesthetic value of pottery and jade articles is closely related to their shapes. Although the ancient craftsmen could not explain their art on a theoretical plane, their works themselves serve as a thesis relating their understanding of the beauty of modeling art.

Using techniques of contrast, they distinguished the principal patterns in the design, and made the image of the theme more attractive and harmonious. Under the same motif, they also added some detailed variations to achieve an effect of fullness and implication. The continuation and repetition of a certain design create an echo effect and produce a profound impression. The style in the design of patterns in the overlapped part of two adjoining patterns produces a dual function of the same curve and round point. They also made the same pattern intercross in the design so as to make the whole design centered around a central point, which suggests a feeling of cohesion and pulsation. They set one pattern within another and a flower amidst others to promote a sense of tiers, producing a feeling of magnificence and depth.

China's jade art has now lasted for more than 7,000 years, an event never seen before in the world. The art of pottery has developed into the art of porcelain, becoming an ever-blossoming flower in Chinese art. The art of bronze works, appearing in a later period, inherited the traditions of the art of pottery and jade articles in terms of variety, shape and design.

Section 4 Original Carved Marks and the Invention of Chinese Characters

During the era of Huangdi, Cang Jie was the most distinguished man who devoted his utmost efforts to the invention of Chinese characters. Of course, many others made their contributions as well to the endeavor. Chinese characters were a product of a period, not invented by some individuals alone.

As a symbol record language, Chinese characters have three elements: the form, sound and meaning. Where did they come from? It has been said that they derived from the eight trigrams used for divination, and some people believe this today. However, this is groundless. There is convincing evidence that most Chinese characters originated directly from carved marks.

A carved mark with a meaning and in a relatively fixed form possessed part of the elements of writing. But it could not be pronounced and so it must be regarded as a precursor of characters, not a character itself. Many of the discovered prehistoric carved marks were left on bone and jade articles. Most were on pottery ware.

Most carved marks have been discovered on the pottery articles of Yangshao Culture (5,000-7,000 years ago) and Majiayao Culture (4,050-5,300 years ago). Of Yangshao Culture, most marks were carved on the painted black wide band around the mouth of earthen bowls with a round bottom. Fewer marks were left on the bottom or on the external side of a basin. Most marks were a vertical cut. Fewer marks were cut in two vertical lines, or in the shape of a X, a Z, a hook or a T. There were various other shapes, such as the shape of a plant. In Majiayao Culture, about 10 shapes of marks were commonly used such as +, –, X, O, +, 卐 and I. These marks were generally cut in black on the lower part of a painted earthen pot.

The carved marks on the earthenware of the Yangshao and Majiayao cultures appear in a separate and independent form, not in a linked form of written language. This makes them very hard to read or understand. Some specialists have tried to explain some of the carved marks. They think that "X" may stand for the character "Five," "^" for "Man" and "↓" for "Grass." Some others believe that most of such marks represented the symbols of a family system, a blood lineage, a clan or a branch of a family tree. There are some basic facts in favor of this presumption. Many such marks discovered in relics in a certain concentrated area may indicate the symbol of a clan. However, the majority of the marks to be taken as a symbol of a clan are hard to be explained. If scores of, even more than 100, varieties of carved marks are all taken as a symbol of a clan, the number of families or clans in the same relic would be that many. In fact, it is impossible. Inhabitants of different communities discovered in distant and different relics cannot be taken as the members of the same family system or blood lineage or clan. But the same carved marks have been unearthed in different excavations several hundred *li* (one *li* = 0.5 km) apart, according to some archeological materials. How can these marks be a symbol of a clan or a family?

We believe that marks on pottery ware were used to record something. Carved records appeared in the history of various ethnic groups. This is readily found in materials of ethnological studies and has also been confirmed by prehistoric archeological materials. More than 40 pieces of recording tools made of bone were found in 1976 in the prehistoric tombs in Liuwan, Ledu County, by a Qinghai archeological team of the Chinese Academy of Sciences. They were made of strips of bone, 0.3 cm wide and 1.8 cm long. On the upper part or the upper and lower parts of the strips, one or two or three marks were carved. This type of record remained a record by using something, but it developed on the basis of records made by tying knots on a rope. With the emerging popularity of pottery ware, it was natural for people to carve marks on pottery. Marks found in different areas usually featured a general similarity. Several most commonly used marks have been found in different excavations, showing that some marks were used across a wide area with generally accepted meanings. As such, they bore the intrinsic elements of Chinese characters.

Pottery marks found in the late period of Dawenkou Culture in the lower reaches of the Yellow River (4,500-4,800 years ago) differ in style from those of the Yangshao and Majiayao cultures. Dawenkou marks are much closer to being images of things. A total of 16 specimens have been found, on which 18 marks in eight varieties of shapes were carved. Two specimens each have two marks, the others having only one mark and the whole or part of some marks being made in crimson. Most marks were laid on the outside of the neck of pottery wine vessels, while some were placed on the outside near the bottom.

Other unearthed relics include: 1. A large-mouthed pottery wine vessel of Nanjing's Yinyangying Culture (5,000-6,000 years ago), with incomplete decorations that can be clearly perceived. 2. Four jade articles of Liangzhu Culture (4,200-5,300 years ago), now in the Freer Gallery of Art in Washington, D. C, USA, including a "jade arm ring" and three Bi (a round flat piece of jade with a hole in the middle, used for ceremonial perposes. The Bi were each carved with a combined mark showing a bird perching on a mountain-top. 3. Two large Cong (a long hollow piece of jade with rectangular sides) now preserved in museums in China. One, in the Capital Museum, was carved with two marks, one of which also shows a bird perching on a mountain-top. Researchers believe it is a relic of Liangzhu Culture. The other, in the Museum of Chinese History, is said to have been unearthed from Shandong Province. According to researchers, it may be a relic of either Dawenkou Culture or Shandong's Longshan Culture.

Researchers have different views about the nature of marks left on the pottery and jade articles of the late period of Dawenkou Culture. Most believe they are primitive characters. For instance, they believe the mark " 凸 " stood for "dawn" or "soul"; " 查 " for the complicated type of "soul" or the blend form of the two words of "soul" and "mountain"; and " 𠂤 " for "catty." Others believe that these symbols are still limited to being simple pictures of things, being symbols to represent some individuals or a clan. Whether they are primitive Chinese characters or not remains to be determined. For example, a bird perching on a mountain-top is too complicated to be a character and is very much like a picture, hardly resembling the shape of a character. Such picture-like carved marks are more likely a symbol of a family or a lineage. However, all these were predecessors of Chinese characters. During the period of the development of Chinese characters, most of these symbols might have been developed to become characters. As evidence for this, many symbols for families and lineage left on bronze articles of the Shang and Zhou dynasties have developed to be characters used as family names.

Reliable clues about the birth of Chinese characters have been discovered from Longshan Culture (4,000-4,900 years ago). In Yangcheng, Henan Province, a black and thin-bodied, flat-bottomed piece of earthenware was unearthed, on the outside of the bottom of which a " 𢆉 " shaped word was carved. This mark is composed of two hand-shaped parts on both sides with something in between. This is an ideographic character meaning "publicly owned" to denote the clan that owned the article. The key evidence is a piece of pottery sheet of Longshan Culture. This is a shard of the flat bottom of a large basin made of polished clay. It is 4.6-7.7 cm long, 3.2 cm wide, and 0.35 cm thick. There are 11 characters arranged in five lines on the inside of the shard. In addition, on its upper left corner, there is a very shallow incised mark. Some people believe that this is also a character. On the lower left corner, there is a short downward incised line. The 11 characters are separated as independent words with fairly smooth strokes and arranged as a whole in a regular form, with the workmanship of carved characters well organized. All this shows that people had broken with the past practice of simply carving marks or picture-like marks. This shard is believed to be a relic of the late Longshan Culture of about 4,000 years ago. And it is the closest tangible evidence of embryonic Chinese characters invented during the era of Yandi and Huangdi.

The advent of characters pushed forward Chinese society into an era of civilization. According to ancient records, during the late prehistoric period, two rounds of religious reform occurred. One came in the period of the grandson of Huangdi, called Zhuan Xu. The other happened in the period of the fifth-generation grandson of Huangdi, called Yao. These two reforms stripped ordinary people and conquered tribes of their power to communicate with the deity. Such a power was to be monopolized by a special class of society. This special class was socerers, the earliest religious professionals. Later, they became the socerers' group in the history of the Shang and Zhou dynasties. These socerers were said to have communicated with the deity and ancestors by way of characters. The socerers in the periods of Zhuan Xu and Yao presumably used characters as the means to monopolize such a power.

In ancient China, different schools of scholars had diverse opinions on the invention of Chinese characters. Taoists held that the invention of characters would bring about cunning, hypocrisy and intrigue. These cunning people could even frighten the spirits.

Confucians and Mohists saw the invention as a tool for the accumulation and teaching of culture. They stressed that only characters could pass down the words and deeds of the ancient sage-kings, and hailed the invention as a great achievement. Despite the differences in viewpoints, all were conscious of the great significance of the invention.

Although we cannot know today how socerers employed characters to communicate with the deity in the prehistoric period, we can presume that their power must have been greatly promoted through the use of characters. Since all the productive experiences and cultural knowledge of any clan society had been accumulated through ages and handed down within the same society, the accumulation and dissemination of experiences and knowledge would have been greatly limited both in time and space, if characters were not available. When characters came into use, such limitations were lifted to some extent. Socerers who had mastered the use of characters were able to become the best-informed people of their time. Equipped with the power of religion, they inevitably grew to be authorities in society. Such authority readily combined with political forces. This combination of authority in the use of characters, theocracy and political power was a historical characteristic of China as it entered its era of civilization and had a profound impact on the development of traditional Chinese culture. What is more important is that the ancient Chinese civilization has been handed down from generation to generation through the carrier of characters.

Section 5   Dragon — a Symbol of the Striving Ethos of Chinese Culture

Many mountains in China contain "dragon" in their names, as in Longgang (dragon hill), or Longling (dragon ridge). The same is true of the names of rivers, such as Longjiang and Longquan (dragon river and dragon spring). Numerous towns, villages, gardens and temples are also blended with the word "dragon" in their names. Dragon dances are usually performed during the Spring Festival, and the Year of the Dragon is the most important of the 12-year cycle. Images of dragon often decorate walls, pillars, tables and desks in halls of royal palaces. Mirrors, caskets, hairpins and combs, costumes, tapestries and curtains are also decorated with the images of dragon. Sculpture has created numerous shapes of dragons. The sound of a dragon can be often heard in poems, music and dramas. Philosophers preach the wisdom of the dragon while religion boasts its power of deterrence. In traditional Chinese culture, dragon symbolizes auspiciousness, power and prosperity. Hence Chinese culture is also known as dragon culture. Dragon has become a symbol of the striving ethos of Chinese culture.

The descendants of Yandi and Huangdi, whatever their ethnic group, beliefs and birthplaces, are all proud successors of the dragon culture.

The "dragon" came into being along with the birth of the Chinese nation and its culture. Many archeological finds have provided convincing evidence of this. A group of prehistoric excavations and relics, dating back about 4,000-6,000 years, has been found decorated with dragon images, including jade, pottery and designs and patterns made from clam shells.

A pottery basin with a design of painted coiled dragon, unearthed in Shanxi Province, is 8.8 cm high, with a mouth diameter of 37 cm and a base of 15 cm. On the inside is a coiled dragon and snake body, painted in red and black. It has a pair of ears, and its mouth is partly open with two rows of small teeth and a forked tongue. This pottery basin was produced about 4,000 years ago.

One large dragon-shaped jade carving, unearthed in Inner Mongolia, is colored dark green. Its body coils like the letter "C" and its height is 26 cm. The work remains intact. Its snout stretches up and forward and its mouth is tightly closed. The tip of its nose is flat, on the upper side of which is a clear-cut horn. The flattened nose tip is an oval, on which there is a pair of round nostrils. Its protruding eyes are shaped like two shuttles, with upturned and tapered ends. Its forehead and jaw are decorated with delicate and thick chequer patterns and the bulged grids are shaped like a small diamond. Over its neck and back grows a long mane, extending 21 cm or about one-third of the total length of its body. The mane is thinly cut into flat sheets with shallow grooves and sharp and curved sides. The cross section of its body is in the shape of an oval with a diameter of 2.8-2.9 cm. Its tail turns inward. On the back, there is a hole with a diameter of 0.95 cm outside and 0.3 cm inside. When it is hung up by a cord through the hole, the dragon's head and tail balance on exactly the same level. This work was carved in the round from a single piece of jade. Polished all over, it looks rounded and bright and clean. The whole piece is so vividly made that it seems to be able to move flexibly and vigorously with its flaunting mane. It is estimated that the work was produced more than 5,000 years ago.

News of the discovery of this dragon attracted widespread attention, but the real bombshell was the excavation of four sets of clam-shell dragon patterns in Xishuipo, Henan Province in late 1988. One set had been destroyed, but the patterns of the three others remained clear. In the first, a dragon and a tiger were laid carefully with clam-shells on either side of the remains of an old man. On the east side, the 1.78-meter-long dragon preparing for flight was laid with its head to the north and its tail to the south. To the west, the 1.39-meter-long tiger opens its mouth to show its teeth, with its legs braced as if it were about to jump down from a mountain. Both animals have their backs turned to their master. To the north of the remains, a scoop design was also laid with a heap of clam-shells and two pieces of leg bone.

The second pattern involves a dragon, a tiger and a deer (not yet identified). In the third, the pattern (a running tiger and a man astride a dragon) is arranged from north to south along a meridian line in the shape of the capital letter "I." The four patterns are from Yangshao Culture. Other relics include houses, caves, ash pits, pottery sites, ditches, a great deal of pottery, jade, bone and clam-shell articles. According to a survey and analysis of the stratum and the relics, the patterns were doubtlessly produced by forefathers of Yangshao Culture. The data from a carbon test for these relics show that these patterns have ever been, so far, the earliest, largest and the most vivid images of dragon discovered in China. It dates back to 6,000 years. Specialists honor it as "China's first dragon."

Despite much study, opinions are still divided on the origin of dragons and archeologists have widely differing views, based on different materials and different viewpoints.

Some believe that the pig is one of the origins of the dragon. Some jade dragons have a long snout, studded nose, and long mane on the neck and back. Others have a forward protruding snout on a wrinkled face, a big head, flap-ears and a big fat body. Some specimens even have ferocious protruding teeth. All these show the features of a pig, demonstrating the close relationship between the original dragon and primitive agriculture. Pigs were the earliest and most commonly domesticated animals during the prehistoric period. Pig-raising had an important place in socio-economic life. The creation of a dragon image was based on people's own lives and productive activity rather than merely imagination.

The image of a dragon may vary in shape. But its body is always in the same shape of a snake. During the prehistoric period, the climate was warm and humid, and vegetation flourished. The mysterious and forbidding snake was commonly seen. At first frightened by the animal, people came to make it a part of the dragon as an object to worship, wishing to escape from harm and to ensure a good harvest.

Some other scholars believe that the clam-shell dragon patterns discovered in Xishuipo, can be explained from the astronomical viewpoint. Chinese forefathers divided up the skies into the east, south, west and north palaces. In each palace, the major constellations were conjured up in the shape of an animal and named as such. So the East Palace was called a green dragon, the West Palace a white tiger, the South Palace a red bird, and the North Palace a black turtle or a combination of turtle and snake. There was also a Central Palace called Big Dipper. In the Xishuipo tomb, on the east side of the excavation is a dragon pattern, and on the west side is a tiger design. To the north, beside the man's feet are two pieces of leg-bones together with a design of a scoop-shaped Big Dipper. This design of patterns conforms entirely with the natural astronomical phenomena in the skies. As they knew nothing about astronomical chronicles or clocks, people of this time could not but look up to the sky and watch the movements of the stars. This led them to gradually master aspects of astronomy. When astronomical chronicles and time-pieces came into use, astronomy as a science was only studied by a few. Most people, however well educated, were only able to use astronomical chronicles without knowing where they came from.

The clam-shell patterns are designed in the shape of the green dragon of the East Palace. This assumption is also evidenced by the style of the tomb itself. In ancient Chinese cosmography, heaven was described as a dome above a square ground (Earth), a pattern which is reflected in the shape of the tomb. Looked at from above, it looks like the head of a man, semi-circular in the south, square in the north and with something like ears on two sides. This agrees with the ancient concept of the heavens being in the south and the earth in the north, the mode of this tomb. It is more evidence of the origin of the dragon image being closely related to astronomical phenomenon.

It is much harder to trace the dragon to its origin through literature and records of the past because dates and periods in most literature and records about prehistoric times are frequently confused and contradictory. Complications also arise due to many alterations that have been made in the literature and records as they have been passed down through the generations. Archeological excavation sites and relics can be scientifically tested to determine a relatively precise time, but we cannot do the same with ancient writings. However, we should still value historical literature and records and make good use of them.

According to ancient literature, the dragon might have the head of an ox, a deer or a bear. Its body might originate from a snake or an earthworm. Its variety included dragons with wings, dragons with scales, and those with or without a horn. Different descriptions of dragons may reflect the differences in development as well as geographical differences. Although the original dragon images may have been produced on the basis of common animals, inhabitants of different areas would know more than one kind of common animal, hence the diversified shapes of dragons. Moreover, different materials used in the creation of dragons must have influenced the style of the products. One cause of the great difference between a jade dragon and the clam-shell dragon was the different materials being used. It was almost impossible to carve out such a complicated pattern as the clam-shell dragon design on a piece of jade at that time. We should not forget that archeology in China is as yet too immature to know how many more potential relics remain underground. Some legends have been demonstrated by unearthed materials and relics, but the fact that some legends have not yet been confirmed does not mean that they can be completely denied. As more and more new relics are excavated and studied, we will be able to reach new understandings beyond simple imagination.

Nevertheless, the study of dragons has already provided us with substantial and confirmed knowledge. The literature and archeological materials that we have studied can demonstrate that the birth of dragon was closely related to the development of primitive farming production. Its grotesque image was derived from more than one animal. It is an artistic product created by the ancients with the mixed-up features of many animals. At the very beginning, as the symbol of tribes in a clan society, the dragon image reflected the Chinese ancestors' knowledge of biology, astronomy, meteorology and other natural phenomena and embodied the importance given to nature in Chinese culture. As a prehistoric cult, the dragon reflected endeavors to achieve ideals and repel suffering. As the various tribes and clans have merged, the dragon image has developed into a wonderful and more perfect design with a deer's horns, an eagle's head, a tiger's claws, and an ox's ears. It has become an almighty symbol, capable of roaming the four seas, and taking a commanding position everywhere, and capable of "appearing in the light and in the shade, becoming small or large, short or long, ascending to the skies at the vernal equinox and submerging into the deep water at the autumnal equinox." It is one of many reflections of the great aspirations of the ancients to explore the mysteries of the universe.

Chapter 2

Chinese Philosophy — The Soul of Traditional Chinese Culture

Section 1 The Study of the Universe and Man

The study of the universe (Heaven) and man is one of the primary themes of Chinese philosophy, particularly of ancient Chinese philosophy. Sima Qian, a famous thinker and historian of the Han Dynasty (206 BC-220 AD) held that only by studying the relationship between the universe and man and expounding the nature of "Heaven" (universe) and the functions of man and his position in it, could scholars make academic achievements.

The discussion about the relationship between the universe and man focused on whether "Heaven" was regarded as a supreme god with its own will, or whether it was simply nature with neither will nor purpose. If man regarded "Heaven" as a supreme conscious god, he would be destined to worship and obey it with no possibility of changing it. In face of nature, man would have been reduced to nothing, except as appendices and slaves to nature, inevitably leading man toward religious beliefs and superstition. If man took "Heaven" simply as nature, with a close relationship with himself, he would try his best to understand it and its laws, and act accordingly, protecting it and making good use of it, ceasing to be passive in the relationship and gradually become the master of nature. These two different attitudes toward the nature of "Heaven" are products of the consciousness of anthropocentrism, and they also show the development level of such a consciousness.

In ancient China, thinkers began to know "Heaven" through their studies during the Xia (c. 21st century BC-17th century BC) and Shang (c. 17th century-11th century BC) periods. From the Western Zhou Dynasty (c. 11th century-771 BC) two contradictory concepts of "Heaven" appeared. One regarded it as a supreme god, the mandate of the god, or the manifestation of the god's will. The other regarded it as only a celestial body in the universe, and as the vast and distant sky. *The Book of Changes* is an example of this. *The Book of Changes*, which made its first appearance in the period between the Shang and Zhou dynasties, is a book of divination of the changes in nature and society by means of the Eight Trigrams. In its text, Heaven above and the Earth below are described as two opposite celestial bodies and a natural phenomenon. However, few records such as this have been found, and most contents of the records are about the will and Mandate of Heaven, looking upon Heaven as a conscious, supreme god.

In *The Book of History* (a collection of historical documents and works about the events of ancient times), for example, the term "Mandate of Heaven" is very commonly used.

Records such as this indicate that the conception of the Mandate of Heaven was the dominant and prevailing idea in society during the three dynasties of Xia, Shang and Zhou. At that time, the relationship between Heaven and man meant that the Mandate of Heaven determined human events. All that man did was entirely based on the manifestation of Heaven's will; the social order, the rules for human conduct and human ideals were all underlined by the manifestation of this will. From this time onward, Chinese thinkers of different times, under different historical conditions, have constantly challenged the will of Heaven and the manifestation of this will through different modes of thought, as follows:

Firstly, stressing the importance of human activities over the manifestation of Heaven's will. During the late period of the Western Zhou, the corruption and darkness of the government led people to become skeptical about theocracy. This tradition of "skepticism of Heaven" continued during the Spring and Autumn Period (770-476 BC) and developed into an ideological trend in society.

For example, once, in the State of Song, five meteorites fell from the sky and six aquatic birds flew over the capital against the wind, appearing to be flying backward. Duke Xiang of the State of Song asked Shu Xing, the royal secretary of Zhou, about this phenomenon. Shu Xing replied that this was the interplay of Yin and Yang, and was neither a good or bad omen from Heaven. "Good or evil fortune are determined by man himself," he said. At another time, following unusual astronomical phenomena, fire broke out in the states of Song, Wei, Chen and Zheng. The officials of the State of Zheng hurried to offer jade treasures as a sacrifice to Heaven in an attempt to extinguish the fire. Only Zi Chan, the executive minister, refused to do so, saying "the way of Heaven is farther away than the way of man and is beyond our reach." Refusing to offer sacrifices to extinguish the fire, he at once took a series of emergency measures to prevent further disasters occurring. As a result, no more fires broke out. This is a typical example of the significance of emphasizing man's activity over the will of Heaven. It has produced a profound and far-reaching impact on the following generations, both theoretically and practically.

Stressing the way of man over the way of Heaven, means that man should on the one hand negate such superstition as the will of Heaven; and on the other, he should bring his talent into play, making use of favorable conditions provided by nature and the earth, to realize his anticipated target, and to gradually emancipate his mind from the fetters of the deification of nature to become the master of his own destiny. In this respect, the military strategists of the late Spring and Autumn Period made important contributions. One such strategist, Sun Wu, first proposed the use of favorable climatic, geographical and human conditions in his book *Sun Zi's Art of War*. By favorable climatic conditions he meant the principles of Yin and Yang, hot and cold weather and the four seasons rather than the consciousness or will of Heaven. By favorable geographical conditions he meant the span of distance, the coverage of area, the importance of position, and favorable or adverse circumstances. By favorable human conditions he meant the support of the people and knowledge of one's own strengths as well as those of his enemy. He believed that only by the availability and making good use of these three conditions, could one possibly win a war. Similar ideas can be found in the later book, *Sun Bin's Art of War*.

In another example, Fan Li, a high-ranking minister of Gou Jian, the king of the State of Yue (r. 497-465 BC), also paid particular attention to the three conditions in war, on which he founded his profound military theory. He held that whether a state was strong or weak, in safety or in danger, and whether it could succeed or fail in a war or win or lose in a military action, were related to the proper or improper use of these three conditions. He once advised Gou Jian that if he wanted to maintain a powerful state, he must adapt himself to favorable climatic conditions. If he wanted to turn the situation from danger to security, he must win over the support of the people. If he wanted to achieve accomplishments, he must observe the actual geographical conditions. Gou Jian, however, turned a deaf ear to the advice and rashly acted against these laws. As a result, he was defeated by the State of Wu. In later years, Gou Jian repented his mistakes, beginning to follow Fan Li's strategies and tactics. He also worked hard to make his country strong, and led a self-imposed life of severity, sleeping on brushwood and tasting bitter gall every day in order not to forget the national humiliation. Eventually he conquered the State of Wu.

During the Warring States Period (475-221 BC), Mencius advocated that the three conditions were integrated as a whole, indispensable with each other. But the human condition was the most important. In a book of ancient military science, the significance of the human condition is also expounded repeatedly. The Taoist school of Huangdi and Lao Zi (the legendary co-founders of Taoism) regarded the human condition as the key link of the three conditions. All these new conceptions about the relationships between Heaven and man have shown that during the period from the Western Zhou to the Warring States, many philosophers had been aware of the values of man himself, signifying the awakening of man's consciousness of being the master of his own.

Secondly, the natural law of Heaven. Good or bad fortune is determined by man, not by Heaven. But what is after all the nature of Heaven? Confucius made a study of the nature of Heaven. He held that Heaven was something without will and its nature was like the changes of the four seasons and the endless growth and development of everything. Therefore, man's survival must be based on his own hard work. This conclusion was the beginning of the theory of "the natural law of Heaven."

Lao Zi, the founder of Taoism, was the first to propose the natural law of Heaven. He believed that the nature of Heaven was natural. According to him, "being natural" is the theoretical summary of all natural phenomena, and is known as Tao (the Way). Heaven, Earth and Man are all natural beings unified within Tao. Giving a representation of Tao, he says: "'Something' has been mixed up to first produce Heaven and Earth. Still and solitary as it has always been, it evolves endlessly, operating as the parent of everything in the world. I know not its name. So I call it 'Tao.'" Tao, as nature, is every natural being and phenomenon including Heaven, Earth and Man. Heaven, as a natural thing, is not necessarily to be worshipped. Mankind is also a natural being, and so Heaven and humanity are equal. This idea of "the natural laws of Heaven" not only has provided a noumenal basis for the belief that good or evil fortune is determined by man himself, but also regarded man as an independent part relieved from the fetters of Heaven.

Zhuang Zi inherited the tendency of Lao Zi's thought, believing that Heaven was the largest of all the perceivable things in the universe. In most cases, by Heaven, he meant nature or the natural environment. He maintained that, by acting against the laws of nature, Man would lose the freedom of action. Man should therefore act according to the laws of nature. He gave the example of a skilled butcher. The butcher dismembered an ox for Lord Wen Hui with skill and almost magical craftsmanship. His knife was operated at a pace as if in accord with the dance steps to the beat of the movement of "Shuang Lin" and to the rhythm of the movement of "Jin Shou." The butcher said that he was able to dismember the ox so dexterously only because he had a thorough understanding and knowledge of the veins, texture and structure of its body, "according to the natural laws of Heaven" and "its intrinsic constitution." He could adroitly use his knife between its joints and bones without contacting them and smoothly dismembered it. Zhuang Zi told this story to show the fact that only by observing the objective and natural laws when dealing with human relations and affairs, could people achieve their goal successfully with satisfactory results. This idea further developed the concept of "the natural laws of Heaven" conceived by Lao Zi.

While stressing the significance of the natural laws of the universe, Zhuang Zi, however, negated the role of the subjective activity of man, regarding man's subjective endeavors as a destructive force against nature. In his opinion, the relationship between man and nature is similar to that between a piece of iron and a blacksmith. The blacksmith can produce whatever he wants with the piece of iron, and the iron cannot have its choice. Heaven and Earth (the universe) are a large melting-pot, nature is the master blacksmith and man is nothing but a piece of iron. Man's whole life is completely subject to nature. He denies that man's efforts can reform nature, but attempts to bring about the return of man to and his identification with nature through recognizing that "man is no match for Heaven." In fact, this is utterly impossible. The following story told by Zhuang Zi suggests that he himself might have been conscious of this. Zi Shang was starving and tried to find out the cause of his suffering: "Is it caused by my father? Or mother? Or Heaven, or man? He thought that it could not be his parents. Nor could it be Heaven. Could it be possibly be man? He had raised the question, but he could not find out the real cause of man's activity in his answer. He concluded that starvation had been caused by man's fate. Thus Zhuang Zi negates on the one hand the will of Heaven, while on the other preaching the inscrutable "fate" of man. Nature, or Heaven, as the final target, after which he had strenuously sought, proved nothing but the irresistible "fate."

Thirdly, man independent of Heaven's will. During the late Warring States Period, Xun Zi first established the philosophical doctrine proposing that "man is independent of Heaven's will," on the basis of summing up the doctrines of various schools, absorbing their strengths while discarding their weaknesses.

He particularly disagreed with Zhuang Zi's glorification of heaven (nature) and rejection of human endeavor. By "man being independent of Heaven's will," Xun Zi by no means intended to separate man completely from nature, or "Heaven." Man, he said, apart from having the general properties of a natural being, also has other different properties transcending a natural being. He said: "Water and fire have *qi* (vapor or energy) but no life. Grass and plants have life but no senses. Animals and birds have senses but no *yi* (morality, or what is right or in order). Man has *qi*, life, senses, and *yi*, and is the most valuable under heaven." He classified the material world into four categories: Water and fire, grass and plants, animals and birds, and man. Man is not only endowed with intelligence, but also has rules for proper conduct. In the relationship between man and Heaven, man is the primary and key aspect of the two opposing parts. Therefore, Xun Zi repeatedly stressed the significance of human activity, rejecting the idea that a state's order or chaos, prosperity or decline was determined by the will of Heaven. He also rejected the idea that an individual's good or bad luck, poverty or fortune were determined by the will of Heaven. He further pointed out clearly: "Heaven cannot impose, if man develops agriculture and practices thrift, poverty on him. Heaven cannot impose, if man is adequately clothed and fed, and works and plays in time, illness on him. Heaven cannot impose, if man always observes the rules of government whole-heartedly, disaster on him." Heaven, he said, has no will. It takes its own course in its movement and change. The important thing for man to do is to know, control and make use of it. In his philosophical teaching that man's will, not Heaven, decides, he said: "Rather than exaggerate the functions of Heaven and admire it, treat it as a thing and control it. Rather than submit to it and laud it, master its laws and make use of them. Rather than sit idly, waiting for providence to bring provisions, make use of the four seasons and till the land. Rather than leaving animals and plants to reproduce and grow by themselves, develop the ability to promote their growth. It is better to have a deep understanding of the nature and properties of everything under heaven so as to control it than conjure up the control of all. In other words, to worship Heaven and disdain the role of man was irrational.

Fourthly, the reciprocity and interaction between Heaven and man. Before the Tang Dynasty (618-907), thinkers confined their arguments to the themes of "the unity of Heaven and man," "the natural laws of Heaven" and "man independent of Heaven."

Liu Yuxi (772-842), a thinker and writer of the Tang Dynasty, free from the bondage of traditional thought, discussed the relationship between Heaven and man from a different point of view. He proposed a new approach, of "reciprocity and interaction" between man and Heaven, based on the differences and interelatedness between them.

According to Liu Yuxi, although both Heaven and man exist in the material form, and are the most distinguished of all things, yet they have their own special strengths, and one cannot replace the other. Their properties and nature are different. Of all the material things, Heaven is the largest. But it is also the smallest in terms of its material form of existence. Hence Heaven is the universe, a unity of both infinite and finite materiality. Man is the most intelligent and most distinguished of all creatures. Moreover, he is able to create in society something more than he has been endowed by nature, a system of laws. Therefore, "man cannot do everything that Heaven can, and Heaven also cannot do everything that man can." Heaven and man must play their respective roles. Additionally, the law (or way) of human society is different from the laws of nature. Natural laws embody the birth, development and varia-

47

tions of all the things in the world. This process is realized through the strong preying on the weak, or becoming weak themselves. Human society is different from nature. The productive and social activities of human creation embody the establishment and perfection of various institutions. The function of such institutions is to set up criteria in law for what is right and what is wrong in people's conduct. All these show that man is man, Heaven is Heaven and they cannot be the same. Man should not impose his will on nature. What is right and what is wrong are to be determined by man himself, and have nothing to do with Heaven. Liu Yuxi wished to take universal laws and social functions to illustrate the distinction between "the way of Heaven" and "the way of man." This is a further development of Xun Zi's concept of "man independent of Heaven."

Another new idea conceived by Liu is the reciprocal relationship between Heaven and man. He believed that man could choose to act according to natural laws. Man could sow seeds in spring, till the land in summer, harvest crops in autumn and preserve them in winter. He could also fell trees, tunnel through hills and smelt metal. He could reshape nature in the process of production to meet the needs of man. On the other hand, natural changes could bring about good or bad effects upon man's production and livelihood. Man's task was to understand and master the internal and external interrelations in nature and their tendencies so as to reduce the risk of harm inflicted upon man by nature.

In Liu Yuxi's view, man himself had imposed a veil of mystery over Heaven, and this was a mistake in cognition. As far as social conditions were concerned, he classified the legal system or social order into three categories: good order, bad order and a complete failure of order. He said that in a society in which good order prevailed, rewards and penalties will be meted out properly and right and wrong will be treated with justice. "Goodness and decency will be surely rewarded with happiness, but wickedness does not go altogether unpunished." People are confident of their own strength and capability, without having to deify "Heaven," and they will not be ensnared by theism. If the legal system is partly demolished, then right and wrong will be confused, resulting in unjust punishments and rewards. Under such circumstances, people are diffident of their own strength and capability and are liable to believe in Providence. If the legal system is totally demolished, then right and wrong are reversed and sycophants will be rewarded, while upright people will be punished and the laws on rewards and penalties will be invalid. In such a society, people will be diffident of their own capability and will be forced to entrust their destiny to the so-called "Heaven" or Providence, becoming a theist. Therefore, Liu came to the conclusion that man created gods for worship only in times when he was unable to control his own fate. The truth is that there are no gods that can determine man's destiny.

So far as the level of man's knowledge of objective reality at that time was concerned, Liu Yuxi believed that the situation could be divided into two parts. One was that man knew the laws of nature and could make use of them. The other was that man did not yet know the laws of nature, which remained incomprehensible to man. Under such conditions, it was not surprising that man did not trust his own strength and was resigned to the control of the will of "Heaven." To illustrate this contradiction, he gave the example of travelling by boat. On a small river, a boat can be controlled easily. If there is a storm, there is no swell or high waves. The boat may sail smoothly and fast through man's correct handling. If it capsizes or gets stranded, this is due to improper handling on man's part. Passengers on the boat would not attribute any of this to the will of Heaven because man has had a good knowledge of it. However, when a boat sails at sea, it becomes harder to control. A breeze can create a swell and dark clouds can blur the view from direction. So a misled perception arises that the boat's safety depends on the will of Heaven. Whether it sinks or survives after undergoing all manner of hardships and risks depends on the will of Heaven. All the passengers on the boat believe this because man does not have sufficient knowledge of the laws of nature.

To sum up, Liu Yuxi, applying his new concept of "the reciprocity and interaction between Heaven and man," studied the relationships between man and nature, between society and natural laws, and the leading role of man in the understanding and remaking of nature. In particular, he surveyed the epistemological origin of theism and atheism, making a great contribution to the philosophical problem in China of the relationship between Heaven and man.

Section 2 The Study of Changes

The study of changes is another important subject discussed in Chinese philosophy.

The idea of unchangeability arose along with the formation of the theory of the Mandate of Heaven. The people of the Shang Dynasty (c. early 17th century-11th century BC) held that the Mandate of Heaven was unchangeable and that everything depended on the steady Mandate of Heaven. On the eve of the collapse of the Shang Dynasty, the tyrant King Zhou was still certain that the Mandate of Heaven was unchangeable and that his rule over the state would not be forfeited and terminated.

The idea of changeability of things (nature and human activity) arose around the time that the Shang Dynasty ended and the Zhou Dynasty began. During the Spring and Autumn and Warring States periods it developed into a fairly complete and systematic theory, which became an important ideological basis of the study of changes (or the study of dualism, or the opposites) for the following generations. Two books from that period illustrate this:

Firstly, *The Book of History*, in which various important historical events of the Shang Dynasty and the early Zhou Dynasty were recorded. Among them are contained many discussions of the changeability of both the Mandate of Heaven and the government. For instance, Heaven is always searching for a suitable sovereign for the state. At first, the Xia were selected, but descendents of the early kings of the Xia Dynasty abused their power and maltreated the people, instead of working for the benefits of the people. As a result, Heaven dismissed the Xia and ordered that the Shang replace them as rulers of the state." For centuries, King Tang and the succeeding kings of Shang worked hard to make their country strong and prosperous through diligence and frugality and so their regimes survived. Eventually, however, the last kings of the dynasty began to seek sensual pleasures. The last king of the dynasty, King Zhou, committed all manner of evil and the dynasty was overturned by Heaven in favor of the Zhou. The Duke of Zhou demanded of the nobles of Zhou that they learn from the honorable and brilliant kings of Xia and Shang, and remember the fatuous and incompetent kings who had lost the trust of Heaven and the people. The conquered Shang tried to take advantage of the faults of the new Zhou regime to overthrow the Zhou, saying that this was the "evil imposed upon the state of Zhou by Heaven." Those holding the reins of the Zhou government were well aware that if the Zhou did not overcome their mistakes, their regime would collapse and they would be reduced to slaves. This was the idea of changeability of the Mandate of Heaven summed up by the statesmen of the early Zhou from their political practices.

Second, *The Book of Changes* (*I Ching*) which appeared at the time of the transition from the Shang Dynasty to the Zhou. The book uses arrangements of eight "trigrams" (three solid and/or broken lines forming patterns which represent Heaven, Earth, thunder, wind, water, fire, mountain and lake) through which natural and social changes can be foretold.

In the book, many opposing categories are recorded, such as auspicious and inauspicious, good luck and ill luck, big and small, entry and exit, incoming and outgoing, forward and backward, up and down, taking and giving, life and death, internal and external, safety and danger, profit and loss. These opposing categories mean the whole world is replete with contradictions. And the world is composed of contradictions that interchange and interact. Something big is sure to come after something small has gone; a plain may rise to become a hillside; present time is a continuation of the past. There is nothing at all that is unchangeable and steady forever in the world. Everything has its own contradiction(s). Everything changes from its own contradiction(s). This outlook on the world may be regarded as the early beginning of the study of dualism, or opposites (dialectics).

During the Spring and Autumn and Warring States periods, people deepened their understanding of the ideas of change and of opposites. A series of works expressing this understanding appeared. With the appearance of *Sun Zi's Art of War*, *The Analects*, *The Book of Lao Zi*, *The Book of Mo Zi* and *Explanatory Notes of Changes*, the study of changes in Chinese philosophy was promoted to a new height of its development.

The main substance of the study of changes was as follows:

First, the concept of motion and change. Ancient Chinese philosophers gained an understanding of this concept only after they had observed a great deal of natural and social phenomena. That is to say, they discovered and inferred the generality of the motion and changes of things from the observation of the individuality of the movement and changes of things. For instance, Lao Zi, as an official historian, saw many changes of things in society such as "no ruler of a state can be in office forever and no positions for rulers and subjects without changes." He also observed such natural phenomena as "highland changes to be valley and valley changes to be high hill." From these observations, he saw that nothing in the world is unchangeable. He said: "A hurricane never lasts a whole morning, nor a rainstorm all day. Who is it that makes the wind and rain? It is Heaven and Earth. And if Heaven and Earth cannot blow and pour for long, how much less in his utterance should man?" Using this instance he wants to explain that both nature and human society are moving on and changing ceaselessly. Confucius, observing the rotation of the four seasons, and the growth and decline of everything, came to know that the world moves on just like a running river. His disciples recorded: "The Master standing by a stream, said, 'It passes on just like this, ceaselessly day or night.'"

This conception of the motion and changes of things was further developed in the *Explanatory Notes of Changes*. The sun, the moon, and the constellations, the four seasons and hot and cold weather, ancient and modern times, and thoughts and ideas are all in a state of motion and change. The same is true of etiquette and penal code and the laws. Nothing in the world is unchangeable. Things change when they reach the extreme. Change will promote development and development will bring about creation. Infinite development is a process full of vitality and a multitude of variations.

That things are always in motion and change is agreed upon by most ancient and modern thinkers. But opinions differ in the relationship between motion and motionlessness, mainly because there exist two kinds of one-sided view about this question.

The scholars of the metaphysical school of the Wei Dynasty (220-265) and the Jin (265-420) exaggerated the functions of stillness, holding that the thing-in-itself (noumenon) is always motionless. Motionlessness is absolute. Motion comes from motionlessness. All the things in motion will ultimately return to the static state of the thing-in-itself. Taoists held a similar outlook. Chinese Buddhism, however, exaggerated the functions of motion, denying the distinction between motion and motionlessless, regarding all things and phenomena in the world as constantly changing and in an endless cycle of life and death.

A comprehensive conception of motion and motionlessness was not proposed until the Song (960-1279) and Ming (1368-1644) dynasties. For example, Zhou Dunyi (1017-1073) of the Song Dynasty conceived the doctrine of the reciprocity of motion and motionlessness. Zhang Zai (1020-1077) likened motion and motionlessness to the opening and shutting of a door, expounding the unity of opposites — motion and motionlessness — from being of daily life. He proposed such ideas as "motion in motionlessness" and "motionlessness being in the course of motion," confirming the relativity of motionlessness, and "ceaseless motion" as the absoluteness of motion. Wang Fuzhi (1619-1692), a thinker of the Ming and Qing dynasties, also opposed the ideas of motionlessness without motion or motion without motionlessness. He considered that "motionlessness involves motion, and motion involves motionlessness," regarding motion and motionlessness as two states of existence of things in motion and change.

It is necessary to point out here that different views still remained as to the relationship between matter and motion. Many Taoist and Buddhist scholars separated matter from motion, believing motion could exist independent of matter. This had been argued repeatedly since the Han Dynasty by those who advocated that primary elements (or vitality) formed Heaven and Earth. They believed that things were in constant motion and change and the material *qi* (vitality) that constituted everything was also in constant motion and change. They pointed out that in the world, there was no motion without matter, nor there was matter without motion.

Secondly, "opposites" are the source of the motion and change of everything. This is the nucleus of the study of changes, and its most brilliant aspect. *The Book of Changes* was probably the first book to conceive the idea of opposites. It held that the cause of motion and change lay in opposites, or the interaction of opposites. However this idea was expressed through the form of divination. The question had not been discussed with a genuine philosophic point of view until the appearance of such books as *The Book of Lao Zi, Sun Zi's Art of War*, and the *Explanatory Notes of Changes*.

Lao Zi systematically expounded the interdependent relationship between the two opposites of things. He enumerated a number of things in the category of opposites such as beauty and ugliness, difficult and easy, long and short, high and low, something and nothing, profit and loss, hard and soft, strong and weak, happiness and misfortune, wise and foolish, smart and stupid, big and small, life and death, win and lose, offense and defense, advance and retreat, light and heavy, honor and disgrace, and motion and motionlessness. If one of the two opposites does not exist, the other will also disappear. The interaction and interdependence of the two opposites are the cause of change and development of things.

The idea of "opposites" conceived by Lao Zi is further developed by *Sun Zi's Art of War*. A weakness of Lao Zi's thesis is that, for him, the change or shift of opposites is unconditional. Therefore, people cannot predict the prospects of the development of things. Meanwhile, in dealing with the theory that "the weak originates from the strong," a theory of interchanges of opposites, the description in *Sun Zi's Art of War* is more profound than that of Lao Zi, because the former has pointed out the precondition of changes. Without certain conditions, the weak will remain weak, and cannot overcome the strong. Of all conditions, man is the most important. For Sun Zi, this means the full performance of the commander's subjective initiative and the soldiers' discipline and valor.

It is said that Sun Zi went to the State of Wu to persuade the king to follow his art of war. The king inquired of him how an army should be commanded. Sun Zi immediately gave him a demonstration by ordering the royal palace maids to form a parade. He divided them into two columns, led by two of the king's favorite concubines. Each time Sun beat a drum to give out his orders, all the women burst into laughter. He then ordered that the two leaders be beheaded. This startled the king and he asked that the women not be executed, but Sun said: "On the battlefield, the orders of the king will not necessarily be accepted by his generals." He then killed the two leaders and assigned two others in their place. Now, when he gave his orders, all the women performed properly and acted as one. Sun told the king that this sort of army could be sent to brave all dangers. The king of Wu then appointed Sun as his commanding general.

The *Explanatory Notes of Changes* further points out that the reason why two opposites of a thing can interact each other and promote the change and development of a thing lies in the opposing property or nature of opposites. Change and development are the logical outcome of the "interaction" and "friction" of the two opposing forces. The author of the *Explanatory Notes of Changes* holds that the interaction and inter-friction of Yin and Yang, hard and soft, motion and motionlessness gave rise to Heaven and Earth, the sun and moon, the four seasons, night and day, cold and hot weather, man and woman, good omens and bad omens, happiness and misfortune, survival and extinction, and life and death in nature and human society. The motive force of changes of things is not outside the things themselves, but lies in the internal interaction and inter-friction of the opposing forces within.

If the study of opposites had reached a peak before the Qin Dynasty (221-206 BC), a new upsurge reappeared during the Song and Ming dynasties when science and technology had further developed. The philosophers of this period inherited and developed previous understanding of opposites, while also absorbing and remodeling the dialectical way of thought in Buddhism, thus making new contributions to the "study of opposites."

"Opposites," as a philosophical thesis, was first proposed by Wang Anshi of the Northern Song Dynasty (960-1127) and Zhu Xi of the Southern Song (1127-1279). This is a new summarization of various previous categories of opposites. Zhu Xi expressed the idea clearly, saying that everything in the world has its opposite, everything contains its own opposite, and each part of the two opposites has its own opposite. Zhu Xi combined his ideas, akin to the essence of dialectics, with the ideas of the Northern Song philosophers Shao Yong and Zhang Zai that "one is divided into two" and "one thing can be halved." From here, he continued, saying that the study of opposites and "one is divided into two" are one and the same. "One is halved, and the half can again be halved, and so on through to infinity." He considered that "one is divided into two" is the general law of the motion and change of things.

Thinkers of the Song and Ming also made new findings in their study of the innate causes of motion and change. For instance, applying their natural science knowledge to the study, Zhang Zai and other thinkers proposed that "motion comes within itself," and "the cause of motion is internal." The internal cause of motion is the imbalance in the development of the opposites of things and the interaction that this produces.

For Zhang, the opposing nature of opposites conceived by earlier philosophers is the imbalance in the development of the "two extremes." It is not only things in different categories which have such opposing extremes; so do things of the same category. Even so is in the case of a thing. For instance, man has two similar hands, but one is on the right and the other on the left. And each hand has five fingers, but they are different in length. Even the hair on a man's head is not completely alike. Simply because of this opposing nature of opposites, the "two extremities" of things can achieve the inter-absorption as well as inter-repulsion between them. As a result, the reproduction of man himself, the progress of society and the change of nature can happen.

Thirdly, there must be one aspect of the two opposites which plays the leading role. As early as more than 2000 years ago, Chinese thinkers already understood this truth from their daily life. The nature of opposites was abstracted with one aspect as the weak (Yin, or female) and the other as the strong (Yang, or male).

The school of Lao Zi stressed the principal role of the weak aspect, holding that the nature and change of a whole thing are determined by it. They proposed a dialectical ideology based on the importance of the weak and female.

Through farming practice, Lao Zi observed that a seedling, though weak at first, could grow up tall and strong. However, when it had become tall and strong, it would begin to approach its death. He held that the best way to deal with life was to place oneself in a weak position, so as to avoid the transformation from weak to strong and eventually to death. Therefore, he believed that if you want to remain whole, be twisted; to become straight, let yourself be bent; to become full, be hollow; and be tattered, that you may be renewed. Those that have little will receive plenty. For this purpose, he urged people to learn the quality of water. Water appears soft and yielding. But it can attack everything harder and stronger than itself, because it can yield to the situation as it flows. Therefore, "nothing under heaven can fight it." This is the essence of Lao Zi's principle of "the weak overcoming the strong."

Contradicting the school of Lao Zi, the school of the *Explana-*

tory Notes of Changes emphasized the role of the strong, believing that "just as the universe evolves on in its own way without failure, a superior man (or a man of virtue) must strive constantly to make himself strong and capable as the Way of Man requires." Their dialectic ideology emphasized man's constant endeavors to make himself strong and capable.

The *Explanatory Notes of Changes* chiefly studies how to keep the strong aspect constantly playing the leading role without being replaced by the weak aspect. However, although the strong aspect is dominant, its action must be moderate in the whole process of motion. Any exertion beyond a certain limit will bring about a result contrary to its aims. Therefore, by absorbing part of Lao Zi's thinking, the book advocates that the strong aspect should play the leading role, supplemented by the weak aspect. If necessary, the strong aspect may be even placed in a secondary position to achieve its aim for the eventual "full development of the Tao."

So far as the weak aspect is concerned, the book holds that if the weak aspect plays the leading role over the strong aspect, the results will be bad. The book compares the weak to the category of "earth" or the female (Yin) nature. These can play their due role only when they are attached to the strong aspect or play their subdued part in contrast to it. For example, during the reign of the tyrant King Zhou, darkness overwhelmed the whole state. King Wen of Zhou was imprisoned and subjected to great suffering. King Wen, however, had a great store of inner strength and virtue, while externally employing the way of the weak, and finally overcame the disaster. When a sovereign was fatuous and incompetent, decent and honorable ministers were sure to suffer. Ji Zi was reduced from being a minister to a slave by his lord, the tyrant King Zhou of Shang, and was put in prison. He protected himself from harm by pretending to be mad and hiding his wisdom and ability. Though he suffered great psychological trauma, his rectitude, decency and integrity remained unshaken. This shows that under certain conditions, one may turn danger into security by yielding in the right way.

The two different dialectic ideologies of Lao Zi and the *Notes* are two different approaches to knowing and dealing with things, both of which reflect a certain aspect of objective dialectics.

Through the ages all Confucian scholars have favored the *Notes* because it demonstrated such ideas as superior and inferior, nobility and baseness and high and low positions through the concept of the weak being subordinated to the strong, which corresponded more closely to the social reality of the time. This was especially true of Dong Zhongshu (179-104 BC), a philosopher of the Western Han (206 BC-25 AD), who applied this idea to the demonstration of the "Three Cardinal Guides"* of feudal society. Dong Zhongshu identified rulers, fathers and husbands as Yang, while subjects, sons and wives were Yin. Yang was superior while Yin was inferior. It was because these concepts had long been dominant among thinkers, the functions of the interchange of the strong and the weak aspects, which the *Notes* tried to avoid, were thus covered up.

As to Lao Zi's idea of "the weak overcoming the strong," although it denies the value of man's activity, its objective dialectical aspect has still not been properly researched, and a need for its deep implications and truth to be further developed still remains.

The primary feature of the study of changes is for practical use. It is not an armchair philosophic theory. As a way of thinking, it is intended to be used for avoiding one-sided views, and upholding an overall point of view. This is the "setting it forth from one end to the other" that Confucius spoke of. Other dialectic methodology approaches suggested by many other thinkers to deal with such opposites as safety and danger, joy and sorrow, obscurity and insinuation, feeling and reason, knowledge and practice constituted the main substance of the study of changes.

It can also be applied to social activities, including politics, military affairs, economy and culture. Through centuries of practice and evolution, people have come to realize that it is imperative

---

*The ruler guides the subject, the father guides the son and the husband guides the wife.

to learn and use the Chinese knowledge of changes if one wants to achieve success in one's career. Many scholars and military strategists abroad have also come to this conclusion, and have earnestly studied *Sun Zi's Art of War*. This is a practical way of studying the ancient Chinese learning of opposites.

Sun Zi's Art of War is the classic of the "learning of opposites" to be applied to military science and human activities. Its expositions of subjective and objective conditions, the relationship between politics and economy, the union of analysis and synthesis, the need to carefully examine oneself as well as one's enemy and to develop one's strong points and attack the enemy's weak points have made the book an encyclopedia of the learning of opposites with its undying theoretical vitality.

Section 3 The Learning of Absorption and Assimilation

The vitality of ancient Chinese philosophy, like water ceaselessly flowing from a spring, came from a unique self-developed course in which it was always able to absorb and assimilate the merits of various schools of philosophy. In spite of their different viewpoints and forms, all schools sought to seek the truth, conducive to promoting human knowledge of nature and society. The absorption and assimilation of various viewpoints had therefore been a marked feature in the development of ancient Chinese philosophy.

A basic facet of this feature is the mutual debate and absorption between different schools. Each school could find the other's weak points as well as its strong points, and could maintain its theoretical principles while overcoming its own deficiencies.

During the Spring and Autumn and Warring States periods, no thesis could be established without debate and no authority could exist without being tested through argument.

Taoists advocated a return to nature, negating human desires and knowledge. Confucians upheld the self-valuing role of man in the universe, proposing that benevolence (Ren) and righteousness (Yi), or virtue and morality, are the general law of everything under heaven. Taoists criticized the Confucians' ideas as being arrogant and ignorant. An example they gave was Xi Shi whose beauty caught the eye of everyone. But birds would still fly away and fish dive deep in the water when they saw her. So birds and fish do not accept man's standards of beauty. People like to live in luxurious houses while eels like to bury themselves in the mud and monkeys climb up in the trees. So animals do not accept man's standards for dwelling place. How, then, can it be asserted that benevolence and righteousness are the general law of everything under heaven? When Confucians criticized the Taoists as being "indulgent in Heaven while ignorant of man," they also confirmed the theoretical findings achieved by Taoists in their study of the way of Heaven. They were conscious of the need to know Heaven while knowing man. They therefore advanced their unique principle of the way of Heaven on which their doctrine of the cultivation of the mind was based, and made a series of creative explorations into nature and the way of Heaven (see first section of this chapter). While rejecting the overemphasis of the human role by Confucians, the Taoists also recognized their merits in the study of this role. Later Taoists tried to reconcile the conflict between their concept of the natural way of Heaven and the Confucians' concept of moral cultivation and to absorb the latter's findings on the knowledge of man.

Mutual debate and mutual absorption occurred not only between different schools, but also within each school itself. Zhuang Zi took different sects in different schools for example. He said there were four sects alone in Taoism. While he had no disagreement with Lao Zi's doctrine, he either confirmed or criticized the doctrines of other sects, even including those of Zhuang Zi himself. Of the sects of Peng Meng and Sheng Dao, he said that they maintained justice and fairness, selflessness and being free from desire were adaptable to change, without prejudice and personal bias and preserved a calm mind amid the bustle of life. But their views on the way of Heaven and the human mind were incomplete. This was because they believed in distinguishing right from wrong, while Zhuang Zi himself basically denied such distinctions. He believed that he had a fairly profound understanding of the way of Heaven, but he also acknowledged that he was not perfect in dealing with the problems of human life.

In another example, Xun Zi, an exponent of one of the Confucian sects, criticized, among others, the sect of Zi Si and Mencius, the most influential sect of the Confucian school at that time. He argued that although their teachings mostly followed the way of the ancient sage-kings, they did not really understand the way of the sage-kings. They had high aspirations but lacked ability. With extensive knowledge, having studied events of remote antiquity, they came up with the five principles of benevolence, righteousness, courtesy, intelligence and honesty which were esoteric and impossible to understand. By today's standards, Xun Zi's criticisms may not seem appropriate. But this example shows that there were diverse opinions among different sects of the same philosophy, and when this occurred debate and criticism would arise.

Debate between various schools and absorption of each other's theories continued throughout the whole process of the development of ancient Chinese philosophy.

When Buddhism was introduced into China and modified with Chinese characteristics, the development of its tenets was mainly credited to the debate within the Buddhist world. To spread its doctrine, Buddhist temples often gave classes on the Buddhist scriptures and classics. During the class, the lecturers, usually learned monks, gave a teaching on the main points of the tenet and explained the scriptures. The audience was allowed to raise questions, which the teacher had to answer. No question could be refused. Moreover, temples often held congregations at which various sects and dissenters were allowed to discuss the arguments or topics brought up by the congregation. This promoted the development of various sects of Chinese Buddhism.

In the development of ancient Chinese philosophy, there was a continuous mutual debate and absorption between the Xuan Xue, or Metaphysical School (a philosophy combining the Taoist thought and Confucian doctrine) and Buddhism, and between Buddhism and the Li Xue, or Neo-Confucianism, of the Song and Ming dynasties. Buddhists asserted that Buddhism's description of the spiritual ethos and its mode of presentation were superior to those of Confucianism. But they also acknowledged their agreement with some elements in the moral philosophy of Confucianism, such as its doctrine of cultivation of the mind, which emphasized the importance of the subjective functions of the human mind. Chinese Buddhism absorbed these and remodeled them into Buddhist doctrines, creating a new theoretical system different from the indigenous Indian Buddhism. For instance, the saying that the Buddha-nature is within everyone is similar to the Confucian teaching that everyone can become like the ancient sage-kings Yao and Shun.

Another important aspect of ancient Chinese philosophy is the absorption and assimilation of the tenets of various disciplines and developing their theories.

In view of the formation and development of the basic doctrine of Confucianism, whatever its conception about the way of Heaven or the moral concepts of Confucianism may be concerned, they have kept a close relation with the development of natural science.

An important reason why the early Confucians could advance the idea that of all creatures, man is the most intelligent and that man's rational and moral faculties are the standards of value for all things under heaven lies in the accumulation of the natural science knowledge at the time. In astronomy, for example, in the latter part of the Spring and Autumn Period, a quarterly-divided calendar appeared, that divided the duration of a tropical year into 365.25 days. The system established a 19-year cycle, seven years of which contained intercalary months. Calendric science had thus entered a stage of maturity, independent from the past practice of time reporting only by astronomical observations. During the Warring States Period, six different calendars existed in the various vassal states. All were divided into four quarters, but they differed from each other in terms of the first day and month of each year.

Thus, with this knowledge it was now possible to fairly accurately predict future calendric events.

In the field of medical science, after much exploration and experimentation, people learned the medicinal value of many herbs and materials and built up a comparatively rich and systematic knowledge of the nerves and veins in the human body. Through practical experience, they established many medical formulae and principles for health preservation.

A fairly rich knowledge of chemistry, mathematics and physics was also acquired.

With man's capabilities and scientific knowledge constantly expanding and growing, Confucians concluded that man has the capability to know and to teach the truth of things. This recognition in turn further deepened people's understanding of their own position and duty in society. Confucians, however, were unable to put forward any practical and effective proposals as to how to reform society. They laid their hopes on "sage-kings and illustrious ministers" and stressed the obligations of man to society. But they neglected the rights man should enjoy in society.

It was not only Confucianism which absorbed and assimilated elements of other disciplines or schools; so did Taoism and Buddhism (see Chapter 4).

The absorption and assimilation of foreign culture is the third important aspect of Chinese philosophy. For details, see Chapter 4.

In modern Chinese philosophy, absorption and assimilation of foreign culture is more conspicuous than ever before. For instance, Li Shanlan (1810-1882) translated the last nine books of Euclidean geometry. The first six books had been translated during the Ming Dynasty (1368-1644) by Xu Guangqi. A complete and new method of deductive reasoning was thus introduced into the Chinese philosophical world. Li also translated Loomis, J. Herschel, William Whewell, and Newton's works. All these had a great influence on the development of modern Chinese philosophy and natural sciences.

Yan Fu (1853-1921), a modern thinker, began to translate *Evolution and Ethics* in 1895, written by British biologist T.H. Huxley. This book had a profound influence on modern Chinese thinkers. Sun Yat-sen (1866-1925) used the book as one of his main ideological weapons in his call for a democratic revolution to overthrow the reign of the Qing Dynasty and establish a republic. It is worth noting that when the theory of evolution was applied to modern society in China, it was not in a biological sense. Elements were selected, modified and blended with the ancient Chinese concept of changes, another example of the ethos of absorption and assimilation. By absorption and assimilation, we mean that any culture and ideology which are useful are to be taken in and assimilated by Chinese culture. This is something that the Chinese have been good at since ancient times.

This ethos can be seen in many well-known personalities in modern Chinese history, such as Wei Yuan, Hong Xiuquan, Hong Rengan, and Zhang Taiyan.* These people earnestly studied Western religion, history, political systems, ideology and academic studies so as to apply them to China. Moreover, such scholars who made academic accomplishments were not complacent and conceited. Most of them were experts in Chinese as well as Western studies, and in combining the two.

In short, the study of Heaven and man, the study of changes, and the study of absorption and assimilation are the main components and characteristics of the Chinese philosophy. They have been reflected, directly or indirectly, in various aspects of traditional Chinese culture.

---

* Wei Yuan (1794-1857), a thinker, historian and writer of the Qing Dynasty.

Hong Xiuquan (1814-1864), leader of the Taiping Revolution. As the contradictions in Chinese society intensified after the first Opium War (1840-1842), Hong Xiuquan absorbed the ideas of equality in human relations from Christianity and founded the Society of God Worshippers. In 1851, he launched an uprising against the Qing regime and established the Taiping Heavenly Kingdom. In 1864, he was defeated by the joint suppression of the Qing government and foreign aggressors.

Hong Rengan, (1822-1864), one of the leaders of the Taiping Heavenly Kingdom, who supported the learning of science and technology from the West, political reform and the development of a capitalist economy.

Zhang Taiyan (1869-1936), a modern democratic revolutionary and thinker.

Chapter 3

Ethics and the Humanities

Section 1 Traditional Virtues

China has always been known as an ancient civilization, and a land of propriety and righteousness. It abounds in historical heritage, including ethical and moral theories advanced in various stages of history and a myriad of moral codes and rules. These have had a profound influence on traditional Chinese culture, and constitute the principal contents of the study of history and literature.

First of all, we have to mention Confucius who lived in the latter part of the Spring and Autumn Period (770-476 BC). He was well versed in the historical records and literature of previous generations. Although he declared himself as a man "interested in ancient learning," he was not a man who swallowed ancient learning without digesting it, but one capable of advancing new theoretical ideas on the basis of assimilating the cultural heritage of the past. Confucius was the first thinker and educator in Chinese history to advance a systematic body of ethical and moral theories.

The study of human relationships in society was of great importance to Confucius. This was closely linked with the time in which he lived. The social chaos during the latter part of the Spring and Autumn Period caused a drastic change in the relationships between people such as rulers and subjects, ruling princes and ministers, and fathers and sons. The rites of the Zhou Dynasty had deteriorated, leaving people nothing to support their ideologies and actions. As a result, a social problem arose crying out for solution: By what principle should people's thought and actions be guided to achieve social stability? Many thinkers of the time gave their answers to this vital question. For Confucius the answer was clear: this principle was "Ren," or benevolence, or perfect virtue. Many people, before him and contemporary to him, talked about "Ren," but none of them explained it so systematically, theoretically, explicitly and concisely as to be easily acceptable to people as Confucius did.

What, then, is "Ren"? Confucius' answer was simple, it was how to conduct oneself. More specifically, it was the standards by which a "superior man" or man of virtue and high learning should live. A discussion of "Ren" must involve the problems of how to conduct oneself, how to deal properly with the relationships between members of a family, between rulers and subjects and between friends.

Confucius' disciples collected many of his philosophical sayings and compiled them into the book called *The Analects*. This became the most influential and most popular book in the history of Chinese culture. In *The Analects*, although in different circumstances Confucius used different words to define "Ren," the essence was always the same.

When Confucius spoke of "Ren," he did not proceed from ancestor worship, rather he gave plain explanations of how to conduct oneself. Neither did he proceed from protecting one part at the expense of another part, rather he tried his best to attend to the interest of both sides in the human relationship. His pupils asked him on various occasions, "What is 'Ren'?" He replied, "It is to love all men." One aspect of this was: "What you do not want done to yourself, do not do to others." Another was: "A man of perfect virtue, wishing to be established himself, seeks also to establish others; wishing to be enlarged himself, he seeks also to enlarge others." The combination of these two aspects is called "Zhong Shu Zhi Tao" or "the doctrine of loyalty and forbearance," and is regarded as the essence of "Ren."

To adjust such human relationships as between rulers and subjects, or fathers and sons, Confucius required a mutual respect between the two parties in accordance with the principle of loyalty and forebearance. For example, if a father wishes to see filial piety from his son, he should cherish a deep love and kindness for his son. If the son does not wish his father to treat him without love and kindness, he should attend to his father with filial piety. Similarly, if a ruler wishes his subjects to be loyal, he should behave like a ruler and have the moral character befitting a ruler. If a ruler does not behave like a ruler, a subject not like a subject, a father not like a father and a son not like a son, then it will be difficult to maintain stability in a family or in society.

It is clear that Confucius spoke of these in terms of ethics and morality. That is to say, a genuine ruler must observe ethical and moral rules, as must all others. Therefore, by "Ren" Confucius meant morality.

In *The Analects*, it is recorded: "Zi Zhang asked Confucius about perfect virtue. Confucius said, 'To be able to practice five things everywhere under heaven constitutes perfect virtue.' He begged to ask what they were, and was told, 'Gravity, generosity of soul, sincerity, earnestness, and kindness. If you are grave, you will not be treated with disrespect. If you are generous, you will win all. If you are sincere, people will repose trust in you. If you are earnest, you will accomplish much. If you are kind, this will enable you to employ the services of others.'" Here Confucius advanced five moral principles, and the general name of these principles is "Ren." But he did not limit his moral principles to these five. Sometimes, he said the five things were to be "benign, upright, courteous, temperate, and complaisant."

Both Confucius and Confucianism attached great importance to moral character, believing that one should not go against the principles of morality when dealing with matters. Morality should not be forgotten under any circumstances, especially when one is in a desperate plight. The pursuit of fortune is a general desire of man. However, it must be restrained by morality. A fortune is acceptable when the means by which it is amassed is acceptable according to moral rules. But it is never acceptable when the means break these rules. Man lives for morality, not for fortune, and only in this way does life have value. For this reason, Confucius said: "The mind of the superior man is conversant with righteousness; the mind of the mean man is conversant with gain."

According to Confucius, righteousness can be united with gain. However, a superior man should refrain from seeking only gain while neglecting righteousness. In fact, he did not refuse the richness of a state and the ordinary people. When he arrived in the State of Wei, he observed, "How numerous are the people!" Ran You, who was driving his carriage, said, "Since they are thus numerous, what more shall be done for them?" The Master replied, "Enrich them." Ran You asked further, "And when they have been enriched, what more shall be done?" The Master replied, "Teach them."

It can be seen that for Confucius "Ren" in fact was a general name for a myriad of virtues, and a standard for the value of man. At other times, he refers to this standard as the Dao (principle, or truth, or the right way). He said, "A man can enlarge the principles which he follows; those principles do not enlarge the man." Man is the subject, with the ability to understand and promote the truth. It is for this purpose that man set the Dao as the final goal of his whole life. The Dao, however, cannot be easily recognized or understood by man. Only by studying and exploring diligently, can man discover and experience the truth. In this sense, the Dao is more valuable than the life of a man. A man's life is limited but the Dao is eternal. Therefore, Confucius said with a deep sigh: "If a man in the morning hears the right way, he may die in the evening without regret." A man is qualified to be called a man of "Ren," only when he has discovered or experienced the truth. Such a man has transcended his own nature, becoming someone with noble ideals and high morality. Such a man, when the realization of his ideal requires that he sacrifice his life, he will do so without hesitation so as to follow his faith in the Dao. Over the long evolution of history, this outlook on life and death has gradually fashioned a common belief cherished by all the Chinese heroes and men of morality, which has become a spiritual motive force of the ongoing progress and development of the Chinese nation.

The advent of Chinese moral education must be attributed to Confucius. Later, many thinkers and educators came to know that it was imperative to promote the level of intelligence and morality of the people if civilization was to be promoted. Cai Yuanpei (1868-1940) a well-known modern educator, once said: "Moral education is fundamental to the perfect integrity of a man. Without morality, a man, even with a well-developed body and mind, is of no good use, but may take the advantage to venture evils." The Chinese nation has its own traditional virtues, such as honoring the integrity of the nation, reverence to the elderly and respect for teachers, helping and supporting the orphaned, the childless and the disabled and changing prevailing habits and customs.

The reason why the Chinese nation is different from the ancient Greeks, Indians and other peoples in the world lies in its different psychological quality being formed during the past thousands of years. Of the "common psychological qualities," there is the factor of honoring the integrity of a nation. Over the past thousands of years in the history of mankind, China has seen a number of national rejuvenation movements in which many national heroes were produced because of their honoring national integrity. What we mean by national integrity is to have a moral sense of and acting for safeguarding the dignity and independence of the Chinese nation. Particularly, the "noble spirit" advocated by Mencius has encouraged and inspired so many later national heroes to uphold the spirit. Wen Tianxiang (1236-1283), a minister and writer of the Southern Song Dynasty (1127-1279) never wavered when he was put in prison. In his work *The Song of Moral Sense*, he says: "In the universe, there exists a noble spirit. Endowed with it, everything takes its own form of existence. When it lowers, it becomes rivers and mountains. When it rises, it becomes the sun and stars. When man is endowed with it, he becomes a man of noble moral sense. It permeates everywhere, in heaven and on earth." He believed that with this noble moral sense, a man is determined to sacrifice his life at any time for the truth he always seeks. "Since olden days there's never been a man but dies; I'd leave a loyalist's name in history only."

Reverence to and supporting one's elders are also one of the virtues of the Chinese nation. During the Zhou Dynasty, there was "the rite of supporting the elderly," taking into consideration their need for nutrition only because of their getting weak and feeble. When the elderly lost the ability to work, it was only natural and reasonable to take care of them and respect them in society. They had rich experience of life, and the young should seek counsel from them and take note of what was useful in their teachings to educate future generations. There were many works in ancient times on the virtues of respecting and supporting the elderly.

China is a country with many ethnic groups. Changing prevailing habits and customs can help promote cultural exchanges between them. To learn from each other's strong points to offset one's weaknesses is greatly beneficial to the progress of civilization of the whole Chinese nation. Early in the Warring States Period (475-221 BC), King Wuling of the State of Zhao (r. 325-299 BC) urged his people to wear the short-tailored costumes of the neighboring tribes and to learn their skills of horsemanship and archery. In the past, warriors of all the states in central China had used horse-driven chariots, wearing loose gowns with large sleeves when they went into battle. This made action very inconvenient. The king found that the tribes often defeated their enemies using fewer troops, and this was because of their short-tailored costumes and skills in horsemanship and archery. Having realized this, he called on his people to adopt the same customs. As a result, the state was made stronger. At the same time, the success of the State of Zhao encouraged many other states to introduce the same practice. The reform, therefore, brought about a renovation of war tactics in China and increased the merging of ethnic groups. King Wuling was brilliant enough to see and act on the necessity of a change of prevailing customs and ritual system in order to meet the needs of the time.

In the history of Chinese culture, many examples have been recorded of the Han people learning from the strengths of other peoples and vise versa. For instance, Songtsam Gambo (c. 617-650),

71

a most outstanding personality in Tibetan history, initiated a marriage connection with the Tang Dynasty and introduced a series of reforms of the customs and prevailing habits in Tibet such as learning Han culture, working out a legal system, and inventing its own writing system. This not only developed the Tubo Kingdom (seventh to ninth centuries) but also promoted the friendly relations between the Han and Tibetan peoples.

During the latter part of the Warring States Period, Confucian scholars advanced the ideal of "Da Tong," or "Great Harmony." They believed that in such a world of Da Tong, men of talent and ability would be chosen to govern the state. The people would be sincere, and cultivate unity and cooperation. The love people held for members of their families would be extended to those outside their families, so that they would come to love and be kind to everyone. In this world of Da Tong, the elderly would be looked after properly until their death and the able-bodied would be employed and the young would be educated. Widows and widowers, the childless, the orphaned and the disabled would be cared for and properly supported.

In such a world, natural resources would be fully utilized. People would be pleased to make contributions to the prosperity of society. There would be no thefts, no riots, and no wars. For Confucians, Da Tong was the ideal world. To some extent this was unrealistic as there was no way that ancient scholars could have created such a world. However, it demonstrated the ancient people's opposition to the exploitation society in which they lived, and their longing for a good and ideal world.

With the ideal of a world of Da Tong, Confucianism by no means intended to escape from the reality of society and seek after a utopia. Since morality and ethics were so important to Confucianism, its doctrine emphasized the obligations that were due to society and how people really behaved. Taoism, another important strain of traditional Chinese thinking, denies the value of morality, legal systems and knowledge. Nevertheless, it does not advocate standing aloof from the world. Instead, it advocates entering the world by renouncing the world. As for Buddhism, its introduction to China had a great influence on Chinese culture, but it has been modified to such a degree that it has become Chinese Buddhism, in which the content of renunciation of the world has been reduced. Therefore, in traditional Chinese culture, there has never been any genuine philosophy of renunciation of the world.

In ancient China, a maxim which had a great influence on intellectuals was Mencius' statement: "Be good to and serve all when you are well off. Be decent and fulfil your obligations to society when you are poor." A decent person, even if he cannot govern the state and bring peace to it to realize his ideal, should not spare his efforts in cultivating his own morality and should undertake his duty and obligations to family and society.

It has been said that traditional Chinese culture is one of morals and ethics. This argument is not wholly without foundation. All humanistic parts of the culture including its history and literature are permeated with a moral and ethical ethos.

Section 2 The Features of the Chinese Science of History

China has an unbroken written history. Since its civilization began, recorded history has continued without failure. Its numerous historical documents and literature are replete with moral teachings on how to conduct oneself and how to rule a state.

In *The Book of Zhou* are recorded the teachings of Duke Zhao of Zhou to his people. One of the teachings says: "In ancient times, the State of Xia was very powerful and strong, but now it has declined. Its dominance was replaced by Yin (the Shang Dynasty), which also became known for its splendid accomplishments in history. But now it too has declined. We people of Zhou should think seriously of the causes that brought these two states down, and learn lessons of history. Duke Zhou also required his descendents to follow the examples of King Wen and King Wu of Zhou, to learn from their personal quality and integrity and carry on their undertakings. Taking history as a mirror or a lesson, this thought and consciousness in the teachings on how to conduct oneself and how to rule a state in ancient China has constituted an important symbol of the humanistic ethos in Chinese history books and documents.

In a sense, ancient Chinese science of history served as an encyclopedia of ancient Chinese culture and academic studies. It explored the relationships between man and nature, man and society, man and family and state, involving every aspect of culture and academic studies. The humanistic and moral ethos in traditional Chinese culture was prominently reflected in the ancient Chinese science of history.

Ancient Chinese history books and documents contained rich descriptions of man's social life, embracing all the significant aspects of social life, from kings and princes to generals and ministers and ordinary people. The *Spring and Autumn Annals*, compiled by Confucius, covered a history of 242 years of the State of Lu from 722 BC to 481 BC in a total of only 18,000 Chinese characters. All the major political and military events during that period were recorded, including military expeditions, political alliances and sacrificial ceremonies, in addition to marriages and funerals, fortifications and constructions, palaces and housing, hunting and farmland.

Man creates history. Many personalities are involved, and Chinese historians have been skilled at describing the features and characters of historical figures. In *Records of the Historian* by Sima Qian, a noted historian and thinker of the Western Han period (206 BC-25 AD), people from all parts of society are described, including kings, nobles, bureaucrats, men of letters and scholars, merchants, knights-errant, and even people at the lowest rung of the social ladder. Each person has been described so vividly that their personalities have been talked about ever since.

Records of the Historian is full of admiration for historical figures that had struggled against natural adversities and the wicked and evil forces of human society. Beginning with the time of the Yellow Emperor, the book records the harnessing and control of the environment, the amelioration of the soil, the planting of crops, and the invention of tools and instruments. Also recorded are heroes who rebelled against dark political forces and injustice in society, while justice and loftiness are glorified. For instance, it is recorded in the book that Yu the Great was so wholeheartedly engaged in his work of harnessing rivers and controlling floods that he forgot to come back home even though he passed by it on three occasions. It records the construction of a water channel project in the State of Zheng, and how the people studied the conditions and chose the appropriate plans for the project. Other examples include the harnessing of the Yellow River during the reign of Emperor Wudi of the Han Dynasty; the rebellion against the rule of King Zhou of the Shang Dynasty launched by kings Wen and Wu of the Zhou Dynasty; the story of Crown Prince Dan of the State of Yan, who sent Jin Ke to assassinate Emperor Qinshihuang and the heroic aspiration of the assassin; and the uprising launched by Chen Sheng and Wu Guang against the tyranny of the Qin Dynasty.

Records of the Historian also discusses political morality. Sima Qian believed that politics must follow its inherent principles, with the stress on education and supplemented by punishment. The key to good politics lay in rulers setting a good example for their people and cultivating them with virtue. He set out in his book how one could become a good monarch and a good subject.

Of great importance to Sima Qian was the self-cultivation of various personalities with different political views. He praised those statesmen who knew themselves well, and worked for the common good, at the expense of themselves. He also had a very high opinion of those knights-errant who honored friendship, kept good faith, took delight in helping others, sacrificed their own interests for the sake of others, always kept their word and aided people in straitened circumstances. They were upright and firm, and fought for justice without any pretensions to self-glorification or rewards. In spite of their mean social status, their deeds were beneficial to society and worthy of praise. He also told of a story of a Zhao family orphan guarded and cared for by Chen Ying and Chu Jiu, to promote the principles of loyalty and righteousness to be observed in the relationship between master and servant and between friends.

The humanistic spirit of morality is also discussed in the *History As a Mirror,* annals compiled by Sima Guang of the Song Dynasty (960-1279). He believed that the key to mankind's survival and development lay in the moral spirit of Ren, Yi, Li, Zhi and Xin or benevolence, righteousness, courtesy, intelligence and trustworthiness, and this had been demonstrated again and again throughout history. A man must have virtue and talent so as to be able to deal with other people and affairs of the world. Morality must be combined with talent: "Talent is the supplement of virtue; virtue is the director of talent....Thus, a man with perfect talent and virtue is called a sage; a man without talent and virtue is called a fool; a man with more virtue than talent is called a superior man; and a man with more talent than virtue is called a mean man." According to Sima Guang, a sovereign should be good at selecting and using his subordinates. Only by employing aides with talent and virtue could his government be honorable and competent. If the sovereign was a man with no talent and virtue, and his aides were all mean men also without talent and virtue, his government would surely be chaotic. Sima Guang attached particular importance to political morality, believing Xin (trustworthiness) and Yi (righteousness) are the foundations of a state. If the people lost trust in their government, the state would not last long even if it had some temporary achievements. He stressed: "Xin is the great treasure of the sovereign of a state. To win a state, one must win its people. To win the people, one must win their trust. Without trust, a sovereign cannot lead his people. Without people, the state will inevitably be lost. Thus, an ancient king would not forfeit the trust of his people, and the ancient overlord of a state would never bully his neighboring states. A good ruler never abuses his people and a good patriarch never abuses his family. Bad ones do just the opposite."

The ancient Chinese history books, when discussing a historical personage, did so according to   standards and values to establish what contribution he had made to the state and society and whether he had observed moral and ethical principles in his life. From this we can see an expression of the humanistic moral spirit which permeates Chinese history books.

Ancient Chinese historians also held that historians should study the laws governing the development of history. To this end, many historians have worked hard and made great contributions.

On the one hand, ancient Chinese historians strove to understand history as a whole. For instance, the *Records of the Historian* contains special chapters describing and recording socio-economic activities and analyzing the socio-economic development of the times under review. It describes agriculture, mining, handicrafts and commerce as productive and economic activities indispensable to human life which develop according to their own rules. Sima Qian records historical events showing that economic development can induce political change. He confirms the saying that "When people have sufficient food and clothing, they understand the meaning of honor and disgrace. When the granaries are full, they understand the meaning of courtesy," holding that a man's mental outlook is greatly influenced by economic conditions.

On the other hand, Chinese historians probed the complicated relationships between laws and institutions on the one hand and ideology, culture and political life on the other. Thus, the best history books can be almost regarded as encyclopedias of social life. In his *Records of the Historian*, Sima Qian noted the laws and institutions practiced before the reign of Emperor Wudi of the Han Dynasty. In his *History of the Han Dynasty*, Ban Gu recorded these in even greater detail. During the Tang Dynasty, books were specially written on such institutions, such as the *Decrees and Institutions of the Government* by Liu Zhi and *A General Record of Government Institutions* by Du You. Such other specialized books were very popular and prevalent in the later Song, Yuan, Ming and Qing dynasties. The purpose of studying such subjects was to find the origin and development of the institutions so as to know their faults and merits.

Nature is indispensable to human society. From nature come the material means on which the existence and operation of a society depend. Meanwhile, nature may bring happiness or disaster to society. Therefore Chinese history books have registered, in a fair amount of detail, the changes of nature as well as its connection with and effects on man and society. In Confucius' *Spring and Autumn Annals*, for instance, all the important astronomical and geographical changes in a period of 242 years were recorded, including eclipses of the sun and moon, earthquakes, landslides, celestial change, floods, droughts and insect pests. Astronomy and geography constituted an important part of the ancient historical records. These records, which systematically registered all the important astronomical changes, gave later readers a knowledge of the real political life in a certain period, particularly the relationship between agricultural production and the astronomical changes. Of course, misunderstandings and superstitions in the explanations of natural phenomena have also often been involved.

As to geographical records, during the pre-Qin period, both physical and administrative geographical conditions had been recorded distinctly. Xiao He, an important strategist who helped Liu Bang establish the Western Han Dynasty, collected as many books as he could in order to increase his geographical knowledge. During the Western Han period, the humanistic aspects in the contents of the geographical records increased. *Records of the Historian* contains descriptions of local economies, taxation, produce, ways of life, customs and water conservancy projects. In *History of the Han Dynasty*, a special chapter on geography is devoted to records of administrative divisions, the rivers and mountains, folk customs, climate and population, initiating the style and scale of a national annals of localities. During the periods of the Wei, Jin, and Southern and Northern Dynasties (220-589), contents of geographical records were greatly expanded by adding special descriptions about localities, mountains and rivers, customs, temples and monasteries, and produce. From the Sui Dynasty (581-618) to the end of the Ming Dynasty (1368-1644), there were not only national annals of regions, but also chronicles of localities, and the compilation of such chronicles was one of the major functions of histeriographers and scholars at various levels of the government.

In ancient China, historians sought to explore the relationships between astronomical phenomena, geographical conditions and social and political life. Some came to understand and grasp certain relationships between the three aspects. Many exaggerated such relationships out of proportions, talking of "communications between Heaven and man" and other forms of superstition, laying themselves open to oriticism by other historians.

It should be particularly noted that around the time that the Qing Dynasty (1644-1911) replaced the Ming, some philosophers and historians began to understand certain dialectic relationship between the natural environment and social life. They held that the history of nature should be distinguished from the history of mankind, that the history of nature has its own laws of development, that each astronomical or geographical phenomenon is not necessarily linked to human society and the laws of natural changes cannot be made to correspond totally to those of mankind. They also held that one should observe the history of nature being adapted by man to meet human needs. Man not only needs to acquire from nature the material means for survival, but also to reshape it. In the process of reshaping nature, man constantly enriches and develops his knowledge about nature.

Here, we would like to give a brief introduction to the many different styles used by ancient Chinese historians, the most influential being the biographical and annalistic styles. The *Records of the Historian* was the first example of the biographical style, while *History As a Mirror* is typical of the annalistic style. Sima Qian's procedures in writing the *Records of the Historian* are as follows:

1.   Ascertaining the historical facts. An important standard for him was whether they reliably reflected history, or whether they involved important aspects of human life. He scrutinized numerous materials and even made on-the-spot investigations to ascertain their reliability.

2.   Setting the styles. The styles used in the *Records of the Historian* include biographic sketches of emperors, interpretive and descriptive records, biographies of aristocratic families, and collected biographies. Arranged in the order of years, the biographic sketches

of emperors give a brief account of the evolution of history. Military, political and economic matters, foreign affairs and astronomical and geographical events are chronicled using interpretive and descriptive records. Biographies of aristocratic families and collected biographies record communities and individuals that have left important marks in history.

3. Method of description. *Records of the Historian* deals briefly with the past, giving detailed descriptions of the present. The book is filled with the author's strong personal sentiments and gives skilful descriptions of a character's nature and characteristics through typical examples. He was successful in piecing together related events described in various different styles in his book, while combining them as a whole by way of cross-reference.

For example, when Liu Bang, historically known as Emperor Gaozu of the Han Dynasty, was preparing to fight for control of the empire, he employed many of his competent strategists and able ministers. In the "Biographic Sketch of Emperor Gaozu," limitation of space meant that the author could not give a full account of all the merits of the emperor's strategists and ministers. He therefore made a list of all his meritorious supporters and aides, and described their achievements and contributions in other stories such as the "Pedigree of the Grand Minister Xiao He and the biographies of Han Xin and Chen Ping. In this way, he not only linked relevant historical events described in different styles in various parts of the book, but also expressed his views about these events. In the "Pedigree of the Grand Minister Xiao He," which records the merits of the minister, only four important events are included, such as collecting books and the laws and documents of the Qin Dynasty, recommendation of Han Xin as the Commander-in-chief, appeasement of the territory in Guanzhong (now Shaanxi Province), and recommendation of Cao Sen as his successor. His assistance to Emperor Huidi, on the recommendation of Emperor Gaozu's last will, and a much less important event in the whole life of Xiao He, are merely referred to in passing in the account of Emperor Huidi's visit to him when he was dying.

The procedures by which Sima Guang wrote his *History As a Mirror* are as follows:

1. Ascertaining the historical facts. The elements of history that the author selected were those concerning the rise and fall of a state, the life and death of the people, good actions to serve as examples and evil actions to serve as warnings. These involve good and evil politics of imperial dynasties through the ages, and the foods, products, punishments, rituals, ranks and positions, and military affairs. According to these criteria, the author and his assistants collected and ascertained all the relevant materials from official records as well as other documents of the past dynasties. In dealing with different accounts of an event, the author "screened many records before drawing conclusions," "compared different versions" and "used reliable facts."

2. Setting the styles. Sima Guang and his assistants first made out a guide to the styles to be used in the book, including 36 items regarding the phraseology and form. And then they ascertained the year and month in which events happened. They used the year as an entry to a ruler and a ruler as an entry to a dynasty, but only the year and appellation of one ruler of one state was to be adopted when many states co-existed. And then they arranged long chronicles of the events in the order of years, and made a final revision under a unified criterion.

3. Method of description. The cause and the result of an important historical event had to be made clear and consistent. The author often selected one or two of the most important events extending over a long period of time in a particular stage of history or a certain dynasty as the outline of his accounts together with supplementary descriptions of other less important events. Minor historical events which could not be given their own independent entry were dealt with in accompanying or additional descriptions.

Biographical and annalistic styles each have their merits and shortcomings. Zhang Xuecheng, a Qing Dynasty historian, for example, wrote history in the styles of biography, annals, interpretive records and romances in a bid to set up examples for posterity. However, using these methods, the important contents and their developments might not be all included and clearly told. Annals can give a relatively full list of historical events in the order of years, but may omit many of the substantial details and richness of history. The history of anything and anyone, which was marked with a date of time, must be recorded, even those which are not particularly important. But those things and people lacking a date of occurrence, though they had a very important influence on the development of history, might not be given a detailed reflection in history. Different historians disagreed as to which style should play the chief role. Zhang Xuecheng declared that biographies could include some of the styles used in annals, but annals could not use a biographical style. This was particularly true of descriptions of human activities in the evolution of history.

Since history is made up of events and is also a stage for human activities, the two aspects must both be recorded. Therefore, the best suitable style should fully use and develop the advantages of biographies and annals. The advantage of annals lies in their clarity of description, while that of biographies lies in their cross-reference of related events. Ideally, as far as possible, the two styles should be combined.

As to the method of research, ancient Chinese historians stressed that one should understand historical events by thinking deeply about each one and coming to know them as if the author himself had experienced the process in person. In this way, he could make a justifiable judgement about each historical event and figure. Meanwhile, a standard of proof must be observed. Without proof 'facts' were not credible. Through various methods, historians should distinguish the truth of historical materials from the false, laying history studies on the solid and reliable foundation of the materials available.

Ancient historians also discussed lessons to be learnt from historical events. The purpose of studying history is to seek enlightenment therefrom. If the study of history does not serve mankind, then it is of no use. Wang Fuzhi, a great thinker and scholar of the early Qing Dynasty, said: "The value of history lies in its service to posterity as a teacher. When a historian records many historical events in detail but neglects important events that can serve a lesson for the coming generations, what is the use of this historian?" Learning lessons from history, however, should start from the actual conditions of reality, and should not copy blindly what ancients did. "It should be done in the light of each particular event, considering expedient and suitable measures in different occasions. Even in the same generation, the way may be different. Even in one case, things can be different from each other. It is better to doubt what has been said than to stick to it against reason," said Wang Fuzhi who was opposed to subjectivism and biased views. This, however, is not an easy task.

Personal cultivation of historians' own morality and skills was considered to be indispensable to their studies and writings. The Qing Dynasty historian Zhang Xuecheng proposed the idea of "virtues of historians." He believed that historians' virtues and learning inevitably influenced their studies. A historian whose mind and actions were bad would distort history and his knowledge of history would be biased. Other historians, though virtuous and noble-minded, should deepen their level of study because they also sometimes drew incorrect conclusions from their studies.

The meaning and connotations of "virtues of historians" were broad. A historian's honesty and faithfulness were considered to be enormously important. The historian must never distort historical facts, even when subjected to violence and persecution. During the Spring and Autumn Period, Dong Gu, an official historian of the State of Jin, was honored as a "righteous historian" by succeeding historians. In 607 BC, Zhao Dun, the executive minister of the State of Jin, fled his country to avoid being murdered by Duke Ling of Jin. Zhao Chuan, a relative of Zhao Dun, killed the duke. In this case, Dong Gu believed that Zhao Dun was guilty of the crime. Defying his power and influence, Dong boldly wrote in his book *Zhao Dun Murdered His Sovereign*, for which Dong was honored as an upright historian.

Ancient Chinese historians held that only with a lofty moral character and basic professional skills could a historian reveal the truth of an historical event, whether in historical research or in relating a historical event, and only thus could he enable the public to draw lessons from it.

Section 3 The Humanistic Spirit and Artistic Charm of Classical Chinese Literature

China is rich in literary works which artistically depict the lives and feelings of their subjects and have become an important part of traditional Chinese culture.

The moral spirit and humanity of Chinese literary classics is a broad question which we will discuss only in terms of poetry and drama. Ancient Chinese poetry sought after the soul, the eyes, the emotions and the talents of a poem. These were a true reflection of the spirit of morality and humanism.

The soul of a poem. In contact with various natural and social phenomena, a poet has to be moved by something that stimulates him to take up his pen. Why is he so moved? His life experiences, learning and demeanor, and his mind and aspiration, or his entire soul and heart all contribute to the effect. For example, the Tang poet Li Shen (772-846) wrote a poem, the first three lines of which are:

Each seed that's sown in spring,
Will make autumn yields high.
What will fertile fields bring?

Up to here, he has only made a general description of a natural phenomenon, and its evolution and the true social conditions. Watching the scene, some may praise the prosperous and peaceful times, others might eulogize the year's bumper harvest, but the poet concludes his verse like this:

Of hunger peasants die.

The final touch is to the depth of the "soul" of the poem. The poet has advanced a question for thought: Nature's gifts are abundant and the peasants have worked hard, then why is it that they "die of hunger"? The poet does not give a direct answer, but everyone knows that the killer is extortionate taxation and relentless exploitation.

Lu You, (1125-1210), a great poet of the Southern Song Dynasty, was born at a time when the Northern Song Dynasty was fast on its way to extinction. He was brought up in a family full of patriotic spirit. Politically, he was adamant for resistance against the Jin invaders, but he was continually suppressed by those who favored capitulation. In the last years of his life, he retired to his hometown, but he never gave up his faith in the recovery of the Central Plain of China. One of his poems depicts a scene which he saw one night as he walked along a riverbank: Peasants staying up all night watering their farmland and traders preparing for the early morning market. He was moved to sigh: "To earn a living, the people work so hard/I feel ashamed taking a state salary for doing nothing." At that time there was nothing that the poet could do for his country, and he was forced to retire to his hometown. There, he lived on a meager pension, and this small sum weighed on his conscience. The poem shows a poet's noble soul of attachment to others and restraint of his own interests.

The great Tang Dynasty poet Du Fu (712-770), in his verse entitled "My Cottage Unroofed by Autumn Gales," depicts his family's plight when his cottage's roof was destroyed in a storm. So far so good, if he had declared at the end of his poem "Could I get mansions covering a few miles/I'd house all my family members and make them beam with smiles." But he writes: "Could I get mansions covering ten thousand miles/I'd house all scholars poor and make them beam with smiles." And he continues: "Frozen in my unroofed cot, content I'd die." This shows that the poet was selfless in his thoughts of others. The soul of a poem reflects the heart of a poet who loves the people, which is also the artistic expression of Confucius' doctrine of "benevolence."

Du Fu loved other living things as well as the people. During the rebellion launched by An Lushan and Shi Siming in 755-763 during the Tang Dynasty, he suffered greatly in his roving life. His son died of hunger but he took compassion on a sick horse and even a dying tree in his poems. In his "A Bony Horse," he wishes he can help this horse that has been abandoned by troops, but he cannot, so he hopes that someone else will do so.

Not only benevolent to animals, he also laments the sight of a tree blown down in a gale outside the door of his house: "Like a tiger collapsed or a dragon smashed up down to bushes/On its bosom is stained blood and tears." He continues as if missing a lost bosom friend: "Now that I have no one to recite my new verses to/My straw cottage will become colorless from now on."

Meng Haoran (689-740), another famous Tang poet, wrote a very popular poem:

This morn of spring in bed I'm lying,
Not to awake till birds are crying.
After one night of wind and showers,
How many are the fallen flowers!

The first three lines give a general description of the scenes and drowsiness in the spring days. The feelings for cherishing flowers of the writer did not gush out till the last line.

As to cherishing flowers, we cannot but think of Lu You. He loved plum blossoms the best. He wrote many poems about plum flowers. One of them goes like this: "One or two flowers bring back a message of the coming spring/In the breezes more flowers on the southern and northern branches are day by day appearing/But seeing a full bloom I know they will sadly decline in no time/I would rather advise them not to bloom so quickly in the prime."

Generally speaking, flower admirers hope to see a full blooming as early as possible. But the poet thinks differently, wishing plum flowers not to bloom and wither away too quickly. This is intended not only for flowers, but also for the writer himself to have a longer period of time to stay with his fondling. He is sincere and selfless. He is also truly affectionate.

The soul of a poem reflects not only the heart of the poet that shares the joys and sorrows of the people and cherishes everything in nature and society, but also an ardent heart. When his warm and ardent patriotic feelings for his motherland turned to be a lamenting song, Lu You gushed out his feelings like a volcano which bursts into an eruption that shakes the earth. In his "Lamentation," he writes:

"….Even if I am buried five meters deep underground/My bones may turn to dust but not my heart/Will not anybody wish to be the brightest star shining over the vast land?/Will not anybody wish to revenge the predecessors for feuds of past generations?"

Never misunderstand that he had intentions to brag of his heroic action. In his "Testament to My Son," which he wrote on his deathbed, he says, "When royal armies recover the Central Plain/Do not forget to tell your sire in sacred rite," wishing nothing at all for his own posthumous honors. His determination to recover his motherland did not end with his death. His determination would shine forever, inspiring posterity to carry out their duties for the nation. This is the artistic crystallization of the "noble spirit" of the Confucian doctrine.

Lu You was no less loyal to his beloved than to his country. He frequently indulged himself in the passionate memory of his late first wife, Tang Wan, who was compelled by his mother to divorce him and eventually sacrificed her life for him. In his eighties, conscious of his soon becoming a clod of clay beneath the hill, he still revisited the garden alone where they used to meet to find her traces and was beside himself with tears. His heart was not only warm and ardent like a fire but also unfailingly sincere.

The discerning eyes of a poet. A book is a medium of knowledge that a writer finds out from the internal links of things through logical thinking. Like a scholar or a scientist, a poet must also have a pair of sharp and discerning eyes that can see through the appearance to get at the essence of a matter. Besides, they should be able to perceive all the properties and details of the matter. A poet draws all that responds to his aesthetic ideal into his mind and modeled that to his images for his production. Therefore, a poem, whatever its content may be in the reasoning, descriptive, lyric and even argumentation styles, is quite different from any other works.

Zhong Rong (?-c. 518), a scholar and commentator of the Liang Dynasty (502-557) in classic poetry, had given some exemplified contents or themes for poem writing.

For instance, Qu Yuan, a great poet of the State of Chu during the Warring States Period, whose political viewpoints were not adopted by the ruler of his time, was deposed and exiled and finally drowned himself. And also Wang Zhaojun, a concubine of the Emperor Yuandi in the Western Han period, who volunteered to marry the ruler of the Huns, making a certain contribution to the establishment of friendly relations between the Han Dynasty and the Huns. Their suppressed grievance, indignation and passion had to be released by way of poems. That is to say, poetry is the best way to express one's own feelings.

Of course, poetry can also be used to reason, describe and even discuss something, only a bit different in form from scientific and literary works. Ye Xie (1627-1703), a scholar of poetry of the Qing Dynasty, said, "Is it necessary for a poet to give the reasons of anything that everybody can explain? Is it necessary for a poet to describe an event that everybody can describe?" Then, how can a poet reason out such things that ordinary people find hard to explain? In the following example, we quote Zhang Jie of the Tang Dynasty as saying in his verses entitled "The Pit Where Emperor Qin Burned the Classics":

Smoke of burnt classics gone up with the empire's fall,
Fortress and rivers could not guard the capital.
Before the pit turned cold, eastern rebellion spread;
The leaders of revolt were not scholars well read.

This poem is a satire on the burning of books and burying scholars alive by the First Emperor of Qin. The emperor so detested those scholars for their criticism of his policies by quoting the teachings from ancient classics that he had all these books burnt and Confucian scholars buried alive, a step he believed to be the final and vital blow. But he had never expected that before the pit turned cold, so many people would stage revolts in the eastern area. Of all revolt leaders, Liu Bang and Xiang Yu, both giving decisive and vital blows to the emperor, were not scholars themselves. The last two lines tell of a fact worthy of thought, that is, the short life of an imperial dynasty had no connections with either any scholars or any books. Without the confidence of people in a ruler's policy, any maintenance of a lasting and peaceful regime is definitely impossible.

From these examples, we can see that the peculiarity of the materials of a poem lies not in the peculiarity of the theme. In an article, we could explain the reasons why the emperor could not save his regime by burning books and burying scholars alive, couldn't we? Yes we could. Apart from tapping the useful content of materials, materials can simply be employed logically in a poem, even irrespective of such a common method as to deduce a conclusion from premises, by piecing out many terms of images, such as smoke of burnt books, fortress and rivers, ruined palaces, cold pit, revolts and the valiant rebellion leaders. And in a form of flashback, that is, the empire's fall, the poet drew a serious lesson from history. The poet had deep vision.

Materials of a story or for a descriptive theme can also be used for poem writing. But in narrative poems, the arrangement of events is dependent on the flow of feelings. "The Everlasting Regret" is one example, written in the Tang Dynasty by Bai Juyi (772-846). The process and details of the revolt of An Lushan, the Emperor Xuanzong (r. 712-756) of the Tang Dynasty fleeing the capital, and the mutiny at the Ma Wei Slope could take hours for a story-teller or ballad-singer to recount. But in this narrative poem, the poet condensed each of these events to one line: "but rebels beat their war drums, making the earth quake," to describe the rebel leader An Lushan's storming into the Tang capital Changan; "six armies would not march — what could be done? — with speed," to describe the royal soldiers' mutiny; and "until Lady Yang was killed before the steed," to describe the death of the emperor's favorite concubine (Yang Yuhuan). The poet lavishes more detailed and passionate descriptions on the emperor's sorrows and grief after he had lost his beloved. "On western waters blue and western mountains green/The monarch's heart was daily gnawed by sorrow keen/The moon viewed from his tent shed a soul-searing light/The bells heard in night rain made a heart-rending sound." "Fireflies flitting the hall, mutely he pined away/The lonely lampwick burned out, still he could not sleep/Slowly beat drums and rang bells, night began to grow long/Bright shone the Milky Way, daybreak seemed to come late/The lovebird tiles grew chilly with hoar frost so strong/And his kingfisher quilt was cold, not shared by a mate/One long, long year the dead and the living were parted/Her soul came not in dreams to see the brokenhearted." In a word, this poem appears to tell the passions of the emperor for his lost beloved rather than an account of the mutiny. Without passions, there will be no narratives. That is one of the features of the materials to make up a poem.

Poetic materials can also be applied to argument. For example, in his "Recalling the Past," Lu You writes: "Ministers are all thinking about the safety of themselves/Qin Kui is not the only traitor to betray his country/It is hopeless to find an able and competent minister like Guan Zhong [a statesman in the Spring and Autumn Period]/There are also no patriots to lament over the loss of their motherland." The poet not only recalled the bad situation of the early days when the Song Dynasty court fled south, but also condemned those in power who sued for peace and their decadence.

From the above examples, we can see that whatever can be used by the poet to express his love, worry and hatred can become materials for writing poems. But it requires keener vision and observation of a poet.

Poetic emotions. A poet may be strongly moved by any object or event that can form a poetic image in his mind. This image then is developed with the rhymes of his emotions into a poem that can inspire an emotional response in his readers. So a poet is totally affected by his feelings during the whole process of his production.

Humans, without exception, are creatures with feelings. But what are the peculiar feelings of a poet? They may be summarized as ardor, sincerity, typicality and individualization.

First it is an ardent emotion.

Feelings are gradually deposited from one's experience, accomplishment and conviction, which usually remain in a static and potential state. As outside factors light up a resonance of feelings of a poet, his feelings may burst out in the presentation of joy, anger, sadness, happiness, love, hatred or desire. V.G. Belinsky, a literary theorist of Russia in the 19th century, said: "Feelings are one of the principal motive forces of the natural instinct of a poet. Without feelings, there will be no poet."

In the relationship between objective events and the feelings of a poet, on the one hand, events can stimulate and determine the feelings. On the other, a poet paints his works with a color of feelings. For example, in her "Slow, Slow Song," the Song Dynasty lyric poet Li Qingzhao (1084-c.1151) wrote: "The ground is covered with yellow flowers, faded and fallen in showers/Who will pick them up now?/Sitting alone at the window, how could I but quicken the pace of darkness that won't thicken?/On plane's broad leaves a fine rain drizzles as twilight grizzles." Under such circumstances, one cannot but heave a sigh like the writer: "Oh, what can I do with a grief beyond belief!" In another example, Du Fu in his "Spring View" wrote these lines: "Grieved o'er the years, flowers are moved to tears/Seeing us part, birds cry with broken heart." The author expressed his sentiment over the turmoil of the time by means of flowers, the dews on which seemed to become his tears; and by means of birds, whose cry seemed to become the rattle of saber that made everyone frightened. Still another exemplary work of Lu You is "Song of Divination," an ode to the mume blossom, "Beside the broken bridge and outside the post hall/A flower is blooming forlorn/Saddened by her solitude at nightfall/By wind and rain she's further torn/Let other flowers their envy pour/To spring she lays no claim/Fallen in mud and ground to dust, she seems no more/but her fragrance is still the same."

Even blooming at nightfall and in the wind and rain beside the broken bridge and outside the post hall, did plum flowers really have their own solitude and sadness? No. This was but the mood of the author himself, which was alien to plum flowers. As to the praise to the flower, it means the resolute vows of the author not to be conquered and squeezed by those ministers in power who sued for peace.

From the above examples, we can see that the force of a poet's feelings could change the quality and shapes of things. They could change beautiful flowers and charming bird's chirrups into tears and fears, or make anthropomorphize mume flowers to feel sad and have a noble quality.

The ardent passion of a poet can change both the quality and shape of things. There is a folk song, entitled "Parting," going like this:

"We'll never part unless heaven turned to earth! We'll never part unless east turned to west! We'll never part unless officials turned orderlies! Leaving me, you can't be separated from me! Leaving you, I can't be separated from you! Even if we both have to die, we'll never part as separated ghosts."

In this song, a fire of love is burning.

Of course, not all the poems are filled with the feelings of fury, indignation or sorrow. Some are sentimental and languishing. For instance, in his lyric to the tune of "Song of Picking Mulberries," the writer Xin Qiji (1140-1207) wrote: "I know what grief is now that I am old/I would not have it told/I would not have it told/But only say I'm glad that autumn's cold." We can also see the expression of sentiments in Li Qingzhao's lines when she missed her faraway husband: "I fear the parting grief would make me sadder look/I've much to say, yet pause as soon as I begin/Recently I've grown thin, not that I'm sick with wine/Nor that for autumn sad I pine." The passions are either profound or consistent. Frivolity and flightiness are not poetic emotions.

Poetic emotions are typical. Such emotions, or feelings, are commonly shared by the broad mass of people while they are fresh and individualized with a certain characteristic. We have mentioned in the preceding section that the feelings of cherishing people and things, of hatred and worry about the times are all feelings of poetry. But sometimes, the feelings directly expressed in a poem are the feelings of some characters in the poem other than those of the author himself. The feelings of the author are indirectly reflected in his attitude toward the feelings of the characters. In a lyric written by Liu Yong (?-c.1053) of the Northern Song Dynasty, a lady in a city who was missing her far-off husband is described as the following:

"Not a word has been received since my indifferent love left home. If I had known this before, I would not have been regretful now for not locking up the horse. I would have kept him sitting before the window to read and write the whole day. And with my embroidering works, I would have accompanied him to spend the prime time of our lives."

At that time, literati and scholar-officials despised this lyric simply because a woman, according to the feudal tradition, should encourage her husband to seek after his career and ambition in society so as to bring home the glory and benefit for his wife and children. How could a woman have acted like this? In fact, this sort of writing imitating the voices of a resentful and desolate woman, or a husband drafted into the army, a music player, and a female professional singer should be taken as dramatic poems and the writer and narrator should not be confused. The detailed and lively description of the sorrows of an ordinary woman who was forced to confine herself in such an isolated family life and could not but long for a reunion with her husband showed that the poet had sympathy and understanding for the woman. This is truly what we mean by the feelings of a poem.

Typification requires that generality be conveyed through individuality. Hence the typical feelings of a poet should be fresh with a specific character. Generally speaking, for instance, people usually feel emotional when they part from their dear ones and friends, but Su Shi (1037-1101), a writer of the Song Dynasty, wrote of his separation from his younger brother: "Men have sorrow and joy, they part or meet again/The moon may be bright or dim, she may wax or wane/There has been nothing perfect since the olden days./So let us wish that man will live long as he can/Though miles apart, we'll share the beauty she displays."

Meanwhile, Li Bai (701-762), a great poet of the Tang Dynasty, wrote a poem to his dear friend Wang Lun, who was as light-hearted as himself and had seen Li off with a song, not tears. In the poem

Li said, "When he is about to leave by boat/Suddenly Li Bai hears a song wafting from the riverbank/Though the water in the Peach Pool is one thousand *chi* deep/Its depth is far less than the feeling of Wang Lun who sees me off."

While men of letters felt sympathy for singsong girls or courtesans or female performing artists, they generally sympathized with those pretty women for their suffering ill fates. Bai Juyi, a poet of the Tang Dynasty, when he first heard the performance of a female *pipa* (a four-stringed musical instrument) player, was deeply moved by her extraordinary skills and astonished to find that she was hardly known by the public and lacked a comfortable family life. He wrote: "Both of us in misfortune go from shore to shore/Meeting now, need we have known each other before?" So he thought he should put her on an equal footing, sharing her sorrows in her life. Only under such a particular situation, "the exiled blue-robed host" (author) was moved to tears. Such a feeling is striking and full of personality.

The feelings of poetry are sincere.

"Sincere feelings can only be expressed with a sincere heart. And only with sincere feelings, can a true poem be produced." The appeal of Du Fu's poems lies in his honesty. Once he talked about his ambitions in a poem, saying: "Though I was born not clever enough/I wish to become a man like Ji and Qi." Despite the fact that Du Fu had never been appointed to important positions all his life, as had Ji and Qi by the sage-king Shun, we can still assert that his feelings expressed in all his works, such as "Being worried about the broad masses of people in a disaster year/I can only give a deep sigh from the bottom of my warmest heart" were sincere. In Li Bai's verses, we also find that he was not aiming to show off his generosity when he says in a poem: "The fur coat worth a thousand coins of gold/And flower-dappled horse/May both be sold to buy good wine that we may drown the woes age-old...."

Poetic talents. In the foregoing passages, we have discussed about the quality of a poet: having an ardent heart, a pair of keen eyes, and with honest and sincere feelings. However, this is not all that is needed to become a poet. A poet must have a talent for poetry. We have said that a poet should use his or her "faculty of imagination" as a furnace to melt what he or she perceives and feels into images with feelings as fuel. So, what we mean by talent for poetry is to denote first the great faculty of imagination.

When a poet starts to compose a poem, he or she has to transform ideas into artistic images. Though some poems erupt with ardent feelings from a poet's mind like lava from a volcano, without using figurative words, like "Recalling the Past" by Lu You, quoted above, yet most poems were produced from images. The lyric poem "Green Jade Cup," written by He Zhu (1052-1125), a Song Dynasty lyric composer, provides an example:

If you ask me how deep and wide I'm lovesick,
Just see the misty stream where weed grows thick,
The town overflowing with willow down that wafts on breeze,
The drizzling rain that yellows all mume trees!

Here we can see that the author doesn't answer the question "how" with such conceptual words as numbers and quantitative adjectives, but conveys his idea with three images that not only imply meanings of immensity, but also of continuation and vastness. What a wonderful imaginative power the poet had!

Apart from a great power of imagination, a poet must have a strong ability in the use of poetic language.

Poetry is characterized by the most profound and complex emotions to be conveyed by the brevity of expression in words. To write or to read a poem equally requires creative imagination. A "single word" in a poem is intended to help the readers to activate their imagination to enjoy the poetic aesthetics. Theorists of poetry summarized this way as "the key of allusion." For instance, in one of the poems entitled "A Maid of Honor" by Zhang Hu (c.785-852) of the Tang Dynasty, he writes: "The moon casts shadows of a tree on the palace gate/Her longing eyes but saw a heron nest and nothing more/Drawing her jade hairpin, near a candle she came/To save a moth brushing aside the red flame." At first sight, the actions of the maid are discontinuous and sporadic. Now she is outside staring at the nest, then inside brushing aside the flame to save the moth. One image jumps to another abruptly, leaving blanks between them. However, there is a subtle psychological process linking them, which requires the readers' imagination. One may imagine what she is thinking while looking at the nest: in the warm nest a pair of herons are sleeping neck over neck. Waking from their sweet dreams early the next morning, they would fly out wing to wing, soaring high over the palace walls to the blue sky and white clouds. How people would envy such a scene! When she thinks of this, she cannot but be moved, her eyes looked languishing with a lover's desire. Then she finds herself alone in the moonlight, single and lonely, and unable to take a step out of the palace walls. She withdraws to her chamber gloomily. At that moment she finds a moth trapped and tortured by the lamp oil. Like her, it is subjected to misfortune. A feeling of compassion is naturally aroused in her heart and she saves the moth.

The actions of the character in the poem are sporadic and discontinuous. But the subtle and delicate psychological movement of the character is like a subterranean river running silently underneath the lines. Classical theory calls this condensed conceivability.

In some works of great poets, allusions and implications are frequently used. This is called condensed rhetoric. In the poem "On the River," composed by Du Fu, there is the line: "To achieve my ambitions, I have to look into the mirror again and again." What did he look at? Certainly he wanted to see how old he was, and whether he was still able to achieve his ambition. If he found he was still young and bright, then he could give himself an affirmative and encouraging answer, and wouldn't repeatedly look into the mirror. Unfortunately, in the mirror, he saw only a senile and decaying man. If he were resigned to reality, he would look into the mirror no longer. However, he was such a poet that he regarded himself as Ji and Qi (two famous and respected statesmen in history) and had a vehement desire to achieve his ambitions, so he did not give up hope, and looked into the mirror once more. With these few words, he revealed his psychology from his worries to disappointment, then his refusal to resign himself to failure, his sentiment, predicament and ambitions.

This example justifies the poet's succinct and proper wording. Poets not only elaborate on their verses, but also on their wording. For instance, in a line of a poem, Du Fu writes: "All mountains rise and fall till they reach Thatched Gate." A single word "reach" suggests a full dynamic sense of these mountains. In his other verses, he writes: "The boundless plain is fringed with stars hanging low/The moon upsurges with the river on the flow," in which the characteristics of "upsurges" and "hanging" are beautifully and succinctly worded. As the night skies are clean and clear, people's eyesight can reach the horizon. So they can see the stars on the horizon, which seem to hang down from the sky vault overhead. Only by having seen the moon reflected in the river water, heaving and rolling, could people be conscious of the long river that is running. "Upsurges" and "hanging" make the idea and image in the poem dynamic, suggesting a sense of vividness and brightness.

Cultivation of imagination and the capability of expression is required of a poet, as is painstaking training. Lu You taught his son how to compose a poem, saying that "if you are determined to learn to write poems, you have to work hard in many things beside simply writing." That is to say, in addition to the cultivation of skills in the writing, he has to foster a poetic mind, to sharpen a keen vision and to enrich a passion, working hard on the preparations for composing poems.

We have just discussed the humanistic spirit in classical poetry. Now let's turn to a brief discussion of traditional Chinese opera.

There are three kinds of ancient opera cultures in the world. These are Greek tragedies and comedies, Indian Buddhist opera and traditional Chinese opera. According to most specialists, traditional Chinese opera did not fully develop into a perfect form until the Southern Song during the early 13th century. It had taken a long time to develop in its gestation period.

There have been various forms of opera, prevailing and popular in different periods of time and places. Two examples are the northern Zaju of the Yuan Dynasty, and the southern opera of the Ming Dynasty. From around the 1560s, a branch of southern opera singing in Kunshan tune was adapted by folk artists to become the dominant Kunqu Opera for more than 200 years until the 1760s during the mid-stage of the Qing Dynasty. A great number of folk operas also appeared along with dominant forms of opera during various periods of time. But, being local operas, each was limited to a certain area. From the early 18th century to the mid-19th century, these folk operas began to spread and develop. Many of them were even staged in Beijing. Beginning in 1790, four local opera troupes of Anhui Province put their programs on the Beijing stage. In the next 10 or so years, in cooperation with the artists of Han Opera from Hubei Province, and absorbing the melodies and styles of performance from Kunqu Opera and Shaanxi Opera, as well as many other melodies of local folk operas, the four troupes evolved a complete artistic style and a performing system of their own to give shape to the famous Peking Opera, which has become the mainstream of Chinese opera.

Chinese opera is characterized by its unique language. Generally speaking, operatic language requires a smack of poetic flavor, but it does not necessarily need to be in the form of poetry. Operatic language includes tune and speech (dialogue and monologue). Though speech is mostly composed of prose, it requires that the tone must have rhyme. The tune should not only be poetic, but also rhythmic. The tunes or singing verses of operas is another form of poetry. But it differs from a poem in general, becoming a kind of poetry that can give an account of events, convey a feeling, and can be sung and accompany a dance performance. It is a kind of poetry to supplement the speech. Therefore, an opera play-writer has to master the particular requirements of opera language in addition to its general rule.

Theorists of ancient Chinese opera have summarized the three problems of opera language from long practice of the art. They are the problems of true language, literary grace and necessities of stage performance. These problems may be understood today as the problems of realism, artistry and the suitable stage language.

True language means simple and plain language. This is intended for the needs of the audience.

Though a tune is written in the form of a poem, it is different in form from poems that are composed only for recitation. A poem must leave room for taste and imagination and implication is its soul. An opera tune, however, is quite different, since the audience does not have time to ponder the meaning of a single line. The idea must be instilled into audience's mind immediately, and the language must be popular language. Language that is hard to understand will pose a barrier between the artists and audiences.

The required true and plain opera language is like the plain language advocated by Lu Xun (1881-1936), requiring "a true feeling without whitewash, pretensions and artificiality." Xu Dachun (1693-1772), a Qing Dynasty physician who was also well versed in diction and rhyme scheme, pointed out in his *The Conveyance of the Sound of Folk Songs and Ballads in Han Style*: "Plain language must have a taste, its extension must be based on true events and its openness must have a profound implication." True and plain language means straightforward language and it must have a true feeling and taste.

Some people mistake the required literary grace of opera language as loading the composition with fancy phrases. This is contrary to the requirements of a true and plain language. Wang Jide (?-c.1623), an opera theorist of the Ming Dynasty, in his *On Opera* said "there are many taboos in opera such as excessive literary, ambiguous language, a classic and pedantic language, or a language of the literati loaded with learning." Some people doubted that faced with so many prohibitions and requirements, a playwright could produce anything at all. Typical examples are eloquent. In *The West Chamber*, by Wang Shifu, a dramatist of the Yuan Dynasty, the writer's language is rich in literary grace, without any ambiguity and ornate traces. It depicts in detail his characters' personalities and actions with a unique genre and color:

Master Zhang, infatuated with Cui Yingying, follows Hongniang to the outside of the abbot's residence. He abruptly introduces himself to Hongniang, but Hongniang reproaches him.

Master Zhang sings:

"The courtyard of my inn is large, my pillow and my mat are cold. A single lamp casts its flickering shadow upon my books and screen. Even if I should be rewarded in this life with the fulfillment of my longings, how can I endure this never-ending night? I cannot sleep. I move about. Like a hand tossed from side to side, I groan and sigh ten thousand times. I pound and twist my pillow and my quilt five thousand times.

"She is delicate as she blushes. She is like a flower when she speaks. Her skin is smooth like perfumed jade. We met but for a moment. I cannot remember her charming face. I rest my chin upon my hand, lost in sweet thoughts."

Zhang receives a letter asking for another meeting, having been fooled once before. While he waits for her at the West Chamber, he sings:

"I stand in the doorway, my cheeks upon my hands. Time drags by, I cannot know whether she will come or not. It may not be easy for her to elude her watchful mother. I wear out my eyes looking forward to her arrival. My poor heart aches from waiting and I blame myself alone that I learned so quickly, all too quickly, to love and long for her!

"If she is really coming, she has left her room by now. And when she comes she will bring with her springtime to this cold cell. If she does not come it will be as though I had cast a stone in the depths of the great ocean to stir it up — in vain. I count her footsteps as she approaches, and lean on my windowsill. I must speak again with you. Have you forgotten, my beloved, the words we had together, you and I?

"Although you have reprimanded me, I do not let your reproaches go to my head. I rejoice to see that you have changed again, and that your love for me has all returned. It seems a full half-year that I have waited for this night. And all this time my lot has been an irksome one to bear."

The wording is as plain as ordinary speech and accurately and clearly describes Master Zhang's falling in love at first sight with

Cui Yingying, his missing her terribly and his impatience as he waits for her. We can also see a smack of good will smock at the infatuated and crazy bookworm by the writer. The language in this drama can be regarded as exemplary, combining true and plain language with literary grace.

The necessities of stage performance means all the necessary and suitable stage language. Speeches that are not suitable for stage performance, including speeches without personality, a sense of movement, or a flavor of poetry are unnecessary. But here we will just talk about the special contradictions of opera language, excluding the conventional requirements we have just mentioned above and those qualities of straightforwardness and flavor of life of the language. What then should be included in the necessities of stage performance? In short, it encompasses the requirements of melody and speech that are easily sung and understood with an aesthetic effect. For instance, the words which are sung must match the tune and be articulated clearly and accurately to their tones in a well-balanced rhythm. It can also be summarized as "pronouncing the words correctly and in a sweet, mellow voice."

To sum up, Chinese literature is a gem of traditional Chinese culture. A basic knowledge in this respect will bring us wisdom, taste and aesthetic enjoyment.

Chapter 4

The Dominant Religions in Ancient China — Buddhism and Taoism

Section 1 The Introduction of Buddhism into China and the Blending of Chinese and Foreign Cultures

China has been a multi-ethnic country since ancient times. It is not surprising, therefore, that there was an extensive range of objects of worship in ancient China. In remote antiquity, these included the worship of ghosts and gods, as well as totems, ancestors and nature. From the Qin and Han dynasties, Buddhism, Taoism, Nestorianism, Manichaeism, Zoroastrianism, and Islam grew up in China or were introduced from abroad. Among minority ethnic groups Shamanism, Bonism and the Dongba Doctrine were popular. During the Song, Yuan, Ming and Qing dynasties, the Mingjiao (Illumination Teaching), the White Lotus Doctrine, the Yellow Heaven Doctrine, the Eight-Trigram Doctrine, etc., were widespread. There are no detailed statistics in the historical records of the number of ancient religions, but we can roughly estimate there may be more than 100 classifications. Among them, Buddhism and Taoism were the two dominant religions of ancient China, which have prevailed for the longest time and over the widest area, and have been of the greatest ideological and cultural significance.

Buddhism was first founded in India, advocating the "four great voids" (of earth, water, fire, and wind), and believing that humanity is born into suffering. Its supreme goal is, therefore, to pursue spiritual release, or an "enlightenment" from the illusory state in the mortal world. Buddhism was introduced into China from India via Central Asia at the end of the Western Han Dynasty (206 BC-25 AD). In 2 BC, the King of Dayuezhi sent an emissary to teach Qin Jingxian (or Jing Lu), a National University student of the Han Dynasty, the Buddhist scriptures. This is a fairly reliable account of how Buddhism was first introduced into China. One night in 64 AD, Emperor Mingdi of the Eastern Han Dynasty dreamed of a Golden Man who was identified as being the Buddha. He then sent a delegation to India to seek the Buddha dharma. In 67 AD, the Emperor invited two monks named Kasyapa Matanga and Dharmaraksa from Central India to visit Luoyang. They came riding on a white horse, bringing with them a picture of the Buddha and *The 42-Chapter Sutra*, and the White Horse Temple was built outside Luoyang, where the monks lived and translated the scriptures. Thus began the construction of Buddhist temples, the making of Buddha images and the translation of Buddhist scriptures in China. It is said that the Emperor allowed Liu Jun, the Marquis of Yangcheng, to become a monk and several women, including A Pan, of Luoyang to become nuns. They became the first group of monks and nuns in China.

Buddhism was also introduced into what is now the Xinjiang region from India around the first century AD. The king of the Yutian Kingdom built a Buddhist temple. Following this, Buddhism was introduced from India to Guizi, Shule, Shache and Gaochang and Buddhist temples were erected. At the same time, Indian-style grottoes and statutes of the Gandhara style and frescos and Buddhist buildings and arts were developed around Guizi and Yutian.

This shows that Buddhism was introduced into the hinterland and the western frontier areas of China during the period between the Western Han and Eastern Han dynasties. This was the beginning of Sino-foreign cultural communications centered on the exchange of Chinese and foreign Buddhist cultures.

The following points characterize the exchange of Chinese and foreign Buddhist cultures:

First, a long history. Such exchanges covered a great span of time from the period between the Western Han and Eastern Han dynasties, up to the Song, Yuan, Ming and Qing dynasties lasting nearly 2,000 years. Most of the monks studied and preached the Buddhist scriptures for several years, or even decades.

The introduction of Buddhism into China resulted in a great many people traveling abroad to seek knowledge of and preach the Buddhist scriptures. They did not travel to seek wealth or out of curiosity, but were seeking Sanskrit versions of the scriptures, or wished to solve difficult questions in the scriptures and to realize Buddhist ideals. During this period, Chinese and foreign Buddhist scholars traveled to each other's countries through the snow-covered Pamirs, over mountains and across deserts or boundless seas, suffering untold hardships. For example, Fa Xian, a monk of the Eastern Jin Dynasty (317-420), was the first to go on a pilgrimage to India to learn the scriptures and his trip proved a great success. He set off from Chang'an in 399 and after six years he arrived in Central India where he stayed for another six years. His journey home, via the present-day Sri Lanka and other countries, took three years. Over a total of 15 years, he had visited about 30 countries. On his way to India, he trekked through the sand and moraine areas for 17 days, guided only by the skeletons of previous pioneers. He traveled through the desert for another 35 days. By the time he had climbed over one mountain, one of his companions had frozen to death.

In 411, the monk Fa Xian was returning home from Sri Lanka by a mercantile ship, together with about 200 other passengers, when they were suddenly hit by a storm. The boat drifted for 90 days before it reached Java. He stayed on the island for five months. In 412, he continued his journey to Guangzhou on another mercantile ship, expecting to arrive there in 50 days. However, after a month at sea, another storm blew up. The passengers aboard suspected that the monk had brought evil luck to them and attempted to leave him alone on an island. He was spared this fate only because some alms givers on the ship spoke out for him out of a sense of justice.

During the 15 years, some of his companions were unable to continue and gave up. Others died on the way. Only Fa Xian survived all the difficulties and hardships and completed his study, bringing Buddhist classics to China, for the first time ever. He also wrote *Records of My Journey to India*, giving a full and detailed account of his experience on the pilgrimage to the West. This was the first travelogue in ancient China to describe India, Sri Lanka and other countries from personal experience, and served as a guide for future pilgrims. His records also preserved many valuable historical and geographical materials about the states in the Western Regions. English and French versions of his book were later produced, and it has frequently been cited with acclaim by scholars of Oriental studies and archeologists.

In 629, another monk, Xuan Zang of the Tang Dynasty (618-907), left Chang'an for India. After suffering untold hardships on his arduous journey, he arrived at last in India, where, he studied in the famous Nalanda Temple for five years and traveled around conducting research for another four years. In 645, he returned to Chang'an, his journey to and from India having taken eight years. After returning home, he worked on translations in the Greater Wild Goose Pagoda. Apart from the many Buddhist classics that he brought back to China, he wrote *Records on the Western Regions of the Great Tang Empire*, telling of the geography, history, religion, culture, communications, folk customs and ways of life, as well as a great deal of myths, legends and stories of the 100 or so countries and regions he had visited, including Central Asia, Afghanistan, India, Pakistan, and Myanmar. This is an important document for the study of history, Buddhist doctrine and Buddhist relics. In recent years, the ruins of the Nalanda Temple, the site of the ancient capital city Rajagrha, the ancient temple Mrgadava and the Ajanta Grottoes in India have all recovered their brilliance, thanks to Xuan Zang's book. It has been translated into English, French, and Japanese. Later, the monk Yi Jing also went to India and studied in the Nalanda Temple for 11 years, and the monk Hui Ri travelled around India and other countries studying

Buddhist classics for 13 years.

Here we have to say a few words about the monk Jian Zhen who introduced the Lu (Vinaya) Sect of Chinese Buddhism to Japan. Against all opposition, he vowed that "for the sake of this religious mission, I am willing to lay down my life." He and his disciples sailed east for Japan in five unsuccessful voyages, in which two of his companions, Rong Rui, a Japanese monk scholar, and Xiang Yan, his favorite disciple, lost their lives. He himself lost his eyesight, becoming blind. But nothing could stop him and at last, at the age of 66, he succeeded in arriving in Japan. His endeavor took him 12 years.

Scholar monks, being sent from Korea and Japan to study in China, usually stayed there for about 10 years. Thanks to their and their like's long-lasting, arduous, and even life-sacrificing pursuit and propagation of Buddhist doctrines, the quality of Buddhist cultural exchanges between China and other countries was guaranteed and exceptional willpower and unwavering spirit became the cornerstone of the exchanges.

Secondly, far-reaching influence. Buddhist cultural exchanges between China and other countries involved the import and export of culture on a large scale. The influence on the cultures of China, East Asia, Southeast Asia and the South Asian Sub-continent and even Persia was inestimable. The Chinese monk scholars who introduced Buddhist culture into China were able to do so without bias. With the emergence of Buddhism in India, factional strife arose resulting in continual splitting and reorganization of religious communities. Finally, many sects were founded including Mahayana (or Great Vehicle, a doctrine believing it can save all living creatures) and Hinayana (or Little Vehicle, a doctrine that Mahayana believes it cannot save all the living creatures because its doctrine is over-elaborated.) Voluminous Mahayana and Hinayana scriptures, statutes and theories were also established. As the Chinese monk scholars introduced Indian Buddhism into China, they tried their best to do so in a precise, systematic and complete way without being influenced by their individual prejudice and likes or dislikes.

During the Southern and Northern Dynasties (420-589), a geographical division arose of "Yi in the South and Chan in the north." Due to the difference of routes from abroad by which Buddhism had entered the country, and to regional cultural differences, theory and analysis was stressed in the south, while there was an emphasis on asceticism and meditation in the north. However, the different styles of learning in the south and the north both exerted an influence on each other, and their differences were not absolutely clear and definite. In the north, a noted master of the Chan Sect would also be familiar with a certain Buddhist classic as his theoretical principle. In the south, Yi monk scholars who studied the Three Sastras, including the Madhyamaka-sastra (On the Mean), the Sata-sastra (The Hundred Verses) and the Dvadasanikaya-sastra (On the Twelve Points) did not refuse the practices of the Chan Sect.

After the reunification of China under the Sui Dynasty (581-618), this difference in Buddhist style between south and north gradually went out of the picture. The various sects of Buddhism founded by scholars in the Southern and Northern Dynasties, and those set up in later dynasties involved almost all the doctrines of Indian Buddhism. Even the Venerable Xuan Zang of the Tang Dynasty, who was specially devoted to the study of the Mahayana doctrine, also studied the doctrines of many other sects after he arrived in India. He also linked up the divergence between the theories of the sect of Yoga (phenomenal and noumenal) and the sect of Madhyamapratipad (the Mean, or "The Sunya Sect" which makes the unreality of the ego and things their fundamental tenet), demonstrating that the doctrines of various sects of Buddhism were identical to each other in their fundamental tenets. This was praised and appreciated by many Indian masters and renowned monks. Chinese monk scholars introduced and developed the whole of Indian Buddhism into China, not merely a part of it. Thus, by the early 13th century, when Buddhism had declined in India, the original records of many of its sects and classics could be found in China. This is an achievement made by Chinese monk scholars in their introduction and straightening out of Indian Buddhist culture and a great contribution to the Oriental and world cultures as well.

Along with the introduction of Indian Buddhist culture, China also absorbed other cultural products from India, including language, Buddhist arts, medical science, astronomy, mathematics and philosophy. Mutual translations in both the Chinese and Indian languages could be traced back to the period between the Western Han and Eastern Han dynasties. During the Wei, Jin and the Southern and Northern Dynasties (220-589), well-known works of translation included the *Shi Si Yin Xun Xu* by Hui Rui. This denoted all the phonetics and meanings of the texts of the scriptures in both Sanskrit and Chinese to facilitate their reading. The Chinese work *The Explanation of the Great Vehicle* was also translated by a monk from southern India named Bodhidruci (Dharmaruci) into Sanskrit. It was the first Buddhist work translated from Chinese into Sanskrit. Xuan Zang of the Tang Dynasty not only translated a great many Sanskrit Buddhist scriptures into Chinese, but he also translated *The Book of Lao Zi* and *The Awakening of Faith in the Mahayana* into Sanskrit and took them to India. These were all important events in the history of cultural exchanges between India and China.

Chinese monks also learned to carve Buddhist statues and cut grottoes from India. The monks Le Zun and Fa Liang of the Former Qin Dynasty (352-394) carved Buddhist statues out of stone in the caves at Mt. Mingsha in Dunhuang. These were the first statues to be made in Dunhuang's Mogao Caves and marked the start of large-scale construction of statues in caves in China. Later, more grottoes were cut in Dunhuang as well as Yungang and Longmen. There are also stone-cut scriptures to be found in Fangshan where caves were cut into cliffs, their walls polished, and scriptures engraved. Inside the caves, there are texts of scriptures engraved on separate stones. All these are treasures of Buddhist art. In the year 645, a sculpture and painting artisan returned home from a visit to Magadha to make copies of the relics of Buddha and statues. Monks and lay people in Chang'an went to imitate and duplicate all these things, which were later copied and displayed in the newly built temples and pagodas in the city.

During the Tang Dynasty, there were Indian astronomers working at the Directorate of Astronomy. In 718, one of these, Gautama Cida, was assigned to translate into Chinese the Indian calendar book "The Nine Graha" which later became a part of *The Kaiyuan Great Calendar Book*. Thus, Indian culture not only brought Buddhist scholars, but also architects, astronomers and calendar calculators.

Among the thinkers influenced by Indian philosophy, particularly worth mentioning is Lü Cai, a chamberlain for ceremonials during the reign of Emperor Taizong of the Tang Dynasty. After Xuan Zang had completed his translation of Hetuvidya science (a theory of logic) from Sanskrit into Chinese in Chang'an, his disciples considered it to be a secret treasure and vied with each other in making annotations and interpretations of the text. Lü Cai also studied the translation and proposed an interpretation of his own, triggering a fierce debate with the monks. Lü demonstrated the relationship between "wholeness" (*yi*, or primal fluid, primary elements that form Heaven and Earth) and "multiplicity" (everything in nature) by integrating the "atomism" of the theory of "Paramartha-satya-sastra" in Indian philosophy with the Chinese doctrine of *The Book of Changes*. He believed that the principle in *The Book of Changes* that "the supreme ultimate produced two opposites, two opposites produced four symbols, four symbols produced the eight trigrams, and the eight trigrams produced everything" was identical to the theory of atomism in Paramartha-satya-sastra. While the words might have been different, in essence they were the same. Paramartha-satya-sastra is one of the six schools of Indian philosophy. Its principle is based on the duality system consisting of ancient atomism, elementals and logic. Most viewpoints of its naturalism and logic are atheistic. By "extra minimum" it means material elements. Lü used "atomism" to explain the material attributes of *qi* in *The Book of Changes* and the premise that "*qi* makes everything in the world" to denote the birth and development of the world. This attempt to integrate outstanding achievements in Indian philosophy with Chinese philosophy opened a new path for the development of traditional Chinese culture.

Regarding the export of culture, after Indian Buddhism was introduced into China, it was digested, assimilated and remolded by Chinese monks, and very soon disseminated to various countries in East and Southeast Asia, producing a significant impact on the cultural development of those countries. China, at that time, served as a base relaying Buddhism to other countries. Vietnam, Korea and Japan introduced Buddhism directly from China, while Buddhism in Cambodia, Myanmar, Indonesia and Thailand became more popular because of the influence of Chinese Buddhism.

Vietnam borders China with easy access to traffic. At the end of the second century, Mou Rong, a noted Chinese scholar, wrote the Buddhist work entitled *On Truth and Uncertainty* in Jiaozhi (now Hanoi in Vietnam) to propagate Buddhism. During the third century, several monks went to Vietnam to preach Dharma by way of or from China. Thus, Buddhist scriptures printed in Chinese have long been used in Vietnamese Buddhism. The mid-seventh century marked the peak of Chinese Buddhism entering Vietnam. Many Tang Dynasty monks, including Ming Yuan, went to Vietnam to preach Dharma, which led to a number of Vietnamese monks traveling with them to India and other places to pursue Dharma. It was around this time that many sects of Vietnamese Buddhism were established on the basis of Chinese Buddhism. Of them, the latter sect of the Chan school was founded by the Tang Dynasty Chan master Wu Yan Tong in Vietnam. His sect flourished in the country, and now, most of Chan Buddhism in Vietnam is derived from his school.

The Buddhist relationship between China and Korea began in the fourth century, or during the era of the Three Kingdoms (Gaogouli, Xinluo and Baiji) in Korea. In 372, an envoy of the Former Qin Dynasty together with a monk named Shun Dao were sent to Korea to present a portrait of the Buddha and scriptures and tenets to the country. Two years later, another monk named

Ah Dao arrived in the country. In 375, two temples were built in Korea for Shun Dao and Ah Dao to live in. This marked the dawn of Korean Buddhism. Buddhism was also introduced to Baiji in the southwest of Korea and the Xinluo area in the southeast.

By the time of the Tang Dynasty, major sects of Chinese Buddhism had passed over to Korea. The monk Da Xian from Xinluo, who had come to China to learn Dharma, returned to his country to establish the Ci'en Sect of Xinluo. Another monk named Yi Xiang, also from Xinluo, built the Flowing Stone Temple when he returned home from China and was honored as the primary ancestor of the Haidong Huayan Sect. Monks like Ming Lang and others from Xinluo built up the Temple of Golden Light after they returned home from China, becoming the primary ancestors of the Esoteric Haidong Shenyin Sect. The monk Fa Lang of Xinluo returned home from China and became the founder of the Xinluo Nine Mount Sect of the Chan school. Essentially, the doctrines of most sects of Korean Buddhism were introduced from China.

In around the sixth century, Buddhism was disseminated into Japan from China. According to historical records, the earliest monks and nuns in Japan were Chinese and the earliest Buddhist temples there were also built by Chinese. By that time, Buddhism had already been introduced into Korea. So it was introduced to Japan either through Korea or directly from China, thus starting a new stage of Buddhism in Japan.

During the Sui Dynasty (581-618) and the Tang Dynasty (618-907), Chinese Buddhism was introduced into Japan on a large scale. During the Tang Dynasty, envoys were sent to China from Japan 19 times, on each occasion being accompanied by four or five hundred student and scholar monks. With the return of these students to Japan, and preaching there by Chinese monks, various Buddhist sects were gradually established in Japan. The first to be established was the Japanese Three Sastras School, or Madhyamika or Middle School (one of the Chinese Buddhist sects, originating in the Madhyamika of the Indian Great Vehicle). It was jointly founded by Hui Guan, a Korean monk, Zhi Zang, a Japanese-Chinese monk, and Dao Ci, a Japanese monk. Dao Ci built the Great Peace Temple in Japan, modeled on the Xi Ming Temple at Huayan and Chang'an in China, which became the most magnificent temple in ancient Japan. Later, the Faxiang and Vinaya sects were established in Japan respectively by the Japanese monk scholar Dao Zhao, the Xinluo monk Shen Xiang, and the Chinese monk Jian Zhen. In 757, the Japanese Mikado (emperor) granted treasures to the monk Jian Zhen for building a Buddhist temple. Jian Zhen had his disciples build the temple, a task which took two years to complete. This temple, named Toshodaiji, is the base from which present-day Japanese monks of the Vinaya school preach Dharma in the country. Japanese monk scholars Kong Hai and Zui Cheng, having completed their study in China, returned home and founded Japan's Esoteric Zhenyan and Tiantai sects. During the periods of Nara (710-784) and Heian (794-1192), the nationwide new Buddhist cultural movement had direct or indirect links with Chinese Buddhist sects, which continued until the later stage of the Qing Dynasty of China.

Together with the introduction of Chinese Buddhist culture into the above-mentioned countries, Chinese linguistics, literature, arts, medical science, mathematics, classics and history and many other productive skills were also introduced to promote their relative disciplines. We may say that Buddhist cultural exchange served as a "channel" or "window" for other forms of cultural exchange between China and other countries. The part that Buddhism played in these other cultural ties are worthy of further attention and study.

Thirdly, perfect assimilation. After the introduction of Buddhism into China, it began to communicate and merge with the traditional native culture, gradually becoming an important part of Chinese culture. Since Buddhism was among the first of the religions to be introduced from abroad and the first to merge with Chinese culture, its influence on Chinese thinking and culture has also lasted the longest.

By Chinese Buddhism, we mean the blend of Buddhism and

traditional Chinese culture on the one hand, and on the other the merging of various sects and schools within Buddhism. The first merging of Buddhism and Chinese culture can be dated back to the period between the Western Han Dynasty (206 BC-25 AD) and the Eastern Han Dynasty (25-220). It had evolved over seven or eight centuries before it entered on the stage of maturity in the Sui and Tang dynasties. The sinicization of Buddhism can be roughly divided into three stages of development. During the period from the Han Dynasty to the Three Kingdoms (220-280) and the Western Jin and Eastern Jin dynasties (265-420), when Buddhism was first introduced into China, in order to overcome linguistic and conceptual barriers, Chinese Buddhist scholars at the time usually adopted analogies to translate or explain a Buddhist idea or term, by using a corresponding or similar term or idea from traditional Chinese philosophy. Although this approach helped to popularize Buddhism, the analogies were often forced, or even gave wrong interpretations of the scriptures. During the Southern and Northern Dynasties, therefore, Buddhist scholars tried their best to change from merely using analogies of tenets to paraphrasing their true meanings. At that time, the Xuanxue, or Dark Learning (a metaphysical sect based on Taoist teachings mixed with traditional Confucianism) was very popular. As a result, Buddhism was gradually absorbed into metaphysics, and this became known as the historical stage of "Buddhism and Xuanxue." As Xuanxue began to decline, Buddhism had to change its form. During the Sui and Tang dynasties, pushed forward by the Neo-Confucian ideological trend, a succession of sects and schools of Buddhism were founded, and Chinese Buddhism came into being. This was the merging process of Buddhism and Confucianism.

In this process, Buddhism blended with Confucianism both in form and in essence, each becoming an integral part of the other. Specifically, in theory, Chinese Buddhism is mainly characteristic of changing the Buddhagotrasastra (the nature of Buddha) of the Indian Buddhism into the "nature of mind" of Confucianism. That is to say, it turns an external idol of the Buddha into an internal belief of mind. In particular, Chan Buddhism (a school of

Chinese Buddhism, introduced from India, advocating meditation and silent chanting as the way of self-cultivation) stresses that there is no Buddha outside the self, regarding oneself on an equal footing with Buddha. The sect of phenomenal and noumenal of the Great Vehicle of Indian Buddhism dared not advocate this, nor could the Sunya sect of the Great Vehicle. All the sects of the Great Vehicle advocating Sunya dared not recognize the emptiness of the Buddha and Dharma, though they might talk about the emptiness of other things. In their view, if they declared the emptiness of Buddha and Dharma, monks whose existence relied upon Buddha and Dharma would vanish into the void at the same time. Obviously it would be harmful to the development of Buddhism. However, Chan Buddhism, according to the idea of "Buddha only works in one's own mind," overthrew two of the Triratna of Buddhism, the Buddha and the Dharma, while protecting the existence of the Sangha (ego). Chinese Buddhism, represented by Chan, in comparison with Indian Buddhism, gives prominence to individual consciousness. It transplants the belief in the Buddha into the nature of the human mind to illustrate the intrinsic quality of man through self-discovery and personal development. This human-centricism reflects the essence of Confucianism because Confucianism, in essence, is "humanism." So, the basic difference between Chinese Buddhism and Indian Buddhism lies in whether one attaches importance to the Buddha or to man. The shift of the importance of the Buddha to that of man marks the maturity of the Chinese Buddhism.

The doctrine of Chan Buddhism maintains that "the Buddha only works in man's own mind." And its way is to prepare for "sudden enlightenment." According to its doctrine, since "all Dharma resides in one's own mind," one should "realize all at once the nature of unchangeable reality in one's own mind." When man cannot "perceive mind and nature," it is simply because he is "muddle-headed" in belief. If he accepts the basic principles of Chan Buddhism, he can "perceive the nature and become a Buddha at once," just as clouds disappear in the wind. This is different from becoming a Buddha through Dasabhumi (the ten stages in the 52 sections of the development of a Bodhisattva into a Buddha) advocated by Indian Buddhism. But it is very close to the "committing to memory everything one sees and hears silently," the introspective way of experience of Confucianism.

As to its values, traditional Chinese ideology was heavily tinted with politics. Various schools and sects were closely linked with the kingly way of politics through different forms. In particular, Confucianism upheld the practice of "practical administration." Indian Buddhism, however, was marked by its aim of deliverance "from the earthly world." After Buddhism was introduced into China, therefore, Chinese Buddhism was gradually influenced by Confucian values, developing from a pursuit of deliverance "from the earthly world" to a way of living "in the earthly world."

For instance, Master Ji Zang, the founder of the Chinese San Lun (Three Sastras) Sect, stated clearly that it would run against "the primary truth of Buddhism" if the proper rules governing the behavior of a sovereign, a subject, a father and a son and loyalty and filial piety could not be implemented. When the primary truth of Buddhism was lost, one could not be liberated from existence (Nirvana). Here, to practice the programs and teachings of Confucianism was taken as a necessary condition to attain the goal of deliverance. The Huayan Sect taught that Sakyamuni and his disciple Mahamaudgalyayana, who left home to become a monk, were in pursuit of a way of filiality, and it worshiped the "Ullambanapatra Sutra" as its filial classic. The Chan Sect broke down the obstacles, in the practice of self-cultivation, between "from the earthly world" and "in the earthly world," believing that cultivation could be practiced in one's own home without going to live in a temple. It preached the ideal of becoming a Buddha in daily life, totally forgetting the admonishments in the "Will of the Buddha Sutra" about having no involvement in secular affairs.

As to its artistic aspects, the sculpting and painting of images of the Buddha, and the construction of pagodas were introduced from India into China. During the Wei, Jin and the Southern and Northern dynasties, although influenced by India's Gandhara and Upagupta skills in statue modeling, the modeled statues in China were yet produced with a flavor of its own, such as the earlier statues in the Longmen Grottoes, which is characterized by a scholarly and pompous style.

By the Sui and Tang dynasties, Chinese Buddhist art had completed its process of sinification. Many Buddhist statues were produced with the bearing of a dignified scholar. Typical of these is the Buddha Rocana in the Fengxian Temple at Longmen. This large statue of Buddha, dressed in Chinese-style kasaya with a round neck, looks dignified and kind-hearted and has an elegant and plump face with eyes expressing calm and insight. This fully expresses the Confucian aesthetic ideal of seeking a unity of internal and external qualities and virtue and beauty.

To match the spirit promoted by society at the time of developing careers aggressively and a government working hard for prosperity, many reliefs were made with a taste expressing the spirit of working hard for the prosperity of the country and of vigor and strength. In particular, paintings of Buddhas, Bodhisattvas, the devas, and men of strength in the various creatures of Sukahavati all embodied images of health and beauty. This is the reviviscence of the beauty of virility esteemed in *The Book of Changes* in a new form. Other forms of art, such as clay sculptures of the Buddha, and embroidered and wooden carvings of the Buddha and figurines made of butter mixed up with various pigments (art works produced in Tibet) were all domestically made in China. Chinese Buddhist art is "liable to plasticity, not to the nature of the Buddha." This viewpoint of art of "being liable to plasticity" is identical to the theory of "the Buddha works only in one's own mind," as advocated by Chan Buddhism.

The merger of various sects and schools of Buddhism also constituted a part of Chinese Buddhism. This is because the merger embodied the ethos of "absorption and assimilation" in traditional Chinese culture. This is called in Buddhism "the judgement of religious sects" (a judgement made by various Buddhist sects and schools on each other's doctrine and a rating of all the sects thus produced). The general tendency was the merging of various sects and schools with Chan Buddhism.

In principles, Chinese Buddhism advocated "the unification of sects and Chan," and "the unification of Jingtu and Chan." The "sects" means the Tiantai and Huayan sects and Chan means Chan Buddhism. The monk scholar Zong Mi of the Huayan Sect through his judgement of religious sects compiled a collection of Chan teachings about the theory of Buddhism and its roots. He believed that a sudden enlightenment was the final product of progressive self-cultivation over a long period of time. All the teachings of master monks were in line with the purposes of the Buddhist texts. He declared that in the whole collection of the Buddhist texts there were only three schools and Chan Buddhism included only three sects. These three schools and three sects (the Tiantai, Huayan and Chan sects) are identical with each other, which is called "a unified Dharma." Since the Tiantai and Huayan sects were merged with Chan Buddhism, a Huayan-Chan Sect was prevalent during the Tang and Song dynasties.

The "unification of Jingtu and Chan" means the unification of the Jingtu (pure land) and Chan sects. The latter, while attaching no importance to the written words of texts and tenets, stresses the importance of man's mind, which corresponds closely to chanting the name of Buddha to attain the Western Paradise and "regarding one mind as a sect," as upheld by the Jingtu Sect. So in the Song Dynasty, many monks of the Jingtu Sect held that they should practice both the way of the Jingtu and Chan sects, resulting in the emergence of a host of monks who believed in Chan, while at the same time chanting the name of the Buddha, a practice parallel with the Huayan-Chan Sect.

As to the way, all sects were in favor of the simple and easy Dharmaparyaya (or the doctrines or wisdom of Buddha regarded as the gateway to enlightenment) of the Chan Sect, which could be readily followed by everyone. This easy and simple way had been attacked in India, but it was followed in China by the Tiantai, Huayan, Jingtu and Lu sects, in opposition to the practice of Indian Buddhist monks and justifying the typical character of the Chinese Chan school. As a result, since the time of the Tang and Song dynasties, Buddhist monks in China were usually called Chan monks and the Chan Sect was almost synonymous with Buddhism. Because it was deeply implanted in the hearts of literati and ordinary people as a religious belief, the Confucian-style Chan Sect has developed without interruption and it is still very popular in the present time.

The exchanges between Chinese and foreign Buddhist cultures demonstrate that for a foreign culture to be implanted into the soil of China, it must comply with the basic ethos of Chinese culture. At the same time, it is not a dreadful thing for traditional Chinese culture to digest and assimilate a foreign culture. It can serve as an impetus for the development of Chinese culture while eliminating what is false and retaining what is true.

Section 2 The Rise of Taoism and the Blending of Various Cultures

Taoism differs greatly from many religions which tend to be exclusive. Taoism is, in a religious form, a cultural system that has incorporated almost everything in its development since it was founded. As a religion embracing most kinds of cultures, Taoism may be called a "learning of absorption and assimilation."

Taoism was a unique religion in ancient China with the Tao, or the Way, as its supreme belief. Founded in the mid-stage of the Eastern Han Dynasty, Taoism deified Lao Zi and his *Tao Te Ching*, or *Dao De Jing* (*Classic of the Way* and *Virtue*). It worshiped Lao Zi as its founder and his *Tao Te Ching* as the principal classic, to which a religious explanation was also made. It asserts that man can make both his mental and physical life survive forever through a long period of self-cultivation, thus becoming immortal.

Based on religious beliefs in ancient China, Taoism has developed by way of absorbing ideas or ways from various other religious sects and schools such as Alchemist Taoism, Huangdi-Lao Zi Taoism (a legend says that Huangdi matched Lao Zi, who were held in esteem as the founders of Taoism), Jing Xue (study of Confucian classics) and the Mohist doctrine (an important school of thought in the Warring States Period, opposed to Confucianism). It has always been regarded as an eclectic religion.

The cultural compositions of Taoism are of great variety, including Taoist thought, architecture, medicine, music, fine arts and literature.

Taoist places of worship were called "Zhi" in the Han Dynasty and known as "Zhi," "Lu," or "Jing" during the Western and Eastern Jin dynasties. In the Southern and Northern Dynasties, they were called "Guan" 馆 (hall) in the south and in the north called "Guan" 观 (monastery) or "Si" (temple). But during the Tang Dynasty, all were known as "Guan" (monastery). During and after the late Tang, "Gong" (palace) was also used to denote some places of worship. Some buildings used for sacrificial ceremonies for common deities by ordinary people were called "Miao" (temple).

The style of Taoist structures was gradually perfected along with the systemization and standardization of Taoist ceremonial rites. During the initial stage of the religion's development, Taoism was usually practiced in simple and crude huts or caves in remote mountains. These were the "Zhi" of the Han and Jin dynasties.

After the Southern and Northern Dynasties, as Taoism flourished, a great number of "Gong" and "Guan" were built across the country and some of the constructions were large and broad in scale. These constructions were usually composed of four parts: a shrine hall, a dining room, a dormitory, and a garden, which were essentially laid out according to the pattern of traditional Chinese courtyard buildings. The main structure was based on a wooden framework and a single building was composed of several "bays." Several individual buildings made up the courtyard construction. On the basis of several courtyard constructions, various types of building groups were formed. A shrine hall was built on the main axial alignment as the principal part of the whole construction, which was flanked by a dining hall and a dormitory. A garden was usually located in a secluded spot. The four sections were clearly defined with easily accessible routes, suggesting a sense of solemnity, tranquility, refreshment and elegance. The construction was generally uniformly decorated together with various art works and paintings such as frescos, sculptures, calligraphy, scrolls, dedications, poems and essays, and stone-carved tablets of writings. With skillful and well-planned execution, the construction was of a high cultural level with colorful and artistic images.

Taoist architecture is designed to express the ideas of Yin and Yang and the Five Elements (metal, wood, water, fire and earth), and other ideas of auspiciousness and longevity, and the Taoist pursuit of immortality. For instance, for architectural adornments, the sun, the moon, stars, clouds, mountains, water, and rocks were painted to imply a meaning of the radiation of light, firmness and eternity. Fans, fish, narcissi, bats, and deer were made symbols of virtue, affluence, happiness, honor and longevity. Pines and cypresses, glossy ganoderma, tortoises, cranes, bamboo, dragons, and phoenixes symbolize longevity, immortality, virtuousness, the exorcising of evil spirits, and auspiciousness. In addition, mythical stories such as "The Eight Immortals Sail Across the Sea" and "The Eight Immortals Celebrate Their Birthdays" are often adopted as the decorative theme of Taoist constructions.

Construction of Taoist palaces and monasteries flourished in the Tang Dynasty with a total of 1,687 such constructions having been built across the country. Frescos covering about 8,524 bays painted during the Tang Dynasty were preserved and left over to the Song Dynasty (960-1279). But after the middle of the Ming Dynasty (1368-1644), such construction began to decline. Famous surviving Taoist monasteries include the Taiqing Palace in Luyi of Henan Province; the Louguantai Palace in Zhouzhi of Shaanxi Province; the Shangqing Palace on Dragon and Tiger Mountain in Jiangxi Province; the Yuanfu Palace in Maoshan, the Xuanmiao Temple in Suzhou and the Chaotian Palace in Nanjing of Jiangsu Province; the Dongxiao Palace in Yuhang of Zhejiang Province; the Baiyunguan Temple in Beijing; the Qingyang Palace in Chengdu of Sichuan Province; the Yongle Palace in Ruicheng of Shanxi Province; the Chongyang Palace in Huxian of Shaanxi Province; and the Changchun Temple in Wuhan of Hubei Province.

Taoist fine arts developed in tandem with Taoist architecture.

They include sculptures, portraits of immortals, temple frescos, and literary Taoist paintings. At first, they were influenced by Buddhist arts but the images all had a Chinese face. The idea of the creative endeavor was mainly to express the Taoist philosophic doctrine and tenets. They inherited the painting skills directly from Chinese bronze vessels, the Han Dynasty portrait bricks, and portrait-painting skills in ancient times. Specifically, a painting or a portrait was made mainly to express the conceived idea of the maker. With various artistic approaches and the ways of "modeling the image of a god" or "shaping a god's image," artists expressed in their works various desired requirements of the Taoist god images.

The extant famous Taoist stone-carved statues include the 5.1-m-high Lao Zi statue on Mt. Qingyuan in Quanzhou, Fujian Province; the Song Dynasty painted statue in the Goddess Hall of the Jin Memorial Temple in Taiyuan and the Yuan Dynasty statues in the Longshan Grottoes, also in Taiyuan, Shanxi Province. The facsimile on silk of the stone-carved portrait of Lao Zi, kept in the Xuanmiao Temple in Suzhou is the most treasured extant portrait of Taoist immortals. The masterpieces of frescos in Chinese art history include the extant large fresco "Clearing the Way for the God of Mount Tai to Return on His Carriage" in the Tianguan Hall of the Dai Temple at Tai'an, Shandong Province, and the Taoist frescos in the Yongle Palace in Shanxi Province. Literary Taoist paintings will be dealt with in the following section.

Taoist literary works in various styles include poems, lyrics and prose and songs, essays and biographies, dramas and novels. They were composed either by Taoist priests or by literati. Poems and Pian Wen (a sort of rhythmical prose characterized by parallelism and ornateness) were composed to eulogize gods and spirits and popularize necromancy and alchemy. Sometimes the prose form was also used for this purpose. The forms of commentary and prose were used to explain the religious teachings and narrative prose was used in biographies of gods. Mythic legends and stories were written in the forms of dramas or novels.

Taoist literature created a unique style of poem, called the

"Buxu Ci Poem," with five characters in a line and four, eight or 12 lines of ornate stanzas. This style was later developed into the popular literary form of "Tao Qing," a type of verse different from the Ci poem with tonal patterns modeled on tunes drawn from folk music, chanted and performed by itinerant Taoist priests accompanied by a bamboo-made percussion instrument while asking for alms along the street. This type of verse is popular and easily understood.

Although religious life was the dominant theme of Taoist literature, most works were interspersed with the author's concerns and worries about his country and people and a true description about some aspects of the social life at the time, which had some academic and ideological value.

Taoist music includes solos, chorus, and the liberal type of songs sung in various parts of performance such as drumming and piping, and instrumental ensemble staged during Taoist feasts and sacrificial ceremonies. On such occasions, Taoist priests would act as performers and Taoist believers the audience. The musical instruments included percussive bells, chime stones, drums, pipes and stringed instruments. Instruments were usually used at the beginning and end of the ceremony and between the singing parts of a song, or a change of array of a procession, or when a priest conducted a religious rite in special steps. But the vocal part, which made up most of Taoist music, was made up of many brief songs of two or four lines of verses. A large tonal music usually contained up to a dozen verses to be used on different occasions.

Taoist religious music is characterized by its special local flavor. For instance, a special piece of music performed during a particular religious ritual may differ with local variations in melody when it is played in various places. Another example is that a verse to be used in the same kind of ceremony may be tuned to a particular local melody.

Obviously, the Taoist cultural composition not only represents a compositional uniform of various kinds of forms and disciplines, but also a uniform of multilevel substances of each form and discipline. This is the most outstanding feature of the Taoist culture.

The comprehensive Taoist culture created a cultural pattern, combining Taoism and the Taoist school, Taoism and Confucianism, and Taoism and Buddhism.

Taoism established its world outlook of religion on the basis of the Taoist school of thought, making this world outlook a principal part of the Taoist thought. The integration of Taoism with the Taoist school of thought is reflected not only in making Lao Zi its founder and the *Tao Te Ching* the classic of Taoism, but also in the worship of and belief in the Tao (the Way). No Taoist scholar would not preach the doctrine of the Tao. The doctrine comprehends the following two aspects: on the one hand, it carries on the belief of the Taoist school of thought that holds that the Tao is the origin of the universe and the supreme being involving "Heaven and Earth." It believes that the Tao generates everything and all phenomena in the world. But it stresses the mystery of the Tao, personifying the Tao as having ideology, consciousness and temperament. Through several links it makes the "Gods of Pure Trinity" ("Heavenly Treasures Master," "Supreme Taoist Master" and "Supreme Master") the personifications of the "Tao." In this way, the "Tao" is endowed with the implication of immortals creating the world, thus leading the noumenon of the Taoist school to religion.

On the other hand, it developed the idea of Lao Zi about the Te (virtue) and focused on the explanation of "how to attain the Tao." According to its explanation, "Te" (德) is Te (得), or "gain," and to "attain enlightenment" is to gain the achievement of the Tao, and to making the Tao reside in ego and integrating the Tao with "ego" as a whole so as to make ego an immortal, permanent survival of its mortal body and spirit.

The Tao is achieved through internal self-cultivation and external self-exercise, known as "Nei Dan" and "Wai Dan" in Chinese. The way of "Nei Dan" is to make the body a "furnace and boiler" and one's own "vitality" and "breath" the medicine to produce a "sacred fetus" or "sacred elixir" through "exhaling the stale and inhaling the fresh." It involves the way of meditation, tranquility, freedom from desire and worry, concentration of the mind, purification and brightness.

The way of "Wai Dan" denotes the elixir medicines produced through alchemy with lead and mercury. Eating them was intended to produce immortality. During the Tang and Song periods, the way of Nei Dan merged step by step with Fang Shu (a general term for certain professions, especially for medicine, divination, astrology and alchemy). It developed to include the way of Qi (breath) promoting, Daoyin (a method for promoting health and curing diseases by combining regulated, controlled breathing with physical exercises), Pigu (a method for improving health by avoiding grain food, only living on drugs) and control of sex. This is a typical example of the merger of the Taoist school with the Fang Shu school.

By adopting the thought of Confucianism, Taoism created its own religious ethics. This is the Taoist thought of the world. Taoism is a religion of secularity. Since it came into being, it has paid great attention to worldly life. Taoist priests are generally interested in the study of the Confucian "Five Classics" (*The Book of Songs*, *The Book of History*, *The Book of Changes*, *The Book of Rites* and *Spring and Autumn Annals*), creating their ethical system and thought by absorbing materials from Confucianism.

Its ethical system is based on the hierarchy of the imaginary paradise of immortals and the realistic system of priesthood. They introduced the Confucian ethical code into their fast and sacrificial ritual and classified all its true souls including the God of Heaven, God of Earth, ghosts and Taoist gods into different grades. It says that even a Zhen Ren (true man) can be classified into different grades of quality. And it analogized the Taoist true master, true man, true lord, and true minister as emperor, king, and many other officials in the feudal society. A strict hierarchy was created in the Taoist priesthood to correspond to that of the imaginary paradise of immortals. The well-organized hierarchical system was an important step in accelerating the process of its feudalization by way of merging with Confucianism.

Taoism introduced the Confucian ideas of loyalty and filial piety and the theory of life and temperament as a central part of its ethical thought. For instance, disregarding the five constant virtues (benevolence, righteousness, courtesy, wisdom and trustiness) is strictly forbidden. Of the 25 articles on the prohibited actions for a Taoist priest, there are 16 which are concerned with maintaining good ethical relationships. It regards loyalty to one's country, filial obedience to one's parents, honesty to one's friends, being kind to one's inferiors, and absence of arrogance and cunning as the necessary conditions to communicate with the "gods and ghosts." It declares that only with this thought, can one be like the immortals. "Although the immortals do not meet me really, yet we meet as if they would like to."

In particular, the Nei Dan school introduced the Confucian theory of life and temperament into its personal cultivation and exercise after modifications and proposed its double cultivation and exercise theory of life and temperament. The cultivation of life means the cultivation of the spirit, breath and vitality in one's body to meet the requirements of the natural law of growth. This is a development of the Taoist methods of inspiration and expiration, and the Qi-promoting method toward Confucianism. The cultivation of temperament means "no contact with anything" and cutting off any desire from its origin with a clean and bright mind, "doing everything with intelligence," and "not violating the law of nature." That is to say, one has to live up to the ethical standards of being a loyal subject, a filial son or daughter or a decent citizen in one's conscience and behavior.

Taoism completed its religious system by absorbing the thought of Buddhism. In history, there existed a fierce controversy between Taoism and Buddhism. Apart from political factors, the controversy, culturally, was intended to seek a common ground and eliminate the differences. Therefore, in the history of their relationship, the mainstream of its development was a supplement in each other's religious tenets.

In its early stage, Taoism made use of some Buddhist tenets to compile its own Taoist books and imitated the Buddhist commandments to work out its own disciplines and rituals. For example, it has "five commandments of the immortals," that is, killing no living things, eating no meat and, drinking no alcohol, speaking no false words, stealing no things and committing no lewd acts; and the "five ways toward transmigration" including hell, hungry ghosts, animals, human beings, and celestial beings. With a few exceptions in wording, most was copied from Buddhism. Legend says that nine dragons were spitting out water when the Supreme Master (Lao Zi) was born. This is also a copy of the legendary story about Sakyamuni. All these show the fact that Taoism has adopted the Buddhist religious system for its own establishment.

Taoism has also absorbed Buddhist religious theories. Taoism originally pursued immortality, and did not talk of "souls" or "transmigration and reincarnation." But this "transmigration and reincarnation" appeared to promote control over the minds of the people and check bad deeds. Taoist scholars introduced this theory into their tenets, beginning to talk of "paradise" and "hell." They depicted mythical scenes in the "paradise" and in the "capital of ghosts." They also said that "human beings will suffer all their lives, whether they believe Taoism or not. Their lives are bonded to endless sufferings from birth until death." This is much like the Buddhist "Catursatya" (the four noble truths, including "Duhkhasatya," meaning everything on earth is in suffering; "Samudyasatya," the innate causes of suffering; "Nirodhasatya," to get rid of all the causes and to be liberated from existence; and "Margasatya," meaning self-cultivation in Buddhism to attain Nirvana). To meet this requirement, Taoism made some modifications in its ways of self-cultivation and practice. It developed the ways from "training the outer form" to strengthen one's external vigor to "nourishing the vitality and spirits" to cultivate one's mind. In particular, after the rise of the Chan Sect, a trend of thought that combined Taoism and Chan appeared, advocating that the initial step in one's self-cultivation was the pursuit of becoming an immortal and then making good use of the skills of various Buddhas, and finally with the consciousness of Bhutatathata (eternal, impersonal and unchangeable reality), one must eliminate such illusions and fantasy as to take all objective things as the truth, and arrive at one's ultimate desire of taking everything as "void of the world of senses," the origin of noumenon of the boundless universe. It specifically took the teaching of "discovering the truth of Bhutatathata" in the text of the Chan Sect as a key link of its way to achieve the aim of Taoism. On the issues of the nature of mind, Taoism and Buddhism and Confucianism come to the same goal at last from different directions.

Section 3 Chinese Buddhism and Taoism and Traditional Chinese Culture

Buddhism and Taoism have accumulated vast quantities of classics and documents, and left over numerous historical relics and treasures. They have influenced, to varying degrees, both the ancient and modern culture in ideology, science and imagery.

Chinese Buddhism has produced the greatest influence in traditional Chinese ideological culture. Buddhism was part of the mainstream of social thought during the Sui and Tang dynasties, becoming an indispensable link between the past and future in the history of Chinese thought. Buddhism enriched Chinese philosophy. During the Tang and Song periods, Chinese philosophy was far more diverse than in earlier periods because of the influence of Buddhism. Buddhism had raised the subject consciousness theory in Chinese philosophy to a new height. It explained the functions of subject consciousness from the viewpoints of noumenon, theory of knowledge, theory of morality, and theory of time and space. It offered a great number of ideological materials on antagonistic opposites such as false and true, real and unreal, life and death, sudden enlightenment and gradual enlightenment, relative and absolute, finite and infinite, whole and part, temporary and eternal, enriching the categories of Chinese philosophy. A number of new schools of thought arose, such as the School of Principles (Neo-Confucianism) in the Song and Ming dynasties. Buddhism influenced many thinkers in the early Qing Dynasty, who enriched their academic thought by absorbing its rational factors while adapting and remolding them.

In traditional Chinese culture, Taoism has the closest relationship with scientific and technological culture. In medicine, chemistry, and pharmacology, Taoism combined its Nei Dan and Wai Dan theories with traditional Chinese medicinal theories and introduced its health preservation methods such as the regulation of breathing, massage, Daoyin and the Qi-promoting method into medical skills and treatment. Alchemy was used to produce medicines. The essences of the methods have made great contributions to Chinese medicine.

The techniques of Wai Dan are an important part of Taoist medicine. The development of these skills has provided much knowledge for the medical and medicinal industry and promoted the understanding of the origin, properties and use of many mineral products such as lead, white lead, lime, and cinnabar. And it also developed an easy and simple testing method for distinguishing natratite and mirabilite from other similar mineral products. The combination of alchemy and traditional Chinese medical practice brought about the development of ancient chemical skills in the production of medicine and accordingly enriched the content of Chinese pharmacology. No literature has been found on chemical medicines or plaster in the medical documents produced before the Western and Eastern Han dynasties. From the Jin Dynasty (265-420), more and more plasters and medicinal extracts produced by way of alchemy and chemistry were used. They gradually became principal medicines for traditional surgery. Hongshengdan and Baijiangdan extracts, now widely used, were derived from the secret preparations of Taoist physicians. Along with the development of Taoist "diet" practice, herbal medicines were gradually produced together with alchemic medicines. And the varieties of medicines were expanded from mineral medicines to herbal medicines, which promoted the development of the science of herbal medicine. Few of the herbal medicines noted in the *Works of Master Bao Pu*, written by Ge Hong, the *Collective Notes to the Canon of Materia Medica*, by Tao Hongjing, and *A Supplement to the Essential Prescriptions Worth a Thousand Pieces of Gold* by Sun Simiao can be found in the collective books of herbal medicines compiled before the Tang Dynasty. It was on the basis of these books that traditional Chinese physicians compiled their herbal medicinal books.

Nei Dan principles were also an important part of Taoist medicine. Alchemists and Taoist priests followed the practice through self-cultivation as an approach to rise above worldly considerations and achieve longevity. From a religious viewpoint, it explains that the feeling of light with the eyes closed, the feeling of heat in the abdomen when Qi (breath) is promoted, and the feeling of flowing in the air when one sits quietly in meditation are the "internal fire" burning inside to produce "Dan" (elixir) and the signs of ascending to become an immortal. Voluminous works on Nei Dan explored the law of changes of Qi, functional activity of Qi, Qi and blood, channels and collaterals in the body, enriching traditional Chinese medical science and therapeutics. During the Sui and Tang dynasties, the Imperial Medical Office appointed masters of massage to teach Daoyin. In his *Treatise on the Causes and Symptoms of Diseases*, Chao Yuanfan, an imperial physician of the Sui Dynasty, listed methods of Daoyin treatment including Qi-promoting self-practice. The Taoist internal practice and nourishing methods are mostly based on the law of nature. The way of Daoyin for promoting long life is based on the imitation of the natural state of growth of tortoises and cranes and for eating no grain food on the imitation of their way of respiration. Qi-promoting can bring about a state of harmony in the body and exercises can make the body flexible. Respiration can rid the body of that which is stale and draw in that which is fresh. Practice proceeds from easy to difficult together with many other ways. Traditional Chinese medicine follows the laws of nature and regulating Yin and Yang, flow in the channels and collaterals, and Qi-promoting, and promoting blood circulation.

Buddhism and Taoism promoted the development of imagery in traditional Chinese culture. First of all, in traditional Chinese painting, a new variety of Buddhist and Taoist painting made by literati appeared. Most painters were worldly people and the theme of their works was stories about Buddha and Taoism. They pursued the Buddhist and Taoist styles of expression and skills. Among them, the most famous are Gu Kaizhi (c. 345-406) of the Eastern Jin Dynasty, Cao Zhongda of the Northern Qi (550-577) and Wu Daozi (c. 685-758) of the Tang Dynasty. Gu was the founder of literary Buddhist and Taoist paintings, putting emphasis on the "spirit" of his objects and introducing the role of notion stressed by Buddhism and Taoism into paintings. His Buddhist paintings are mostly about people. According to the record in a book, he painted a fresco for a temple. When he was going to add his final touch to the fresco, the temple invited benefactors to view his work for the particular occasion. Within only three days, the temple received a donation of "hundreds of thousands of coins." Through this we can see the value of his Buddhist paintings. His Taoist paintings mostly depicted clouds and dragons because the legendary Lao Zi was a dragon by birth. Since then, clouds and dragons have become one of the characters of Chinese paintings.

Cao Zhongda introduced Indian Gandhara sculpture into Chinese painting. It features the characters in strained clothes. The clothes look as if they are wet and sticking to the body. Though Cao's painting techniques were not passed down to the present time, the standing portrait of Sakaymuni now preserved in the Mrgadava Buddhist ruins in India can provide a glimpse of his style.

Wu Daozi was also a noted Buddhist and Taoist painter. Before the Tang period, Chinese paintings stressed the drawings with lines. Wu began to introduce the Indian concave and convex method into Chinese figure painting and adopted the Taoist concept by letting the people in his works wear a loose and broad garment and belts, moving just like an immortal in the sky. His style of works can be found in the frescos in the Dunhuang Caves. The paintings of these three men brought an entirely new look to Chinese painting. During the Song and Yuan periods, this kind of paintings began to combine with the skills of landscape and flower-and-bird paintings, enhancing the expressiveness of Chinese painting. For example, on a scroll painting, an album or a fan, painters intentionally pursued a state of "inaction" and "ultimate serenity" through the drawing of landscapes, flowers and birds in the paintings, forming a style of art of transcendence, dignity and indifference to worldly concerns, a style which still exists in the present-day painting community. The contemporary painter Zhang Daqian had lived in Mt. Qingcheng in Sichuan Province for many years. He produced a number of Taoist figure paintings which are carved on mountain rocks and regarded as treasures of Buddhist and Taoist paintings.

Secondly, a number of renowned works with a Buddhist or Taoist theme appeared in traditional literature. These works brought with them a novelty of artistic conception, a new style, and a new way of wording. Li Bai, the famous Tang Dynasty poet, was one of the best in his time. He wrote such lines as "Motionless as I sit in meditation/The whole world penetrates my hair." Many of his other poems are full of thoughts of immortals with a feeling of a natural grace. For instance, in his poem "On Mount Taishan," he described his life and self-cultivation experience in his quiet studio like this: "Quiet and serene for as long as three thousand days/On white cloth I wrote the Taoist tenet/When I am enlightened by chanting the text/All the gods come to protect my form/Sailing on the clouds like wind/I flap away as if I had wings." In another poem called "The Antique Style," he again fully expressed his yearning for becoming a hermit and immortal: "One meal is enough to survive ten thousand years/Then I needn't return to my hometown/I'll go with the high wind forever/Roaming beyond the sky as I like." Tang Buddhist poems had a direct impact on poets of the Song Dynasty. The production of Song Ci-lyrics was at its peak with most derived from the stories of Taoism. In addition, many Buddhist scriptures and texts also promoted the creation of novels in the Jin and Tang dynasties. Literary stories and the librettos of ballads adapted from Buddhist sutras had a consequential relationship with the formation of later Chinese popular literature. The quotations from the doctrine of the Chan Sect were not only followed by thinkers of the School of Principles in the Song and Ming dynasties, but also had some influence on the literary works of later popular literature.

In the field of architecture, since most Taoist constructions adopted the traditional courtyard style, closely resembling secular constructions, they have accumulated and provided a great deal of novel designs, layout patterns, techniques, and other unique executions of building for secular constructions. Their architectural design, techniques, and style together with architectural art and philosophy still serve as typical references for modern Chinese architecture.

Chapter 5

Colorful and Stylistic Historical Relics

Section 1 The Cultural Characteristics of Jade Articles

Jade articles produced in ancient China were used in sacrificial ceremonies, rituals, funerals, and adornments. With their solid and smooth quality, and lustrous colors, jade products have always been famous for their beauty and style.

In ancient times, jade was only used for personal ornaments. After the middle and later period of the Neolithic Age, large jade articles replaced small ones. Large jade articles, usually symbolizing a certain political prestige, began to reflect the ideas of the social class system and ancient religions. Until this time, jade pieces had been regarded as merely ornaments, but the stone now became closely connected to a ritual system.

Sacrificial ceremonies occupied a place of great importance to the nobility of the Shang Dynasty (c. 17th century-11th century BC). As well as elaborately engraved and magnificent bronze ritual articles, they carved many colorful and stylistic jade ritual articles. After the overthrow of the Shang Dynasty, the Western Zhou Dynasty (c. 11th century-771 BC) created a sacrificial ceremonial system corresponding to the patriarchal system. This social class system and its ideas were distinctively reflected in the use of jade ritual articles. The rules of this system laid down the use of "green *bi* as a tribute to worship the Heaven, yellow *cong* to worship the Earth, blue *gui* to worship the East, red *zhang* to worship the South, white *hu* to worship the West, and black *huang* to worship the North." Jade articles were also produced in various shapes of *gui* to represent six official ranks: *zhenggui* for kings, *huangui* for dukes, *xingui* for marquises, *gonggui* for earls, and *gubi* for viscounts and *pubi* for barons. Thus, jade articles used in ritual ceremonies for worshipping deities were strictly classified and those to be used by nobles of different ranks were also strictly distinguished from each other. Jade articles became marks of different classes in the Kingdom of Heaven and the world of man. During the Western Zhou period, grand sacrificial ceremonies promoted the development of jade article production. However, confined by the conceptions of the social class system, jade articles, though produced in great quantities, were limited in variety.

During the Spring and Autumn Period (770-476 BC) and the Warring States Period (475-221 BC), drastic changes took place in social, political, economic and ideological spheres. As a result, the functions of jade articles changed accordingly. Jade ritual articles began to play a role in paying respect to the king, making vows, marriages and funerals. By now, the concept that the conduct of people being of greater importance than gods was gradually growing and developing. Jade articles were used more frequently to illustrate the moral aspects of man. In *The Book of Rites*, jade is described as "mild, smooth and lustrous like the virtue of a kind and decent man. It is fine, precise, and solid, just like the virtue of a wise man. It is cut with angles and corners, but will not hurt anyone, like the virtue of a righteous man. A jade ornament worn as a pendant is like a benign, modest man of good manners. When it is struck, it gives a clear, resonant and lingering sound which lasts till it comes to a sudden stop, just like the attitude of a man of virtue toward music. The beauty of a piece of jade co-exists with its flaws which are not covered up, like the behavior of a loyal and honest man. It is crystalline and transparent and shiny, like the quality of purity which springs from the bottom of a good man's heart.

By the beginning of the Han Dynasty (206 BC-220 AD), although *gui* were still being used as ritual articles, other jade articles at the time were used only as ornaments. Hardly any *zhang* and *cong* had been found from this period, and those that had were refashioned out of older ones. Vestiges of the ritual system surrounding jade articles gradually vanished. The production of jade articles in the Han period, having broken from the traditional influence of the ritual system, had entered a new stage of development. The jade articles of the Han period were produced with a vigorous, firm, bold and unconstrained style, pursuing an artistic beauty free from vulgarity, which reflected the lofty aspiration of the unified Han empire and marked the transformation of jade article production from being merely ornamental to works of art.

During the periods of the Three Kingdoms, the Western and Eastern Jin dynasties and the Southern and Northern Dynasties (220-589), when Taoism had grown in strength, people believed that jade had medicinal properties that could make them live longer, resulting in a temporary craze for eating jade. This, however, did not affect the further development of the use of jade for decoration.

Jade is a natural substance, but when it is processed and crafted by man into ornamental and ritual articles it becomes stamped with the mark of society and becomes a part of culture. As an old Chinese saying goes, "Until jade is cut, it is not jadeware." By fashioning the stone into an article to be used by man, man's thinking and feeling are instilled into it. It becomes a symbol reflecting the evolution of social life, from its use in ritual to its use as an ornament. The achievements of human civilization can be embodied either by a "thing" or an "idea." Superficially, they have nothing to do with each other, but in fact, they have a common point. The evolution of jade production demonstrated a change within Chinese philosophy from theism to humanism.

Ancient Chinese jadeware reached a very high artistic level. The jade articles of the Shang period embodied a combination of carving skills inherited from previous times such as concave and convex lines, relief, and round carvings. All these skills were employed naturally and dexterously with skillful coordination, delicate and clear patterns and regular and balanced shapes. A large quantity of jade articles was produced, particularly during the latter part of the Shang, mostly engraved with smooth lines and complicated patterns of high aesthetic value. More than 1,900 jade articles were unearthed from the Fuhao tomb, and these are typical of those produced in the later Shang period. They can be classified into two categories: flat and round ones. The flat ones have similar and symmetrical patterns on both sides, harmonious and perfect, an expression of the essential spirit of traditional Chinese culture (see the "Introduction" to this book). Flat articles are fan-like or circular-shaped with arc circumference. Their outward edge is convex and the inward edge is concave, suggesting a dynamic sense of movement. Their exactly cut contours give a full presentation of the features of the work with the effect of a papercut, hence known as "papercut-style jade engraving art."

The round ones are produced in the shape of a cylinder or a cube. They include *cong* (a kind of jade articles produced in ancient China, with a round hole in the center of a rectangular-shaped jade) and *gui* (a food container with a wide and round mouth and two ears) and other shapes with animal and figure designs. *Cong* and *gui* are produced with a style of solemnity and dignity, and those with a bird and beast design are grotesque and full of imagination and romantic taste. The only two turtle-shaped pieces of jade that have been handed down to the present time are produced with the original and natural colors and grains of jade. The material's original deep dark color is retained to make the shells of the turtles and their eyes and claws stand out in sharp relief against the white and gray colors of the other parts, showing a more realistic image with a wonderful and naturally-made effect. Later, many artisans and craftsmen followed after the skills of the craftsmanship, known as "beautifully colored jade articles." These two jade turtles are the jade articles so far discovered in the country.

The artistic style of jadeware produced in the Western Zhou Dynasty tended toward simplicity. A unique craftsmanship was created by using coarse block lines or delicate intaglio cut lines while maintaining the way of drawing an outline with double lines, a skill passed down from the Shang period. Patterns were usually expressed by simple and robust cut lines, and the typical patterns include that of *kui* (a one-foot bizarre dragon-like beast in ancient legend) and phoenix. The shapes of jade articles produced in the Eastern Zhou (770-256 BC) were of a great variety. But they had a conspicuous feature, that is, they pursued a spiritual likeness of things. Most of the jade articles produced at this time contained decorative motifs. Such motifs as those of phoenix and *panhui* (a kind of viper) derived from that of *kui* were very common. During the Warring States Period, patterns of clouds and grains were very popular. At the time, gold and silver articles were very commonly inlaid with jade.

Along with the improvement of tools and techniques in the making of jade articles, such articles as those with raised relief and round carved patterns were produced in great quantity. And more hollowed-out cut articles and vessels appeared as well. Their patterns and decorations were rich and colorful, such as grains, cattail leaves, whirls and clouds and designs of dragon, phoenix, *taotie* (a fierce and voracious beast in ancient legend) and *li* (a kind of dragon without horns in ancient legend, the image of which was often used as decorative pattern on art works) and tiger. The jade figurines, galloping horses and jade *pixia* (an ornament to ward off evil spirits) round carving works typical of the Han style, are novelties, superb in design and craftsmanship with lively looks. They are unique in China's ancient carving art. They have not only inherited the tradition of the round carving skills passed down from the Shang and Zhou dynasties, but also absorbed the romantic style of the Chu culture, fully expressing a vigorous, firm, bold and unconstrained style.

Though less in number, yet each of the jade articles of the Tang Dynasty (618-907) was exquisitely produced. Their style was closely linked with the delicate style of gold and silver articles and the full and bold style of sculptural art and the refined and detailed style in painting. The way of expression was realistic with round carving and relief to show the outline of the product and rough intaglio cut lines to show its looks and appearance. The skills in the making of jade articles of this stage reached the acme of perfection. Image articles were usually produced with well-designed images and good and lively appearance, marking jade art beginning to scale a new height of development.

During the Northern and Southern Song dynasties (960-1279), designs of jade articles pursued a target to show the common psychology of society and the designed shapes were mostly imitating the images of flowers, grass, birds and beasts commonly seen in daily life. The way of expression mostly used was hollowed-out carving, with either complicated and beautiful patterns or fresh and graceful designs, all attaining a high degree of unification of life and art. During the time, since the rise of epigraphy and the popularity of a tendency of favoring antiquity, imitated antique jade articles appeared. The craftsmen of the time, to copy the ancient products, invented a way to make products dyed with flaws. With its wonderful hollowed-out skill and vivid and lively patterns of flowers and birds and its new imitated antique articles, the jade carving craftsmanship of the Song period produced a far-reaching influence upon the later development of jade articles. Meanwhile, the clearly and simply designed articles with a strong realistic style produced in the Liao period and the Jin Dynasty (1115-1234) products characteristic of using *chunshan* and *qiushui* jade are also of high value of art.

Jade articles of the Yuan Dynasty (1279-1368) adopted the skillful hollowed-out craftsmanship passed down from the Song and Jin periods. And the relief technique was also dexterously applied. The main patterns were flowers, birds, landscapes, *li* and tigers and sea animals. The jade articles with flower and bird patterns are characteristic of the Chinese trumpet creepers, with a quite different model and design from those of their preceding times. Particularly, the Dushan large jade sculpture, which was produced with a feeling of magnificence and a style of simplicity, robust and bold and unconstrained, is the best representative product of all the Yuan products.

Jade article production of the Ming (1368-1644) and Qing (1644-1911) periods incorporated all kinds of the craftsmanship of the past ages. The jade articles made in the Ming period featured a modeling of roughness and boldness and vigor with such themes as ordinary people and animals and plants. Hollowed-out skill was very commonly used. On a piece of flat jade, craftsmen could cut out different patterns on the upper and lower levels of it and could properly administer the harmonious balance between the superficial and internal parts. Decorations included flowers and birds, animals and auspicious designs, figures and stories. The products were clear and graceful with a strong taste of painting and the curves and lines are stout, firm and clear-cut. The imitated antique products of the time were produced as good as their originals. Jade products of the Qing period are characteristic of large size, great quantity, and fine quality. The craftsmanship of traditional intaglio cut and line, relief and hollowed-out cut was fully developed into an acme of perfection. Lines were cut as straight as a rule and a circle as round as a full moon. Hollowed-out cut products were crystalline and all the detailed parts were carefully and elaborately done, suggestive of a feeling of harmony and satisfaction. Landscapes, figures, flowers and birds, legendary and mythical stories, and such designs and inscriptions as auspiciousness, longevity and wealth and rank, which were cut on pieces of jade, had attained a high level of artistry. Particularly, those designs of landscape, flowers and grass and figures and stories that sought a painting effect had reached an art realm of combining poetry and painting. In the Qing period, its imitated antique products also attained a peak of perfection in terms of their aesthetic value. Meanwhile, its techniques to produce beautiful jade also reached its peak of development. Bright and colorful jade products of the Ming and Qing periods have drawn a satisfactory full stop for China's jade article production.

Jade articles induced by a primitive and hazy sense of beauty appeared and have undergone twists and turns in their development of more than 7,000 years from simple decorations to sacrificial ritual articles in ancient times and to symbolic fittings for lofty morality, and finally to art works of various types and varieties. They profoundly reflected the social consciousness of different historical stages. Especially in a certain stage of development, people made the natural properties of jade moralized, enabling it to play a special role in political, religious, ideological and cultural spheres and develop a unique function that other art works could not do. In the world cultural history, this cultural phenomenon has never been known in other countries and regions, and embodies a distinctive national character.

Section 2 The Cultural Value of Bronze Mirrors

In ancient China, bronze mirrors were both functional items and works of art. Over the course of more than 4,000 years, the shape and patterns of bronze mirrors continued to develop to become a rich bronze mirror culture.

The development of bronze mirrors occurred much later than other bronze articles and jadeware. Therefore, as compared with the culture of the former two, the latter contains more mundane culture, an important feature of the bronze mirror culture.

There were decorative patterns of dragon, phoenix or fish on bronze mirrors. They were totems in immemorial times. But on bronze mirrors, they were no longer totems, but a symbol of auspiciousness. Fish patterns first appeared in a time as late as the Jin Dynasty (1115-1234). Wishing that they could have a prosperous and prolific family with more sons and grandsons, people liked to use fish patterns to symbolize "having more roes" and "affluence" because in Chinese "fish" is pronounced as "yu," which is homonymous to another Chinese character meaning "surplus" or "affluence."

Such patterns as the sun and moon and Heaven and Earth were often found on bronze mirrors. This is simply because they had a close relationship with the traditional ideas of Heaven and Earth and gods. But they chiefly mean what people knew about nature. The measured and scaled patterns on the bronze mirrors produced in the Han period reflect that people had known that the Heaven was round and the Earth was square. And stellar patterns were used to show the four directions and four seasons. The pattern of a chain of arcs meant the beams of the sun and moon and the vault of Heaven. The eight-trigram patterns on the mirrors produced in the Tang and Song periods meant the organic combination of Heaven, Earth and man. Sometimes, characters were cast on the mirrors, for instance, "when the sun shines, it is bright daytime," and "as bright as the sun and the moon."

During the Han Dynasty, the patterns of "four gods" (green dragon, white tiger, red bird, and black tortoise) and the 12 animals (rat, ox, tiger, rabbit, dragon, snake, horse, sheep, monkey, rooster, dog, and pig, representing the 12 Earthly Branches) appeared on bronze mirrors. But they became obsolete in the Song period. They reflected ancient people psychologically seeking the protection from gods and taking animals as an auspicious symbol. These patterns also reflected their knowledge of geography, seasons, and the level of their understanding of nature.

After the Tang period, patterns of flowers, grass and trees began to occupy a prominent position rather than served as embellishments in the design of bronze mirrors. Since the prime stage of the Tang, bronze mirrors with flower and grass as the main decorative patterns had appeared. The flower-and-bird mirrors, auspicious beast mirrors, and lucky bird mirrors were also matched by many flowers, grass and twig patterns to make animals and plants complement each other, to present a colorful picture as a whole. Patterns of flowers and grass and trees on bronze mirrors produced in the Song Dynasty were simple and graceful, and the pictures were clear and fresh, full of an idyllic tang.

Human figures had appeared on bronze mirrors of the Warring States Period. During that time, people set great store by martial qualities. So on bronze mirrors there were images of warriors clad in armor. During the Han Dynasty, mythological stories were widely prevalent. Adaptations from fairy tales were commonly seen on mirrors. The images of fairies were often interwoven with the scenes of hunting, riding a chariot or a horse, and dance, strongly reflecting people's keen admiration of the life of a fairyland and the earnest pursuit for the life of the existing world. A fierce polo contest was vividly produced on Tang Dynasty bronze mirrors. The ball-kicking scenes on Song Dynasty mirrors and the weaving maids on the mirrors of the Jin Dynasty also reflect some aspects of the social lives of the time.

To sum up, the greatest characteristic feature of Chinese bronze mirror culture is to reflect completely and artistically people's realistic lives and their yearning for a bright future. This can be evidently seen on mirrors produced in the Tang period, because at the time the socio-economic and cultural development had advanced and the prosperity of Sino-foreign cultural exchanges and the growth of the mutual influence of various cultures had appeared, enabling the bronze mirror culture and its artistic level to be promoted to a new height. For instance, the "twin-bird mirror" was quite popular in the prime and middle stages of the Tang Dynasty. A pair of birds carrying a ribbon in their bills expressed the people's expectations for good luck and happiness. The "hunting-scene mirror" vividly showed the hunters riding horses to hunt after deers. Hunting was an important event in social life at the time, because Emperor Taizong of Tang attached importance to hunting so much as to the prosperity and unification of the state. He took these three things as his great happiness and merits, something quite different from the hunting in later times as a pastime. The "immortal riding a flying cane" mirror was an artwork reflecting the Taoist mythological thought at the time. It may be said that the social life was very widely and extensively reflected in bronze mirrors.

There are also inscriptions on the mirrors. On the mirrors produced in the Han Dynasty, the implications of many love affair inscriptions were more than the love affair itself, embodying a profound social presentment. Other inscriptions directly expressed people's longing for a peaceful life.

Philosophical ideas were usually induced from bronze mirrors in ancient China. According to the earliest records about bronze mirrors, almost all took mirrors as a means to learn a lesson from. And they were extended in meaning to learn a lesson from someone. A story in the *Strategies of the Warring States* says that one day when an official named Zou Ji of the State of Qi looked into the mirror before he went to pay respect to the king, he thought he was not so handsome as the noted handsome man Lord Xu at the time. But all his wife and concubines and friends said he was more handsome than Lord Xu. From the flattery Zou thought one should not be fooled by praises from his kinsfolk and should have self-knowledge. He told the king of the reasons. When he heard his explanation, the king felt he had learned something. He ordered that all his subjects should constantly make self-criticism about their own mistakes. And this had brought about a good influence politically. Later, an inscribed board with the words "a bright mirror hanging high above" was put up in the halls of many government offices, suggestive of pursuing a policy of drawing a distinctive line between right and wrong, and of justice and self-lessness. Tang emperors often granted bronze mirrors as an award and encouragement to those officials who had achieved merits in their work and were honest in working style. Some mirrors had such inscriptions as "honesty will always be maintained by my descendants," "as a traditional family's heritage, honesty shall be kept in mind forever," or "good manners or not, good will or not, one's appearance and mind can be examined through the mirror as well." All these expressed an earnest wish of Chinese people seeking for an honest government and a lofty personality.

In ancient times, Chinese bronze mirrors through trade or donation found their way overseas through the "Silk Road" or by sea. Mirrors made in the middle and later stages of the Western Han were unearthed in Korea and Japan. During the Three Kingdoms and the Western and Eastern Jin dynasties, as well as bronze mirrors, some Chinese craftsmen and even a great deal of materials were sent to Japan to produce mirrors there. During the early stage of the Tang Dynasty, in Chnag'an, as an economic and cultural center of the time in the world, exchanges between China and other countries took place very often. Tang mirrors were often found overseas, most of them in Japan. These are the best evidence of Sino-foreign cultural exchanges. Bronze mirrors have been also found in Korea, Mongolia, the former Soviet Union, and Iran. This proves how popular Chinese bronze mirrors were. At the same time, patterns like grapes and twin birds on Tang mirrors had a similar style to that of the patterns on Persian silk goods, showing that Chinese bronze mirrors had absorbed foreign culture to enrich itself when it was exported to other countries. The wide spread of Chinese mirrors abroad promoted the friendship between China and various other countries.

Section 3 The Cultural Connotation of Gold and Silver Articles

Gold and silver articles include all the vessels and ornaments made of gold and silver. Since gold and silver are precious metals, such articles are produced much less in quantity than those of bronze, jade and pottery and porcelain. But the former ones are finely produced with a higher cultural value. Beliefs and religions, life and customs and national cultural features in ancient society are usually reflected in gold and silver articles.

The earliest Chinese gold articles were found in the Shang Dynasty. And silver articles were found a little later than gold articles. After the Shang Dynasty, gold and silver articles were also produced in various periods and left to the present day. These products produced in different times show different characteristics of their own.

Gold articles produced in the Shang period were small ornaments, though not great in quantity and variety. During the Zhou Dynasty, particularly in the Spring and Autumn and Warring States periods, the quantity and variety of gold and silver articles apparently increased and the earliest gold ware appeared.

During the Qin and Han periods, the craftsmanship of gold and silver products was improved, becoming an independent trade separated from the traditional production of bronze articles. Gold filigree and welding skills were commonly used and gold plating technique was also very popular. Apart from gold-vessels, there were also articles with animal designs and other ornaments. Seals made of gold and silver were also found.

Not many gold and silver vessels were found dating back to the Three Kingdoms, the Western Jin and Eastern Jin dynasties, and the Southern and Northern Dynasties, but the few that had been found all have their own style. Except small ornaments, many vessels were unearthed that had been imported from Persia in the Sasanian Dynasty. They show the cultural exchange between China and foreign countries at the time, particularly in the period of the Northern Wei (368-534), was very frequent.

Since the economy of the Sui and Tang periods was prosperous, groups of the Tang gold and silver ware were unearthed on several occasions. The products produced in this period were various and rich in variety, including cups, boxes, plates and pots, even coffins and Buddhist pagodas never found before. They also included articles in such designs as dragon, phoenix, heavenly horse and heavenly lion. The patterns on the products included peony, lily lotus, honeysuckle, pomegranade, in addition to musicians and singers, female figurines, frolicking children and hunters and horses. With all kinds of patterns, the vessels suggest a feeling of pleasantry and gracefulness. At the time, casting and foundry, welding, cutting, polishing, riveting, plating, punching, carving and hollow cutting were widely used in the production of gold and silver vessels.

During the periods of Song, Liao, Jin and Yuan, urban economy and commodity production were well developed. At the time, gold ware hitherto being exclusive products of the upper class of society had now become commodities on the market. They were not only owned and enjoyed by nobles and ministers, but also possessed by ordinary but rich families and appeared in many entertainment and public houses and brothels. Their style had changed from sumptuousness to simplicity, with the tang of life or poetic flavor. Gold and silver products of the Liao period are full of ethnical style. There are not many gold and silver products of the Jin period unearthed, but many of the Yuan Dynasty products were unearthed, most of them in the south part of China, justifying the well developed craftsmanship in the south. Many products made in this period usually contained inscriptions and signatures of the makers. Many others were even inscribed with poems or essays. These products providing accurate written materials can serve as standard materials for research.

Few novel products were found in the Ming Dynasty. But in the Qing Dynasty, production of gold and silver was developed as never before. The variety of gold and silver articles covered a wide range from decrees to sacrificial vessels, headdresses, daily-use articles, horse gears, furnishings and Buddhist ritual vessels. And a great deal of gold was used. In the 45th year of the reign of Emperor Kangxi of the Qing Dynasty (1715), a set of 16 gold bells was produced with a total weight of more than 460 kg. A gold pagoda enshrined in the Zhongzheng Hall was 5.33 meters in height and 350 kg in weight. The social function of gold and silver vessels further expanded at the time with models and patterns well developed. Such new techniques as attaching enamel to gold vessels and a mixing of filigree and enamel appeared. The full development of the production of gold and silver products during this time reflected the wanton extravagant life of the ruling class, as well as the socio-economic prosperity and upgraded sci-tech level of the time.

To make a general survey, the development of Chinese gold and silver vessels in ancient time contained affluent cultural contents. Generally speaking, they included:

First, worship and belief. There are many gold and silver articles that reflect the worship and belief of the ancient people. The unearthed gold facial cover is one of the evidences that show the idea of worship. It was found covering the face of a bronze man, possibly used in some ritual in a sacrificial ceremony. After the introduction of Buddhism into China, and since the Northern Wei Dynasty (368-534), gold and silver vessels had been used to hold Buddhist relics enshrined in the chamber of the basement of a pagoda. During the Song and Liao periods, many gold and silver vessels were also unearthed from pagoda basements. But it should be noted that not all gold and silver vessels reflect a religious worship and belief. And the later the time came, the less religious content they contained.

Secondly, the idea of hierarchy. Gold and silver articles had always been used as a symbol to show the social status of the owner. There were gold batons and gold crowns to symbolize power. For example, an unearthed "three-star gold baton" is a gold product of the Shang period, 142 cm in length, 2.3 cm in diameter and 780 grams in weight. According to archeologists, it was probably used to symbolize the status and authority of a tribal leader. The prince's gold seals of the Eastern Han period were the very thing to show one's power and status. After the Song Dynasty, the quantity of gold and silver products increased and mostly were used to show the wealth of the owner. Along with the progress of social life, gold and silver products were more and more used in people's daily life, such as gold box, silver box, gold and silver cups and silver pots. These products were welcomed by the people for their usefulness and artistic value.

Thirdly, a clear reflection of the folk style and customs.

This feature has been more apparently shown in the products made by ethnic minorities. Archeologists found the Huns and Xianbeis liked to make gold and silver vessels with animal patterns, particularly such ones as a fight between a tiger and a wolf — a presentation of the nomadic life of these peoples. Qidan nobles had a unique funeral custom, using gold and silver masks to cover the faces of the dead and colorful brocade to bind their hands and feet. Gold and silver masks found by archeologists are convincing proofs of this.

Gold and silver products found in the Central Plain were usually decorated with animals and plants that symbolized auspiciousness and good luck, suggestive of good wishes for a happy life. The patterns of dragon and phoenix were quite often used to symbolize the great propitiousness, sheep good luck, mandarin ducks affection of a loving couple, wild goose propitiousness, paradise flycatcher longevity, and pomegranate the proliferation of a family.

Fourthly, the craftsmanship of the products is also of unique artistic level.

Gold and silver products in early times were small and simple.

During the periods of Han and Tang, gold and silver products were produced in great variety and in unique shapes. During the periods of Song and Yuan, the style gradually became simple and elegant. For instance, a silver fruit container made in the Song period had been popular at the time and in later periods for its usefulness, delicate modeling and suggestion of good luck and peace. In the periods of Ming and Qing, products made of gold together with jade increased in number. And their models suggested a dignity, boldness and vigor, like a gold ball with pearls made in the Qing period, which is 82 cm high with a diameter of 30 cm. It is a model of the heavenly body, reflecting the magnificence of the Heaven and Earth and the cosmos of the time, and helping people to know the universe. It is a product of people's knowledge of the universe and a stylistic art work as well. Obviously, gold and silver products have a high value of art and cultural virtuosity.

Section 4 Bronze, Pottery and Porcelain Ware and Ancient Chinese Culture

1. The Cultural Connotation of Bronze Vessels

The periods of Shang and Zhou were famous for their production of bronze vessels, so they are called "the bronze era."

Bronze came after the discovery of copper. Copper, a natural mineral ore without any processing, has some metallic luster and the property of extension. It was discovered by the primitive man when he sought stone material to make stone articles. In the late stage of the Neolithic Age, people could produce small tools and ornaments with copper. The discovery and use of copper had contributed to the accumulation of skills and experiences for the creation of bronze, laying a foundation for the transition from the stage of using copper together with stone to the stage of using bronze.

Bronze is a green-gray alloy of copper and tin. It has a lower melting point than copper, but it is harder. The earliest bronze articles found in China are the small knives of the Majiayao Culture unearthed in Gansu Province, dating back to 4,000 and 6,000 years. In the later Qijia Culture tombs, some bronze farm tools and ornaments were also found. The way of production included cool foundry and metallurgy which showed a primitive bronze industry had appeared at the time.

A few bronze products including *jue* (wine vessel), *jia* (wine container), halberds, barbed arrowheads, awls, and small knives were unearthed in the tombs of Erlitou Culture in Yanshi, Henan Province. They might have been produced in the Xia Dynasty (c. late 22nd century to early 17th century BC) and the production had developed to become the culture of the early stage of the Shang period discovered in Erligang in Zhengzhou and the Yin ruins of the later stage of the Shang period found in Anyang. All these have clearly shown the development of bronze production from lower to higher levels in China.

The Shang and Zhou periods are known as the prime stage of bronze culture in China. At that time, large workshops for bronze production had appeared. Some of them covered an area of about 1,000 to 10,000 square meters, or even up to 120,000 square meters. People had learned how to promote the hardness and tenacity of bronze products, by changing the percentage of contents of copper and tin in the composition. The products of the time involved farm tools, weapons, sacrificial vessels and musical instruments, of which the last two represented the highest level of craftsmanship of the time.

Bronze products were first used by ordinary people in their daily life during the Spring and Autumn and Warring States periods. The style of the products also became simple and the pattern ingenious with shallow and simple engravings. The decorations varied, and such decorations as fighting and banquets also appeared. During that time, iron products began to be used in daily life instead of bronze products. The latter was no longer a significant mark of the era.

What is the culture presented by bronze vessels?

First we may see religious and ancestral worship reflected in bronze vessels. The Shang tribe regarded that "large birds" had been ordered by Heaven to become their original ancestors. Consequently, ancestors, Heaven, constellation, winds, rains, thunder and lightning, spirits and ghosts became the objects of worship. The rulers of the Shang Dynasty put a great deal of bronze vessels in their ancestral temple — the most sacred place — for worship and sacrificial ceremonies. After they died, these vessels were buried with the dead for them to use in the nether world. Types and patterns of the bronze vessels were also designed to show the idea of religious worship. Looking at the motifs of *taotie* (a mythical ferocious animal), people of today may have a mysterious and terrific feeling. Other designs like the so-called *kuilong* (a kind of dragon), *kuifeng* (a kind of phoenix) and *chixiao* (a kind of owl), as a certain symbol, reflected the idea of some superpower of nature in people's minds.

During the Western Zhou Dynasty, there were also mythical tales about the origin of its clan. A complete system for sacrificial ceremonies for worshipping gods had been established at the time, with a set of strict rules on where they should be held and what kind of bronze vessels to be used. However, as uncertainty about the Heaven grew and virtue began to be held in esteem, the mythical witchery and deterrent force of these bronze vessels mainly used in sacrificial ceremonies began to decline at the end of the Western Zhou. Since then, the religious flavor of bronze vessels has been greatly reduced.

Secondly, let's make a review of the ritual functions of bronze vessels.

From the bronze vessels unearthed from tombs, we find that the number of wine vessels to be buried with a dead member of the Shang nobility shows his or her status and position. Since the mid-period of Zhou, the number of cooking vessels and food-containers gradually increased. *Ding* (a cooking vessel) became the principal symbol of one's status and position. And a strict system of the use of *ding* was introduced. For instance, nine *ding* were required to be used in the ritual ceremony for a Son of

Heaven, seven for a vassal state ruler, five for a senior official, and three for a senior serviceman. At the same time, *ding* were used together with a certain number of *gui* (food container) in a ritual ceremony; for example, four *gui* and five *ding*, six *gui* and seven *ding*, and so on by analogy. There were other rules on the number of plates and pots to be used. Still other bronze ritual vessels were regarded as a symbol of state power. Whoever came by such a vessel was considered the ruler. It can thus be seen that bronze vessels represented and symbolized the rigid hierarchy of status and positions and the idea of maintaining such hierarchy in the periods of Shang and Zhou.

Finally, the artistic value of bronze vessels should be taken into consideration.

Exquisiteness of the modeling of bronze vessels was one of the basic requirements in the making of the products. The bronze products made during the Shang and Zhou periods had refined and exquisite shapes. All the parts were well-treated, perfectly balanced and in line with standards. As an integral whole, they were natural and full without roughness.

Magnificence was another requirement. The Si Mu Wu rectangular *ding* made in the Shang period weighs 875 kg. Two large *ding* of the Western Zhou, the Da Yu and Da Ke, weigh 153.5 kg and 201 kg respectively. The weight of a number of musical instruments is also surprisingly heavy.

The patterns of bronze vessels are bizarre and vivid. Apart from the mythical and beautiful *taotie*, *chixiao* and *kuilong* designs, there are many other designs full of human interest. After the Warring States Period, the patterns brimmed with a deep love for life.

The inscriptions on bronze vessels are honored as the "art of lines." Inscriptions of the Shang period are vigorously carved in a plump style. The starting or ending strokes are usually sharply cut, while some of the inscriptions have thin, but vigorous shapes, bearing evident marks of oracle bone inscription influence. The inscription styles of the late Shang period were inherited by the early Western Zhou, with natural and varied presentations suggestive of a sense of elegance. During the mid-period of the Western Zhou, long inscriptions stressed the art of composition and the long-shaped or round-shaped characters were cut with a mellow style, suggestive of a sense of solemnity and elegance, having a comparatively high aesthetic value.

As one of the major carriers of ancient Chinese culture, Chinese bronze vessels contained decorations, shapes and inscriptions that represented the inflexible pursuit of beauty by the people of the time, which have produced a significant impact on the later arts of sculpture and calligraphy and become an important part of the history of ancient Chinese culture.

2. The Humanistic Ethos of Pottery and Porcelain Products

Pottery and porcelain products were the most common articles used by ancient Chinese in their daily life. Pottery articles were made of clay together with sand and charcoal cinders baked by fire. The materials, such as Kaolin, used to make porcelain articles are better and finer in quality than those used for making pottery articles. The baking temperatures are much higher, usually over 1,200 degrees Celsius. The rate of water absorption is also lower. Pottery article production has a longer history than that of porcelain products, dating from 9,100-8,200 years ago. But the earliest porcelain shards that have been so far found were probably produced about 4,000 years ago.

The pottery products of the Neolithic Age vary in kind. The most particular one is the painted potteries. For instance, a pottery basin with an exquisitely painted human face and fish patterns has two groups of black-colored designs around the inside of the basin. Each group contains two patterns set in symmetry. In addition, the unearthed painted pottery artifacts such as those with dance patterns, stork and stone axe designs, are all outstanding products of the Neolithic Age. There are also many other pottery products, such as the eggshell black pottery products of Longshan Culture in Shandong, shining and bright as lacquer with even thickness. Some are as thin an eggshell, but are as hard as a stone.

Some of the pottery artifacts of the Neolithic Age are produced in the shape of animals, such as owl-shaped *ding* (cooking vessel), dog-shaped *gui* (cooking vessel), and rooster-shaped *yi* (wine vessel). Some are made in the shape of a human being such as a human-shaped painted pottery flask on which, as well as color patterns, there is a nude figure. Some jars are designed with a mouth in the shape of a human head and a round and pot belly in the middle like a pregnant woman. Both animal and plant patterns are used in the designs. Some variations include triangles, trellises, waves and billows, circles, nets, zigzags, strings, stars, and petals. Craftsmen were so skillful in the composition of a point, a line or a surface and highly conscious of the aesthetics of the swivel patterns and curve lines that they already had a certain understanding of nature and human beings. Their imaginations and beautification of and worship for nature were also presented in the designs. A vague idea of "man" being the subject in the perception of the world in the struggle against nature began to emerge at the time. This is the dawn of the Chinese culture of humanism.

The Shang and Zhou periods were historical stages marked by bronze vessels. During those periods, pottery production adopted some strong points from the production of bronze vessels and made much headway in subsequent development. The success in the making of white pottery clay articles with carved patterns was a landmark of pottery production. The combination of white and plain models and beautiful patterns is very pleasant and charming.

During the Spring and Autumn and Warring States periods, pottery products were mainly used in building and in sacrificial ceremonies for the dead. At that time, when large-scale construction was being carried out in the various vassal states, a great demand for materials made of pottery was needed. A section of pottery pipe unearthed from the ruins of the State of Yan was shaped like a tiger's head in front with an upturned nose, wide-open eyes and erect ears. It represents the state-of-the-art of that time in the building sector. In the Qin and Han dynasties, pottery production boomed, being known as a stage of "the bricks of Qin and the tiles of Han."

As pottery vessels gradually replaced immolated humans and

animals buried with the dead, pottery making improved greatly. The life-sized terracotta warriors and horses unearthed around the mausoleum of Emperor Qinshihuang present a vivid and lively picture of the mighty legion of the Qin empire. The mood and expressions of the soldiers are also skillfully expressed according to their status and age. Some appear to be in deep meditation, others express worry, sadness, uneasiness or resolution. The designs of funerary potteries in the Han period cover a wide range involving daily-use articles, houses, pavilions, wells, cooking ranges, even soldiers, officials, slaves and musicians in various postures. A pottery entertainer unearthed from a tomb ruin of the Eastern Han in Sichuan is typical of those figurines of musicians. With his naked bust and plump and full muscles, a typical and lively musician figurine was thus produced. The tri-colored glazed pottery, the glazed pottery warrior, and the Tianwang (heavenly king) glazed pottery of the Sui and Tang periods are also treasured products. The tri-colored glazed potteries are made of white clay and coated with yellow, green and blue glazes fired at low temperatures of 750-850 degrees Celsius. With gorgeous-colored patterns they are produced through traditional skills such as printing, applique, engraving, and sculpturing. After the Tang period, pottery production began to decline, being gradually replaced by the growing porcelain production. However, there have remained many exquisite funerary pottery artifacts in various ages.

The shapes of pottery products made in the period from the Shang and Zhou to the Han and Tang were mostly derived from images of humans and things in society, the former being the main theme of modeling and design. The terracotta warriors mentioned above reflected the might of the State of Qin and the gallantry and bravery of its soldiers. Various models of other pottery products unearthed from the ruins of Han tombs reflected the various aspects of social life of the Han period. The figurines of officials, musicians, dancers, acrobats and many others are also fine art works reflecting the cultural and economic development of the Tang period. Moreover, many colored glazed pottery works modeled in the shape of horses and camels in the Han and Tang periods showed the use of animals at that time, profoundly reflecting people's understanding of nature and humankind and the humanistic spirit in the periods under review.

Although porcelain production dates back to the Shang and Zhou dynasties, it did not come to maturity until the Eastern Han period. A celadon sheep, unearthed from the ruins of a tomb of the Three Kingdoms period in Nanjing, was glazed all over with pale blue color, even and flawless. It looks calm and in a casual mood. And the patterns on it are smooth and beautiful, quite distinct from porcelain products made before the period of the Three Kingdoms. A celadon pot with a dish-shaped mouth unearthed from the ruins of a tomb of the State of Wu (222-280) in Nanjing adopted the then new technique of using underglaze color, an evidence of the earliest painting skill being applied to utensils, combining porcelain production and painting art which laid a foundation for the formation of the underglaze color techniques for the blue-and-white porcelains of later times.

The appearance of white porcelain broke the dominance of celadon. Techniques of white porcelain production made further improvements in the Sui period. In the Tang period, a distinct division in porcelain production appeared, with celadon in the south and white porcelain in the north. White porcelain production reached its peak during the Tang period. White porcelain produced by the Xing kiln was the most famous of all at the time, honored as "white as snow." The Yue kiln was famous for its celadon and it built an extensive system to compete with the Xing kiln products. The special *mi se* (olive green) porcelain produced by the Yue kiln was exclusively used for imperial ware.

During the Five Dynasties (907-960), in the stable environment under the regime of Wuyue, the production of the Yue kiln made much headway. A comprehensive skill of decoration was developed including carving, underglaze color, and gilding. Later, the celadons produced by the Cai kiln won great popularity for "its color blue as the azure sky, bright as a mirror, thin as a piece of paper, and resounding as a chime stone."

Porcelain production skills further developed during the periods of the Song and Yuan. Celadons were exquisitely produced in the Song Dynasty, especially by the Longquan kiln in the south and the Ruzhou kiln in the north. The official kiln in Kaifeng, Henan Province, imitated the products of the Ruzhou kiln and improved on its techniques. The Jun kiln later became a new and outstanding producer. In the Song period, celadon production reached its prime stage of production with perfect skills. White porcelain production was also further developing and spreading into the south with the Ding kiln in Hebei as the most famous producer. During the Southern Song, Jingdezhen became the principal maker of white porcelain. Its products with a high degree of whiteness and translucence were regarded as one of the representative products of the Song period. In the Yuan Dynasty, Jingdezhen became the center of porcelain production. Based on the white porcelain production skills of the Song period, skills were developed into a technique for producing colored porcelain. The well-known blue-and-white porcelain of the Yuan Dynasty was produced with blue paintings made on white porcelain.

Porcelain production reached its acme during the periods of the Ming and Qing. During the period of Yongle (1403-1424) of the reign of Emperor Chengzu of the Ming Dynasty, the body of white porcelain products was as thin as a piece of paper and as clean as jade and its glaze was so transparent that it seemed there was no body. It was also known as *tian bai* (sweet white) porcelain. During the period of Xuande of the reign of Emperor Xuanzong (1426-1435) of the Ming Dynasty, the quality of blue-and-white porcelain reached perfection. Great achievements were also made in producing single-color glaze under high temperatures. During this period, the exquisitely produced blue color was very well known. During and after the middle period of the reign of Emperor Kangxi (1662-1722) of the Qing Dynasty, porcelain production steadily developed and fine-ground blue pigment and bright glaze material were used. Western-style paintings were also applied to porcelain products. A blue-and-white porcelain pot with cover, produced during this time and stored in the Beijing Palace Museum, depicts two old men roaming along a mountain path. Heavy and light tone colors present a distinct perspective, contrasting far and near. During the reign of the emperors Yongzhen and Qianlong (1723-1795), color glazed porcelain developed rapidly. Many imitations of ancient porcelain are regarded as lively as their originals in pattern, shape, and style.

Porcelain articles are important Chinese cultural artifacts, a unique creation of Chinese people. China is well known by the world partly due to its porcelain products. In English, china means porcelain. With its unique cultural characteristics, porcelain products can represent China's age-old civilization. The shapes and decorations of porcelain products typically present a panorama of Chinese culture, as follows:

1. The thought of humanity is best shown in the unity and harmony between man and nature since the ancient times. Landscapes and flowers and birds and other animals can be seen in the designs of porcelain products together with human figures, and an unwavering pursuit for the unity and harmony between nature and man can also be discerned. For example, a blue-and-white prunus vase was produced with a beautiful plum flower design in the Yongle period of the reign of Emperor Chengzu of the Ming Dynasty. The plum flowers in the design remind the admirers of a sense of solemnity and elegance as if a communication of feelings between them and man occurred.

2. A sincere feeling and gallant demeanor of human figures in the design make man the genuine image of beauty. All the porcelain products produced in various historical stages give a strong presentation of the beauty of life, reflecting the ardent love and strong conviction of Chinese people toward life. A typical tangible product is a porcelain bottle produced in the Kangxi reign period with the design of "colorfully painted ploughing and weaving pattern," in which there are musical instruments, chess, calligraphic works and paintings in addition to farming and weaving workers. It is a picture skillfully and harmoniously composed of the presentation of various aspects of human life. A careful enjoyment of the product can make people feel the happiness and sweetness of life, rather than a burden of labor. These patterns particularly

convey the traditional Chinese spirit of "joining in the worldly life," indicating that the pursuit for a happy life in the world is possible.

3. Respect for history is embodied in products. Many historical stories are depicted on porcelain products. An historical event or historical stage may be reflected artistically through the products, producing a profound sense of history. A bottle with "a single-color design of human figures" tells a story of Liu Bei, the ruler of the Shu Kingdom during the period of the Three Kingdoms, who married a wife from the Wu Kingdom. Through the picture in which houses and pavilions combine the historical figures, people find history and reality are closely linked.

The spirit of humanity shown in porcelain products reflects the Chinese people's pursuit for a happy life and good things in art and it is really a typical representative of Chinese culture.

Chapter 6

The Cradle of Chinese
Culture — Education

Section 1 Origin and Characteristics of Schools in Ancient China

Education has always been very closely linked with culture. Only through education can a nation's cultural tradition and spirit be spread, developed and renewed. Therefore, if we are to properly understand the age-old Chinese culture and grasp its spirit, it would be helpful to look at some of the characteristics of schools and traditional education in ancient China.

Ever since ancient times, schools have been the primary means of cultivating talents, though schools are not the only form of education. What sort of talents can be trained by schools depends on the nature and type of school and its purpose and content as well as the method of education, in addition to the coordination of the whole society and the practice and hard work of those being taught. In ancient China, there existed two types of school, operated either by government or individuals. Over the course of history, at times one type might predominate over the other, but mostly they complemented each other, and both accumulated rich experience as providers of education. We shall give a brief account of their origins and make a general analysis so as to find the unique style and appeal of each.

1. Primitive Society and the Dawn of Schools

Over the course of China's long history of development, the

forefathers of the Chinese people acquired various kinds of knowledge and experience in their life and production. Archeologists have shown that half a million years ago, Peking Man knew how to make simple stone tools and how to cook food by using fire. These things seem easy and simple today, but they were closely linked to the lives and development of the people of that time, giving them more confidence in hunting and battling against the challenge of nature. In order to help the younger generation to survive, their elders naturally passed on their experiences in the use of fire and tools to their offspring. The primary form of education was thus established. According to historical records, "Sui Ren taught people to cook food with fire and Fu Xi taught people to hunt game as there were so many wild beasts." Then "people were taught to plant crops by Shen Nong." All these activities might be included in the scope of education. But this was basic and simple form of education for production and living without a regular place of instruction or specific receivers and occurred randomly according to the demands of a particular time and place.

In the late primitive period society advanced into matriarchal clan communes and patriarchal clan communes as the social productive forces developed to a degree where they could accumulate greater wealth. The content of collective life in the clan communes became richer as well. Apart from education for simple production and living, naturally ideological education relating to some aspects of collective ideology, customs and morals appeared. Archeological excavations at the ruins of the Banpo Village at Xi'an revealed 50 houses closely laid out in a commune, in the center of which was a house for public activities. This was a place for the people of the commune to discuss public affairs and conduct ideological education. People elected their leader, discussed clan feuds, and held religious and celebrational activities there, thereby forming their sense of collectivism, customs and ways of life. At this time, however, they had no official organization of education.

Only at a time when human civilization and the spoken and written language had developed to a certain degree and when the first great division of agriculture from animal husbandry had developed into the great division of the handicraft industry from agriculture, particularly when the social product of labor had increased enough to surpass the needs of society, so as to enable a number of people to quit physical labor and work instead with their minds, and when these people felt it necessary to hand down certain special knowledge and experiences to their offspring intentionally and in a planned way, could schools as special educational institutions appear.

2. Slave Society and the Rise and Fall of Government Schools

According to historical records, schools first appeared during the Xia Dynasty (c.2100-c.1600 BC). However, due to a lack of archeological materials, we know very little about such schools. During the Shang Dynasty (c. early 17th century to 11th century B. C.), China's slave society made further progress in politics, economy and culture. The existence of schools can be found not only in historical documents, but is also evidenced by archeological findings, particularly from inscriptions on bones or tortoise shells from the Yin ruins. The schools at the time were called "Xiang," "Xiao" or "Xu." Others were called "Xue," "Da Xue" or "Gu Zong." During this period, official schools appeared and further developed. Writing and mathematics were taught and education in religion, military affairs, rituals and, especially, music were also stressed. The worship of gods and ghosts was important at this time. When people went to war or conducted ceremonial activities, a certain ritual accompanied by music would take place. Education in rituals and music was therefore given great attention.

During the Western Zhou period (c. 11th century-771 BC), a real school system began to develop. At that time, there were two types of school systems: national schools and local schools. National schools were central government schools located in the region of the king and the capitals of the vassal states. Local schools were local government schools, and were located in local administrative regions. National schools included high schools and lower schools. High schools were built in the city of the King of Zhou and in the capitals of the vassal states. They were usually enclosed by walls, and surrounded by water on three sides, with one side leading to a forest. Lower schools were divided into two types. One was for the children of nobles and located close to palaces, and the other was for common people and was located on the outskirts of cities.

According to historical records, local government schools for the children of nobles had appeared during the Western Zhou period, but there was still no widespread local school network.

From the time of the Western Zhou, a tradition of the "unity of officials and teachers" and the "unity of government and education" began in schools. It should be noted that this feature was closely linked with the social nature of such education. Nobles, with support from the government, established schools and special officials were appointed to oversee their operation. In this case, teachers in these schools naturally blended with officialdom. Assuming the role of both teacher and official, they not only taught students in the school, but also conducted various social activities there. In the high schools in the kingly city were often held ceremonial rituals for the worship of gods and ancestors, military meetings, celebrations for capturing prisoners of war, military training and musical performances. Local schools were not only places of education, but also for discussion about local government affairs. This "unity of government and education" produced a significant impact on later generations. Though schools of later periods were separated from the government and teachers worked on a full-time basis, local officials still paid attention to education. This can be regarded as an important feature of traditional Chinese culture.

During this time, education centered around the "six arts," that is, propriety, music, archery, chariot driving, writing and mathematics.

"Propriety" concerned politics and morals and taught the political and moral standards of the hierarchy of the patriarchal society. "Music" included not only music, but also poetry, songs and dances. It was closely related with ritual. Music was said to train the inner passions, while propriety trained outward manners, enabling the acquisition of flexibility in rule, which would bring about a positive effect on social stability and alleviate the acuteness of social problems. Propriety and music were the cornerstone and core of education in the "six arts." Archery and chariot driving were military training courses. Writing and mathematics were basic cultural courses. The "six arts" were the basic courses in government schools in the Western Zhou period. They were compulsory courses in both national and local schools, though the precise content differed according to the school. The purpose of government schools was to cultivate talents, either to safeguard the country with skills in archery and chariot driving or to administer it with capabilities in "propriety and music" and "writing and mathematics."

The beginnings of an administrative system for education were established in the Western Zhou. An examination system was instituted, to be held every other year in national high schools. In the first year, students were examined on their analysis of the classics and their ability in differentiating their aims in studies. In the third year, they were examined on their ability to concentrate on their studies and get on with their fellow students. In the fifth year, they were examined on their ability to continue an extensive study and whether they respected their teachers. In the seventh year, they were tested on their ability to debate, and on their ability to associate with good learners. In the ninth year they were tested on their ability and flexibility in putting knowledge into practice giving them the foundation to live and work. All these examinations stressed the cultivation of learners in both their studies and morals, setting a good example for schools in later years. Those who passed the examinations would be appointed as officials by the Son of Heaven while those who failed, did not respect their teachers and could not be reformed, would be dispatched to a remote place and be permanently denied such employment. A similar examination system with standards for rewards and punishment was also set up in local schools.

To stress the importance of education, the Son of Heaven

would visit schools four times each year to worship forefathers of education and inspect the school. This is the "unity of government and education" in another form, with the highest ruler encouraging his people to observe the existing social order through education and to cultivate qualified talents needed by the nobility.

Government schools had reached their highest level of development in the Western Zhou period. By the end of this period, they began to decline because of the weakness of the royal family and the scramble for power among the various vassal state rulers. As the government school system declined, classics and historical documents which had been held secretly by government offices began to leak out into society. The government being unable to manage schools, a new situation began to appear. During the mid to late Spring and Autumn Period, private schools emerged, and quickly sprang up everywhere.

3. The Unified Feudal Society and Diversified School Network

The outstanding cultural achievements of the Chinese people were created over the course of more than 2,000 years of feudal society, and these were spread, developed and renewed through education in schools. During this long period of feudal society, the school system was quite different from that of the Western Zhou. The long tradition of official schools was preserved, but privately run schools diversified and spread. In many respects privately run academies particularly distinguished themselves.

Government schools.

The government school system in the Xia, Shang and Western Zhou dynasties eventually disappeared along with the collapse of the aristocracy. As soon as this happened, privately operated schools sprang up. With the gradual formation of a unified feudal empire, a new type of government schools was born. The Jixia School run by the State of Qi near its capital Linzi can be regarded as a prototype for the new type of government schools. The old ways of running government schools during the previous three dynasties were abandoned, and the newer, more liberal thought of privately run schools was adopted. This produced a profound impact on the development of the later government school system.

Emperor Qinshihuang, who unified China in 221 BC, decreed that "law is education," belittling the functions of both government and private schools. The first formation of China's feudal government school system dates from the period of Emperor Wudi (r. 140-87 BC) of the Han Dynasty, being perfected over the course of various dynasties. Generally, government schools in feudal society reflected the social stratification of the time and there were a number of such schools of different types. Here we give only a brief account of the various modes of teaching, examination and administration.

The national university (the highest school in the capital) of the Han Dynasty (206 BC-220 AD) introduced a teaching mode in which teaching of classics in class was combined with private study outside of the classroom. At that time, students had to study by themselves after class. During the Song Dynasty (960-1279), a new mode of teaching appeared. Hu Yuan (993-1059), a great educator, introduced the disciplinary teaching mode. He opened two courses — classics and special learning. Six classics were taught to those with a strong ability to handle state affairs. Special learning meant professional skills such as civil and military affairs, water conservation and calendar calculation. Later, Hu introduced this mode of teaching into the national university where he taught. Students were divided into different groups according to their different pursuits of learning. This method was popular among the students because they could fully develop their individual personalities and specialties. Many talented people were trained in this way.

During this period, the organizational form of teaching was a particular characteristic of professional schools. The use of models for teaching and practice were first introduced in the teaching of medical science. Wang Weiyi, a specialist in acupuncture and moxibustion, invented a bronze model of the human body for training in acupuncture and moxibustion. On the model, he marked out all the acupuncture points. For the teaching of medical science, a special garden was planted with various kinds of traditional Chinese medicines and herbs for students to learn to differentiate. A new practice system was also set up, which required the students to make a regular visit to schools to see those who were sick, and take notes on their diseases and treatment.

During the Ming Dynasty (1368-1644), a new type of probationary system was set up in the Directorate of Education (the highest institute of learning). Students studying in the institute would be sent to government offices for a probation period of three months or half a year. Then, after examinations, they would be divided into three groups according to their records. Those who got the highest marks would be selected for office, and the rest would be sent back to the institute to continue their studies. This was a very important means of promoting the quality of teaching and producing more competent personnel.

A strict examination system was also established in government schools in the feudal society. The system of examinations held every other year in government schools during the Western Zhou Dynasty was gradually perfected through long practice in government schools in feudal society. The national university in the Han period paid much attention to examinations, not only to ascertain how much the students understood the classics, but more importantly, to decide the opportunities for students' development in the future.

The typical method of examination in the national university was to answer questions. Two groups of questions were carved on bamboo sheets for students to choose to answer. Students would be assigned to an official position according to their test records. During the Tang Dynasty (618-907), more examinations were regularly held including a quarterly test, a yearly test and a graduation test. The Ministry of Rites would assign positions to those students who proved themselves qualified in the test, or got them participate in the imperial civil examination. During the reign of Emperor Shenzong (r. 1067-1085) of the Northern Song Dynasty,

Wang Anshi (1021-1086), a statesman, writer and thinker, carried out a reform of the examination system of government schools, introducing the "three colleges method." He divided the national university into three parts: external, internal and supreme colleges. Children of high officials above the eighth rank and good and competent children of commoners, after being tested and qualified, would be enlisted as the students of the external college. These students, after an examination, to be held once every two years, and a check on general professional skill and behavior, would then go up to the supreme college to study if they passed the examinations. Qualified students of the supreme college would be directly assigned to official positions. This system also examined the general professional skills and behavior of the students, and so promoted the quality of their studies and morals. As a result, it was adopted by many other professional schools, even in many local schools. Students of local schools might be upgraded after examination step by step to the highest local college and then to the top college of the national university. In this way, government schools and local schools became closely linked for the first time, forming the beginning of a real education system. This was of great significance in the history of education in China.

A school administrative system with its own characteristics was also established in feudal society in China. A certain administrative system is indispensable to a regular school, but what type of administrative system will be established is important. Generally speaking, the government schools had a special educational administrative organization which was controlled by officials of the ritual department in the central government together with local officials. This was clearly not suitable for the coordination and development of all the schools in the country. During the Sui (581-618) and Tang (618-907) dynasties, the directorate of education was set up to control the government schools at the central level. Local government schools, however, did not create special administrative organizations until the Song Dynasty. At the same time, educational fund was also to be guaranteed. As a rule, feudal government schools had strict regulations and other rules for administration. All these show the autocratic aspect of the education. However, there were some aspects that can be learnt from by later generations.

For instance, a strict selection of teachers and a tough examination system were first introduced in national university in the Han period. At that time, teachers of the national universy were strictly selected according to their level of knowledge and morals. During the reign of Emperor Shenzong of the Song Dynasty, the imperial court ordered the creation of an examination system for teachers. Under this tough examination system, the total number of teachers in local schools across the country was only 53. A fairly objective standard for selecting teachers was conducive to guarantee of the quality of teachers. After the Song period, this practice continued without lessening the requirements. Teachers play a very important role in educational achievements. So strict selection of teachers, a traditional practice in ancient government schools, is a practice that later generations can well learn from.

Now let's turn to the subject of privately run schools.

Private schools were a new form of education originating from the decline of government schools under the slave system. Their appearance not only brought prosperity to academic research and culture, creating a flowering of different schools of thought, but also cultivated a great many distinguished and talented people who contributed to the formation of a centralized feudal dynasty. Though they themselves focussed on the operation of government schools, rulers of the various dynasties neither prohibited nor limited the operation of private schools, resulting in the continuation and development of private schools over the course of more than 2,000 years. Private schools developed their own unique features, differing from those of government schools, and to some extent, they helped reduce the burden on the feudal state in the operation of schools. In general, private schools in feudal society were characterized by the following two aspects:

1. A relatively free policy of operation and a unique teaching style were created, which promoted a comprehensive development

of Chinese feudal academic thought, science and technology, culture and education in feudal society.

If the hierarchy and class character of feudal government schools were generally expressed by the unification of its purpose, receivers and content of education, private schools, on the contrary, was characterized by a relative flexibility and freedom in their operational policy, content and mode. This feature was particularly apparent in many private schools run by scholars before the Qin Dynasty. The scholars of different academic doctrines at the time spread and developed their educational thought through teaching. They broke from the bondage of hierarchy created by the entrance system for government schools practiced in the Western Zhou period and introduced open education in society for anyone. Confucius said that in education there should be no distinction of social status, while Mo Zi advocated a mobile educational system to expand his influence of thought. The private schools run by both Confucians and Mohists were known far and wide at the time.

After the appearance of the unified feudal patriarchal society, particularly after Emperor Wudi (r. 140-88 BC) of the Han period actively advocated the exclusive practice of Confucianism, Confucianism became the dominant system of thought through the ages. It influenced society through education in all types of schools. All schools were obliged to teach Confucianism, to a greater or lesser degree. However, private schools had more freedom in their teaching with less interference from political influence and control of thought. When they taught Confucianism, they paid more attention to the study and discussion of its academic aspects, rather than the direct moral and political preaching in government schools. For example, Han Dynasty masters of ancient script classics (a school of Confucian classics research. Ancient script classics were classics of Confucianism written before the Qin Dynasty and explained by scholars of the Han Dynasty) were very interested in the operation of private schools, in an attempt to popularize the texts of the classics and research findings of its investigations and proofs. They were bold enough to contend with the scholars of modern script classics (a school of Confucian classics research, written and explained by the Han scholars) in the politicized national university and promoted the development of classics research and education. There were also various schools of Confucianism in the Song Dynasty due to the booming of private schools. Government schools, limited by their unified teaching requirements, lacked the basic conditions for academic debate. For instance, during the period that Wang Anshi (1021-1086) was in office, he proposed that the teaching content in the national university be unified under the "new explanation of the three classics," and a new policy should be practiced. Cheng Hao (1032-1085) and Cheng Yi (1033-1107), philosophers and educators of the Northern Song, who were political adversaries of Wang, retired to Luoyang to set up private schools, teaching Confucianism in their own way. The Northern Song Zhang Zai (1020-1077) also set up a private school to preach his own doctrine. All these private schools at the time promoted academic and educational thought.

New teaching methods were also introduced in the long development of private schools, such as the method of the most capable student teaching other students. Dong Zhongshu (179-104 BC), philosopher and master of modern script classics of the Han period, adopted the method. Ma Rong (79-166), a classics scholar of the Eastern Han period, also adopted this method of teaching. With 400 students in a school, only about 50 were taught by Dong personally, the others being instructed by this method, which was one way to solve the shortage of teachers, meeting the development demands of private schools and contributing to the spread of Confucianism and its culture.

To meet the demand of the time for philosophical explanations of Confucianism, Song Dynasty masters of the Neo-Confucian School (or School of Principles) focussed more on enlightenment and guidance in their teaching. For example, Zhou Dunyi (1017-1073), founder of the Neo-Confucian School of the Northern Song Dynasty, often raised thought-provoking questions with his disciples Cheng Hao and Cheng Yi. Zhu Xi (1130-1200), philosopher of the Southern Song Dynasty, often took his disciples out after class to ramble in the woods and by the waterways, discussing philosophical problems to deepen their understanding of Neo-Confucianism.

The freedom of teaching in private schools was not only seen in the creative popularization of Confucianism, but also in the diversification of the courses offered by the schools, including quite different doctrines of Confucianism, Buddhism and Taoism. For example, during the Wei, the Jin and the Southern and Northern Dynasties, owing to the social upheaval and frequent wars, feudal government schools began to decline, but private schools mushroomed. As well as Confucianism, Buddhism and Taoism were also taught in schools, bringing a greater variety to academic thought.

Moreover, private schools played an important role in the popularization of ancient Chinese science and technologies and art and literature. Although professional schools in areas such as medical science, mathematics and painting were set up in feudal government schools, their number and scale were limited. Many students who were interested in these skills could therefore only learn them in private schools. The most common way of teaching, however, was the one whereby professional skills were taught and passed down from father to son.

2. Private schools, with some success, undertook the task of primary education in feudal society, supporting the limited effort rendered by the state.

Generally, the development of education is closely linked to the social and economic structure. Along with the development of feudal society and its economy, the scale and types of government schools also expanded. During the Song Dynasty, local government schools at the prefecture and county level were prevalent. After the Yuan Dynasty (1271-1368), the government ordered the establishment of primary schools (community schools) below the county level. But restricted finances and capability meant that the government could not afford all the funds and personnel. These community schools, therefore, were in fact special private schools. The so-called government schools in the mid and late period of feudal society could only be set up at the prefecture and county levels. At lower levels, the government had difficulty in affording the operation of primary schools, so the task was taken over by private schools. These schools formed the foundation of education in feudal society, over the centuries attracting a great many educators who gradually produced a complete set of texts combining knowledge, ethics and interest. They also made valuable explorations in teaching and school management.

The key problem of primary education for many educators was the content of books. They gradually came to understand through practice that texts should be tailored to the immature psychology, physiology and thinking of children. Then they should become acquainted with basic general knowledge, history, poetry, songs and moral principles. Abstract ideas and empty theoretic preaching should be avoided. These ancient rudimentary readings for children can be divided into two categories: general readings, such as *Three-Character Classics*, *The Names of a Hundred Families*, and *A Thousand-Character Classic*, and specialized readings, such as *A Selection of Poems from a Thousand Poets*, *Seventeen Historical Stories for Children*, *The ABC of Nature* and *Ethical Teachings*.

Whether the content was general or specialized, all these books stressed the combination of knowledge, moral principles and interest, sometimes specially illustrated with fine pictures. Some of the contents concerned feudal ethics which are obviously out-dated now, but many teachings on learning, making friends, and discussion are still useful for education today.

It cannot be denied that serious corporal punishment was practiced in the primary education in feudal society. But it should be noted that genuine educators who understood how to teach a child refused to do such things, pursuing instead creative ways of cultivation, taking into consideration the child's age. Cheng Hao and Cheng Yi proposed that teachers should stimulate the interest of a child. They proposed that ethical principles could be written in the form of jingles for children to sing and memorize. Children would enjoy singing them and, through daily repetition, they would be gradually influenced by the teaching.

Zhu Xi also noted the features of the age and mind of children.

He advocated that a child's mind should be influenced through figurative stories and proverbs. Wang Shouren (1472-1528), philosopher and educator of the Ming Dynasty, pointed out that "generally a child likes to play rather than being constrained." He said that education should take full consideration of a child's temperament, interest and psychology. At the same time, educators of ancient times also emphasized that education should maintain strict cultivation and training in good behavior with high morals. In this respect, Zhu Xi proposed strict requirements of dress, language, hygiene, reading and writing, and so on. Certainly some of the requirements were unreasonable, being affected by feudal ideology. But some were sensible. For example: "A person who is reading aloud, is required to do three things: concentrate the mind, focus the eyesight and move the tongue and mouth. If a person's mind is not present, then he cannot see properly what he is reading. Without the concentration of the mind and eyes, one cannot memorize anything even though reading aloud. As to writing, no matter how well one can write characters, he must first of all write each character distinctly and right, and never scribble."

Wang Yun (1784-1854), a primary educator of the Qing Dynasty, stresses in his book *The Methods of Teaching Children* the importance of rudimentary training, pointing out that each stage of training, for example, learning to recognize characters, writing, reading, and composition, should be "strictly carried out step by step." Such education should bear in mind the features of a child's body and mind, and at the same time remember to set strict requirements for them. These were the two major problems that many primary educators of ancient China wanted to solve in their teaching.

Finally, a few words about academies (Shu Yuan).

Academies were a unique form of higher learning, which appeared gradually after the late Tang period. At first, they were government offices to collect, store and revise books. Sometimes, out of vanity, individuals called their private studio or study an academy. Later, due to the inadequacy of government schools, academies began to become places of teaching by private scholars.

Genuine teaching academies appeared in the later years of the Five Dynasties (907-960). Through their initial stage of development in the Northern Song period (960-1127) and their flourishing in the Southern Song period (1127-1279), a number of well-known academies, such as Bailudong Academy, Yuelu Academy, Chongshan Academy, Shigu Academy and Yintianfu Academy came to the fore. They established their own styles of operation, making an important contribution to the cultivation of talents and the richness of academic studies.

In general, early academies were privately operated by scholars. When they made achievements in education, they would be honored and supported by the government of the time. After the Yuan Dynasty, most academies became government-run or controlled schools. When we talk of the characteristics of academies, what we are referring to were the practices in the early stage of their development. The fact that these were passed down over a period of more than 1,000 years suggest that they established some worthy traditions, which were inherited, spread and developed by many educators. Differing from both government and ordinary private schools, academies were a higher form of private schools with their own unique style of operation.

Firstly, they emphasized the integration of teaching and academic research, and a free atmosphere in debate on academic problems was fostered. Education in ancient China was dominated by Confucianism, and the academies did not abandon the teaching of Confucian classics. However, they differed from government schools, in that academy teachers did not only teach knowledge of the classics. Their teaching methods included research, and so, through teaching, they imparted the results of their own research and also deepened their own understanding. In places where the research work was well developed, so was the academy, and the leading researchers in a place naturally ran the local academy.

Most striking was the creation of a free atmosphere in debate on academic issues and research. For instance, in 1175, Zhu Xi and Lu Jiuyuan (1139-1193), philosophers and educators of the Southern Song period, representing different schools of thought, convened a new type of symposiums in which both criticized each other's viewpoints. In spite of their different academic opinions, they were still intimate and sincere friends in the study of academic problems. Later, when he was sponsoring the Bailudong Academy, Zhu Xi invited Lu to teach in the academy and Lu was happy to accept his invitation. Lu gave a lecture on the subject of "the superior man is concerned with righteousness and the mean man with gain." The lecture was so sincere and vivid that many of the students were moved to tears. Zhu appreciated the lecture so much that he asked Lu to leave the text behind and had it carved in stone.

In another example, Wang Shouren of the Ming period, and philosopher Zhan Ruoshui (1466-1560) taught in the same academy and diligently studied their own academic subjects although their views differed. Gu Xiancheng (1550-1612) and Gao Panlong (1562-1626), of the late Ming Dynasty, both stressed the importance of free debate on academic problems, usually holding a big debate once a year, and a small one once a month. They even agreed to hold discussions on the promotion of justice and righteousness, respect for knowledge, and on critiques of imperial affairs, contemporary personages and current state affairs.

Free debate brought about different views on some problems. But discussions and debate in turn furthered the understanding of the problems. This was commonly acknowledged by many leaders of academies. As a contemporary philosopher put it, "If there is a difference in views, it will be taught and discussed. If all are in agreement, what need is there to teach and discuss it?" Free debate and discussion became a fine tradition that substantially improved the development of academic studies.

Secondly, academies emphasized the combination of students' private studies and guidance by the teacher, stressing the importance of cultivating the students' ability to pursue their own independent studies. This practice of independent study combined with the teacher's guidance dates back to the period before the Qin Dynasty when private academies from various schools of thought prevailed. During the Han period, in the national university, apart from lectures given to big classes, independent study was a primary task of the students. Academies in later periods inherited and developed this precious educational tradition, which had previously been widely practiced. True, academies did give group lectures, but more importance was given to guiding students in their own studies. A teacher's function was that of a guide and a provider of acknowledgement. If any questions were raised, they could be discussed. Zhu Xi would take his students outside to ramble and investigate, giving them lectures freely in a relaxed and beautiful environment. When the students studied indoors, they had enough books and materials to consult in the academy's library. Zhu Xi particularly stressed the ability to raise questions. When a student could not solve a problem after thinking about it deeply, he could go to ask the teachers. Zhu created a "learning method" from his rich teaching experience in the academy, and his students summed it up as "progressing step by step," "learning a thing by heart and thinking about it deeply," "being modest and broad-minded," "personal practice and investigation," "working hard," and "holding respect for others and persisting in one's own goal." These six principles won recognition from later intellectuals and they produced a far-reaching influence. Students in the academies also developed their own independent academic research work, producing theses which were printed and published by the academies.

Thirdly, they aimed to establish an ideal natural environment (campus construction) and a harmonious cultural environment (the relationship between students and teachers), inheriting and developing the fine tradition of students respecting their teachers, and teachers loving their students.

Most of the famous academies were located in remote, quiet uplands amid beautiful landscapes. For instance, Bailudong Academy was built under the Wulao Peak on Mount Lushan in Jiangxi Province; Yuelu Academy, under the Baolong Cave on Yuelu Mountain in Changsha, Hunan; Cangzhou House of Excellence, Zhulin House of Excellence and Kaoting Academy were all located on Mount Wuyi; and Xuehai Hall was located on Yuexiu Mountain.

In addition to the selection of a beautiful natural environment, academies also stressed the creation of a harmonious cultural environment, or an amicable relationship between students and teachers. Confucius set the example for students and teachers of "never being satiated with learning and never being tired of teaching." He also built up a harmonious and profound friendly relationship with his disciples and followers on the basis of pursuing the "Tao" (or the "Way"). As time went on, however, as more worldly practices were introduced into government schools, this friendly relationship between students and teachers dwindled, or even disappeared. "They treat each other like strangers in the street," to quote Zhu Xi. In contrast, students and teachers of academies cherished a sincere affection for each other. They lived together happily, discussing their feelings as well as academic problems. For instance, Zhu Xi studied together with his student Cai Yuanding (1135-1198), a scholar of the school of Neo-Confucianism, in the academy. They would often debate a problem well into the night. When Zhu Xi learned that Cai was demoted and banished from the court, he led more than 100 students to see him off. There were tears in the eyes of the students over the wrong that had been done to him, but Cai remained calm and collected as usual. Said Zhu Xi with deep feeling: "There are two striking strong points about Cai Yuanding: heartwarming fraternity and unfaltering determination," showing the sincere love and care of a teacher for his student.

To sum up, the school system in feudal Chinese society was mainly composed of government schools, private schools and their higher form, academies. Government schools played the main role in feudal society, but when at times they declined, along with the decline of a dynasty, private schools would develop. At other times, under the control of an enlightened government, government schools were developed and the number of private schools might dwindle. Mostly, however, these two types of schools advanced side by side, supplementing and supporting each other, constituting a diversified school network to undertake the lofty task of cultivating talents for the nation.

Section 2 Traditional Chinese Education and Culture

Confucius was the first to advocate moral education. Politically, he advocated the practice of the "rites of the Zhou Dynasty," and in education he urged the re-adoption of the Six Arts formed in the heyday of the Western Zhou Dynasty. However, his "resumption of the Zhou rites" was by no means a simple retrogression to the Western Zhou period, but was intended as part of a reform needed by his own time. His fundamental idea of reform in education was to attain the goal of "recommending outstanding talents" by way of introducing "the best students to officialdom." Here, by "outstanding" and "best" he meant those who had perfected their morality, those who were truly benevolent or virtuous. Moral education was therefore given prime importance in his teaching. He devoted almost all his life to systematically editing and revising *The Book of Songs*, *The Book of History*, *The Book of Rites*, *The Book of Music*, *The Book of Changes*, and *Spring and Autumn Annals*, and compiling them into teaching materials known as the Six Classics.

The Book of Songs is a collection of poems and songs written from the Western Zhou period onwards. Of the original 3,000, Confucius selected only 305. The central idea of the poems and songs he selected conformed with the moral standards of the "rites." Learning *The Book of Songs* was, for him, a matter of great significance. Studying the book could give voice to a person's feelings and ambition, enable one to observe society and understand life, and also promote a consciousness of cooperation. The key was to learn the way and reason of "serving one's father," and "serving one's sovereign." A person who had learned the book, but could not apply the teachings in practice in the world, had only touched the "skin and hair" of the book, not the essence and substance within it.

The Book of History or *Shang Shu*, is a collection of political and historical events compiled by governments before the Spring and Autumn Period. It recorded the important historical events of the

Xia, Shang and Zhou dynasties. The whole collection was said to have had one hundred sections, but only 28 have survived. Confucius believed that to learn the book would not only to enrich one's knowledge of history, but more importantly enable one to master the way earlier kings ruled their kingdoms through moral teachings. He said: "What does *The Book of History* say of filial piety? — 'You are filial, you discharge your brotherly duties. These qualities are displayed in government.' This then also constitutes the exercise of government. Why must there be that — making one be in the government?" From this, it is clear that what Confucius considered most important in *The Book of History* was its moral teachings on filial piety and love for one's brothers.

The Book of Rites is also known as Shi Li or Yi Li. Confucius carefully studied the rites of the Xia, Shang and Zhou dynasties. Of these, it was the rites of the Zhou period that he chose for people to follow. The "Zhou rites" that he selected were those concerned with the spirit of "Ren" or benevolence. He was strongly opposed to the use of the rites simply as a social veneer. For this purpose, he selected 17 works describing the "norms of etiquette" for scholars to learn. These were to be conscientiously learnt by students in order to understand the basis of how to be a good man — "If you do not study the rites, you cannot know how to conduct yourself."

The Book of Music was unfortunately lost during the Qin Dynasty and no one knows what it contained. However, it is known that Confucius' reason for compiling the book was his belief in the moral power of fine music. The best music, he said, should be a harmonious unification of beauty and virtue.

The Book of Changes is also known as *Zhou Yi*. Confucius studied the book relatively late in his life, but during that time he studied it so hard that the bamboo sheets (the leaves of the book at that time) fell out of their binding. While studying the book, Confucius and his disciples wrote annotations and commentaries, generally known as *Yi Zhuan*, explaining the Confucian doctrines of morality, politics and philosophy.

Spring and Autumn Annals is a chronicle of the State of Lu, the native place of Confucius. After Confucius revised the book, it became heavily endowed with political and ethical hues. Through his use of metaphor, he concealed the ideas of "rectification of names," "judgement on people," and "distinguishing virtue from wickedness." It became a very important book for training personnel for the rule of virtue as advocated by Confucianists.

From this general analysis of the Six Classics, the motif of moral teachings of the Confucian classics can be clearly seen. With the exception of *The Book of Music*, they became the basic courses for both government and private schools in feudal Chinese society.

Along with the progress of feudal society, Confucian educators over the ages made different annotations to the classics, which accordingly promoted the development of diversified forms of Confucian educational ideology. The five classics were always maintained as the fundamental courses in schools, though the particular emphasis varied in different dynasties.

For example, when Wang Anshi of the Northern Song Dynasty reformed the national university, he stressed that the newly annotated *The Book of Songs*, *The Book of History*, and *The Book of Rites* should be used as the fundamental courses in the university. After the Song period, Confucian educators added *The Great Learning*, *The Doctrine of the Mean*, *The Analects*, and *The Book of Mencius* to the fundamental courses for both government and private schools. In private schools and academies, more attention was paid to the academic aspects of the classics. In private schools, books such as the *Three-Character Classic*, *The Names of a Hundred Families*, *Thousand-Character Classic* and the *Seventeen Historical Stories for Children* all came to include the introductory knowledge to Confucian moral teachings.

It is worth noting that the structure of courses centered around moral teaching as its core was the main feature of traditional moral education in China as a whole. We can see that moral teaching was also an important part of the fine traditions of Chinese culture. This traditional education also contained a certain degree of natural sciences, literature and arts. In fact, the Confucian classics involved some knowledge of natural sciences, such as the names of some birds, beasts, flowers and vegetation in *The Book of Songs*, the world's earliest record of a solar eclipse in *The Book of History*, and the record of Halley's Comet in *Spring and Autumn Annals*. Along with the economic and political development of feudal China, various professional schools appeared such as the comprehensive school of poetry-calligraphy-painting, and schools of history, mathematics, painting, law, and rites. All of these contributed to the development of diverse sciences and arts in ancient times.

In addition, a number of Confucian educators made proposals and suggestions for the improvement of teaching as the actual conditions required at the time. For instance, Wang Anshi, when he insisted on the introduction of moral education on the basis of the new explanation of the three classics, proposed the adoption of a policy of incorporating all that was good in the diverse schools of thought. Gu Yanwu (1613-1682), Huang Zongxi (1610-1695) and Yan Yuan (1635-1704), educators of the late Ming and early Qing periods, also had similar proposals, advocating the incorporation of education in practical science and technology in addition to Confucian moral education.

In summary, this structure of moral education courses occupied a dominant position in traditional Chinese education. However, natural sciences and literary and art courses were also developed, sometimes faster than other courses and leading to the creation of a number of professional schools. Most of such schools were operated by private individuals or families. This form of education was closely linked to the relative stability of the 2,000-year-long patriarchal feudal society in China. But faced with the emerging science and industry of the modern world, traditional Chinese education was out-dated and had to accept the challenge of the new era.

With the goal of education and the courses to teach having been specified, the question was how teachers should teach, how students should learn and how the relationship between the two should be handled. Over the years, the many educators of the past had accumulated a rich and important body of experience. The key aspects of this are as follows:

1. Respect Teachers and Love Students

The success of any educational activity depends on a harmonious relationship between teacher and student. This can be seen clearly in the fine tradition of "respect teachers and love students."

Confucius, the great educator, knew how to love his students. He recruited students without distinction of wealth and class, and he taught them with sincerity and love. His education principle was, to quote him: "If a man purifies himself to wait upon me, I receive him so purified, without guaranteeing his past conduct." He not only paid attention to students' progress in their studies and moral cultivation, but also to their wellbeing. When someone among his students fell ill, he would go to visit him and when someone was in difficulty, he would offer to help him. This noble integrity and love that Confucius had for his students naturally won him the respect and love of his students. After he died, many of his students observed mourning for their deceased teacher for many years. They were determined to popularize his doctrines and teachings defying all difficulties.

Later generations of educators followed Confucius' good example, forming a fine tradition in Chinese education. Generally, teachers who were devoted to their cause of education and warmheartedly took care of their students' progress would receive the sincere esteem of their students, no matter what teaching style the teacher preferred. For instance, Cheng Hao was amiable and kind in teaching, giving his students a feeling of "being caressed by a spring breeze." But Cheng Yi was known for his seriousness and sternness. When one student went to visit him, the student saw his teacher meditating with closed eyes, so he stood outdoors obediently until the falling snowflakes had piled up a foot high. It can thus be seen that the respect the students held for their teachers stemmed from the inspiration of the latter's moral integrity.

2. Elicitation and Guidance

A teacher needs active responses and cooperation of the students. The psychology of students was of great importance to educators in ancient China, and when possible they inspired them to think.

Confucius never merely instilled his teaching in the minds of his students, instead he guided them in how to proceed in their studies. He skillfully made good use of any opportunities and conditions that would inspire them to use their minds and think independently. The Master said, "I do not open up the truth to one who is not eager to get knowledge, nor help out any one who is not anxious to explain himself. When I have presented one corner of a subject to any one, and he cannot from it learn the other three, I do not repeat my lesson." He provided a free and lively environment for them to speak their mind without restraint and talked to them with charm and wit. Sometimes, he would pretend that he knew nothing about the problem they were discussing, raising all kinds of questions to help the students explore the issue. In this he was similar to Socrates and his "midwifery" method of teaching. Socrates opposed direct teaching of students, preferring to question them and lead them to draw conclusions by themselves.

Many other educators in ancient China also made profound studies of this elicitation teaching method.

3. Teaching Students in Accordance with Their Aptitude

To promote students' initiative in their studies, a teacher must know and master the individual character and psychological quality of each student so as to teach them better.

Confucius had a deep understanding of this. Once Zi Lu, a student of Confucius, asked his teacher: "Should one act immediately upon hearing a good idea?"

"How can you act without first consulting your parents and elder brothers?" replied Confucius. After a while, another student, Ran Qiu, asked the same question, but this time Confucius answered, "Yes! You should." Gong Xihua had been listening, and was puzzled by this.

"Why did you give such totally different answers to the same question?" he asked.

Confucius explained to him, "Ran Qiu is hesitant and needs encouragement. But Zi Lu is rash, and needs to learn restraint."

This method introduced by Confucius has been recommended and used widely in teaching practice. Cheng Yi concluded, "Confucius taught his students using the method in accordance with their aptitude. Some he taught by way of politics, some by way of language and some by way of morality." Cheng himself also used this way to teach his students. Nobody can deny that this time-honored teaching method is still important in present-day education.

4. Proceed Step by Step in an Orderly Way

Educators in ancient times gradually came to understand through practice the significance of teaching in an orderly way and step by step. Thus, the unity of the teaching materials, the order of their arrangement, and the aptitude of the students should be taken into consideration. In practice, it is important to proceed from the easy to the difficult, from that which is near to that which is far, and from the concrete to the abstract. It must be said that ancient educators had varying levels of understanding of this.

Confucius was skillful in applying this principle to his teaching, leaving a profound impression on his students. His student Yan Yuan said with feeling, "The Master has led me forward step by step, using classics to enrich my learning, and using etiquette to guide my acts. I could not give up learning now, much as I want." For students, learning means a growth of knowledge only by means of accumulation. "Only by one step following another can one travel a thousand *li*; only by gathering water from all the streams can there be the ocean," to quote the ancient philosopher and educator Xun Zi (c. 313-238). Zhu Xi spoke of this in his famous article "The Reading Method," stressing that one must read books one part after another and each article and each sentence in a book should be perused. There is no point in lapping up information without properly digesting it.

5. Integrating Learning with Thinking

Learning and thinking are two parts of a whole. Learning

without thinking is merely the piling up of information, while thinking without learning is merely empty daydreaming. Ancient educators understood this well and urged the integration of the two.

Confucius said that learning without thinking is like eating food without digesting it, and is just as useless. But thinking without learning produces nothing practical, so it is also harmful. He was quite right, and this came to be considered as a basic principle for later educators. Mencius (c.372-289 BC), a Confucian thinker, statesman and educator during the Warring States Period, also advocated the significance of learning, but he especially attached importance to thinking. He said: "Man's mind is the organ for thinking. The way to solve a problem can be obtained through thinking, but there will be no way out when you do not think." In his view, learning without thinking leads to being easily misled. He stressed: "When one believes completely what a book says, it is time to throw it away."

The training of a skeptical mind was considered to be of great importance by ancient educators, so as to avoid one-sided viewpoints and promote students' capacity for independent thinking. Debate between teachers and students was particularly common in academies. Zhu Xi especially stressed the importance of questioning in one's studies. He said that "if something is believable, even it is said by ordinary people, it cannot be changed. If it is doubtful, even if it comes from the lips of scholars and great men, it should be carefully examined and thought over." It was this fine tradition of questioning which promoted the development of traditional Chinese educational theories and academic and cultural thought.

Wang Fuzhi, a great thinker of the early Qing period, said, "Learning is not an obstacle to thinking. With extensive learning, one's thinking will reach far. Thinking is helpful to learning and when difficulty arises in thinking, one has to learn harder." Only by closely integrating learning with thinking, can students' learning be guaranteed. This is perhaps the most important lesson left to us by the educators of ancient times.

6. Specialized Knowledge Needs a Broad Base

Specialized and broad knowledge are mutually dependent. To gain broad knowledge with no depth is like acting without a purpose. But depth without a foundation of breadth is unreliable. Ancient educators had a full understanding of this.

In his teachings, Confucius attached importance to breadth of information. But he stressed that at a suitable time, one should sum up one's broad knowledge into intensive knowledge as a guiding thinking. According to Mencius, the logic between extensive and intensive knowledge lies in the full understanding and command of extensive knowledge, which is finally boiled down to intensive knowledge.

Confucian scholars during the Song and Ming periods also paid attention to the relationship between these two parts. Zhu Xi's extensive knowledge had an intensive core of morality. He described those who sought broad information but had no intensive guiding idea as "wandering riders who never go home."

Ancient educators found the contradiction between these two parts and advocated that they should be linked up as a whole. However, they usually took moral principle as the only intensive core, a way of thinking confined by the nature of a feudal society that is quite different from modern explanations.

7. Gaining New Insights Through Reviewing Old Material

Gaining new insights by reviewing old material that one has already learned is also unity of opposites. If these two elements are properly handled, progress can be made. At the very beginning of *The Analects of Confucius*, the first sentence "Is it not pleasant to learn with constant perseverance and application?" shows the importance the Master attached to studying and restudying. He also advocated that when a student finds his teacher's words to be contrary to the truth, he should insist on his own viewpoint. He also said, "He who gains new insights through restudying old material is fit to be a teacher." The educators of ancient China meant here to promote a creative and fact-seeking way of teaching and learning.

Wang Chong (27-c.97), a materialist philosopher of the Eastern

Han Dynasty, actively opposed blind following what teachers and great masters had said in their books. Instead, students should read extensively and have enough courage to challenge the conventional teachings of sages and masters. He left a number of valuable essays such as "Ask Confucius" and "Interrogate Mencius." Zhu Xi wrote a famous poem in which he cleverly reduced the creative spirit couched in the phrase "gaining new insights through restudying old material" to these two lines: "How is it that this brook is so clean/Because there is flowing water springing from its source." Many people of deep insight, both past and present, have been inspired by these two lines.

8. Learning Through Practice

The purpose of traditional Chinese education was to promote the moral level of the people. The doctrines advocated by Confucian educators must be eventually applied to personal actions in line with moral principles. Therefore, practice by both teachers and students was the most important aspect of moral education.

For Confucius, the greatest fault of intellectuals was the use of clever words and boasting that did not match their actions. A man of virtue should regard empty talk as a disgrace. When assessing the moral level of a student, the teacher should not only listen to what the student said, but also observe how he acted. His deeds should match his words. Xun Zi (c. 313-238 BC) also held that learning should not remain in the superficial stage of "listening and speaking," but proceed further to practice through "asking," "perceiving," and "knowing." *The Doctrine of the Mean* described the process of learning as "reading extensively, asking questions, carefully pondering, clearly distinguishing, and conscientiously practicing." This conclusion has become a cardinal principle for later generations in their teaching and learning. In the theory of knowledge, though ancient educators disagreed on whether it was knowledge or practice that came first, they all made moral education the basis of teaching and learning. The combination of learning with practice had been an important feature of traditional Chinese education.

9. Teaching and Learning Complement and Support Each Other

Teaching and learning naturally supplement each other. Teachers and students can promote and help each other in the practice of teaching and learning. Educators in ancient China set examples for us in this respect, providing much food for enlightenment.

The chapter on learning in *The Book of Rites* has a profound analysis and description of the complementary relationship between teaching and learning. The students, having learned and practiced, find that their knowledge is lacking. The teachers, through practice, find that their abilities are also lacking. Because the students have found their weaknesses, they are able to examine themselves and work harder to improve their studies. The teachers, having learnt their limitations, will work harder to improve their teaching skills. In this way, the teachers and students are equal. Through teaching and through learning, each will discover their weaknesses and know where they have to improve. A competent teacher is never complacent in his teaching, and recognizes the need to restudy and improve his teaching skills, and the best source of this knowledge is his students. "Anyone can be a teacher from whom knowledge can be acquired," said Confucius. "If there are three men walking together, one of them is bound to be good enough to be my teacher." This shows his persistence in the pursuit of learning and restudying throughout his life. Once when he was discussing an academic problem with his student Zi Xia, he exclaimed, "You have enlightened me, Pu Shang [another name of Zi Xia]!"

Han Yu (768-824), a writer and philosopher of the Tang Dynasty, summed this up, saying that though the student was a follower of his teacher, he was by no means inferior to his elder if he was stronger in a special field of study. So he concluded: "A student is not necessarily inferior to his teacher, and a teacher is not necessarily superior to his student." The key is to complement each other in the course of teaching and learning.

In ancient private schools, particularly in academies, teachers and students often discussed academic problems together in addition to class teaching. In fact, this kind of free discussion or debate could help promote the further study of some problems so as to facilitate teaching and learning.

We have summarized the main experiences of traditional Chinese education. These experiences are most certainly a part of the important intellectual wealth of traditional Chinese culture.

Chapter 7

Chinese Calligraphy and Painting

Section 1 Introduction to Chinese Calligraphy and Top-Notch Calligraphic Works

Calligraphy occupies one of the highest positions in the rich and colorful treasury of Chinese art. Through the use of a brush to write Chinese characters, a calligrapher can express his or her aesthetic idea, education, thoughts and feelings, personality and temperament in a point or a line. Calligraphy has developed in China over the course of more than 3,000 years. It is a wonderful art, becoming an important part of the best traditional Chinese culture.

The art of calligraphy spread to Japan, Korea, Singapore, Malaysia, and wherever the Chinese diaspora has settled. Its popularity continues to grow.

Two aspects of Chinese calligraphy distinguish it from other calligraphic arts: the nature of Chinese characters and use of the brush. The structure of Chinese characters, each of which occupies a square space, and their rich connotations make them an ideal calligraphic medium. The softness and elasticity of ink brushes make them ideal tools to express the changing styles of calligraphy. A line made with the stroke of a brush may present different tastes of writing styles. This can be completed only with an ink brush. Various types and sizes of characters require different kinds of brushes.

There are three elements in Chinese calligraphy: 1. *Maneuverability*. This requires the dexterous control of the brush, the scientific movement of the fingers, elbow and body and effective use of the ink. The brush must be controlled to move on the paper at the right speed with the required force, quick or slow, light or heavy, lifting up or pressing down to form various types of brush sharpness, mid-way or side cutting, or hidden or exposed point. The lines should be written with force, giving a feeling of substance, like the veins, bones, blood and flesh of the human body. 2. *Structure*. This refers to the layout of the points and the execution of the brush movement. It stresses the balance, escape and supplement, capping and piercing, facing up and the reverse, siding, filling a blank, covering, and increase and decrease, to make the combination of the strokes of each character full of life and animation. 3. *Style*. This refers to the taste, style and quality of the work. It requires the skillful expression of a combination of beauty in form and in quality of the work so as to give a vivid presentation as a result of the producer's inspiration. The maneuverability of the brush and the structure are techniques used to produce a beauty in form and quality. But the style represents the producer's personal accomplishments separate from achievement in calligraphy. Style is the most important, but it cannot be separated from the beauty in form and quality. A good calligraphic work is required to contain these two aspects.

Calligraphy, superficially speaking, is nothing more than writing characters. However, good calligraphy cannot be produced without a good educational foundation. The wonder of a calligraphic work is always based on the depth and breadth of the knowledge of its producer. This involves a process of integrating training in basic techniques with knowledge.

It is very difficult to appraise a calligraphic work. This is because the requirements of a work include the practical function of communicating information through seemingly simple points and lines, the expressive function of communicating feelings, and the aesthetic function. The simpler the expression, the richer the content. The more abstract it is, the deeper its implication. It is a medium for expressing the mood, will, feelings, ideas and the pursuit of beauty of its producer. This requires the appraisers and connoisseurs to have extensive knowledge and keen observation.

Chinese calligraphy is the product of 5,000 years of Chinese culture. Through the ages, a great number of outstanding calligraphers have emerged. Wang Xizhi (321-379) and his son Wang Xianzhi (344-386) of the Eastern Jin Dynasty (317-420) created a beautiful and flowing new style, which has remained very popular in later generations. Ouyang Xun (557-641), Chu Suiliang (596-658), Yan Zhenqing (708-784) and Liu Gongquan (778-865) of the Tang Dynasty (618-907) each created their own types of regular script which have also been followed by later generations. Zhang Xu and Huai Su (725-785), also of the Tang Dynasty, invented a wonderful cursive style of writing. Su Shi (1037-1101), Huang Tingjian (1045-1105) and Mi Fei (1051-1107) of the Song Dynasty (960-1279) were all well known for their cursive hand and running hand. During the Qing period (1644-1911), calligraphers were divided into two schools: the stone rubbing school and the model book school. Yu Youren (1879-1964) blended the two schools into one to create a new school. All these calligraphers established their own unique styles: the "free and natural beauty" of Wang Xizhi, the "strong and robust beauty" of Yan Zhenqing, the "fresh and clear beauty" of Mi Fei and Huang Tingjian, the "bold and flowing beauty" of Zhang Xu and Huai Su and the "exotic and clumsy beauty" of Su Shi and Zheng Banqiao (1693-1765). The brilliant history of calligraphy and the achievements of generations of calligraphers are an important part of the history of Chinese culture.

Chinese calligraphy is an art based on the unique form of Chinese characters which developed from inscriptions on tortoise shells and ox bones to Dazhuan and Xiaozhuan (seal characters), official script, regular script, running hand and cursive hand. If we take writing (in any language) as the first great creation of human culture, then calligraphy is the second great creation of Chinese culture based on Chinese characters. Calligraphy, unlike writing for the sole purpose of social communication, is an art used to express the ideas, accomplishments, and feelings of the calligrapher. It is an expression of the outlook on culture, history and life in various ages, a tangible culture parallel to ideology, and a medium for conveying cultural information of all kinds.

Throughout history, philosophy has exerted a strong influence on calligraphy. Yin and Yang in the doctrine of changes, the Confucian doctrine of the mean, the Taoist doctrine of the Way of nature, and the Chan Sect's sudden enlightenment, meditation and self-cultivation, have all stamped a deep brand upon calligraphic aesthetics. Traditional national philosophical ideas, it may be said, have nourished Chinese calligraphy. And calligraphy, in the form of art, has embodied the meaning of traditional philosophical ideas. Good verses and compositions are copied by calligraphers, so calligraphy involves the presentation of literary works. People can enjoy the beauty of both the calligraphy and literature at the same time. Wang Xizhi's "Foreword to Lanting Pavilion" written by hand is a good example. The literati of the Song Dynasty further combined poetry and calligraphy. Many of the poems and essays written by hand by Su Shi and Huang Tingjian can be admired for the art of their calligraphy. Modern master calligraphers, including Kang Youwei (1858-1927), Guo Moruo (1892-1978), Qi Gong, and Zhao Puchu, have produced many excellent calligraphic and literary works.

Calligraphy integrates the aesthetics of painting with those of music and dance. It boasts the rhythm of music, the posture of dance and the pattern of painting. Form, quality, posture, style and reasoning are combined, making substance abstractive to produce a lasting feeling of beauty.

The following are some examples of masterpieces of calligraphy:

1. The "Foreword to Lanting Pavilion" by Wang Xizhi

Wang Xizhi was born into a noble family. When he resigned from government office, he settled at Shanyin, Guiji (now Shaoxing of Zhejiang Province). During his early years, he learned calligraphy from Wei Furen. Later he learned regular and cursive scripts from Zhong You and Zhang Zhi. He adopted the strengths of each of his teachers to create his own style. His works, using official script, regular characters, running hand and cursive script, surpassed those of master calligraphers before him. He led the development of calligraphy from a natural way to a way of skill training and improved it to perfection. He was famous during his lifetime and esteemed as a "true calligrapher sage" by later generations. Wang Xianzhi, his seventh son, was also a good calligrapher, particularly famed for his running hand and cursive script. Inheriting his father's achievements, he further improved the primitive and clumsy style of calligraphy. He wrote with elegance and boldness and his style had a great influence on later generations. The calligraphic works of the two Wangs are still widely published and the latest edition of *A Complete Collection of Chinese Calligraphic Works*, published by Rongbaozai Studio in Beijing, includes two volumes of their works.

The "Foreword to Lanting Pavilion" is the best-known example of Wang Xizhi's running hand. It is regarded as the "First Running Hand Under the Sun."

It is said that on the third day of the third month of the lunar calendar, in the year 353 (the ninth year of the reign of Emperor Mudi of the Eastern Jin Dynasty), Wang Xizhi and a group of eminent scholars gathered at Lanting Pavilion in Shanyin, Guiji, where, according to the conventions of an old sacrificial ceremony, they drank and enjoyed themselves on the bank of a river. When the wine cup flowing on the water stopped before one of them, that person would compose a poem immediately, otherwise he would have to take a drink. Wang wrote a foreword to the collection of all these poems: the "Foreword to Lanting Pavilion."

The "Foreword to Lanting Pavilion" was a favorite piece of brushwork of the writer himself. It is said that Wang copied the work several times, but felt that he could not reproduce the original effect. It became a cherished family heirloom. Later, it was handed down to the Venerable Zhiyong, a seventh-generation descendent of Wang Xizhi, who was also a famous calligrapher. When Zhiyong was dying, he handed the work down to his favorite disciple Biancai who hid the work in a hole he had made in the center-beam of the hall of a temple. Li Shimin, Emperor Taizong of the Tang Dynasty (r. 627-649), who was very fond of Wang's calligraphy, sent his secret envoy Xiao Yi to get the treasured piece of brushwork from Biancai. Xiao Yi knew that he would not be able to obtain the work by force, so he disguised himself as a scholar. Xiao succeeded in his approaches to Biancai, who invited Xiao to stay with him in the temple. They soon became good friends and made frequent visits to each other. One day, they were discussing calligraphy, and Xiao said that he had studied the two Wangs' regular script, and had collected some pieces of their works. He invited Biancai to see and enjoy them the next day. When Biancai saw the works, he said: "These are genuine works made by the Master. But they are not the best. I have a piece…."

"What is its name?" asked Xiao.

"The 'Foreword to Lanting Pavilion.'"

"How could you get hold of the original copy after all the wars?" said Xiao with a smile. "Surely it's a fake."

"This was handed down, generation to generation, by my master's ancestors. One of them gave it to me on his deathbed. Please look."

Biancai took the work from the hole where it was hidden, showed it to Xiao and then carefully replaced it. A few days later, when Biaocai was out, Xiao stole it from the hole and then went to the prefectural yamen where he showed the emperor's imperial edict saying that His Majesty wanted the calligraphic work. Biancai finally realized that he had been deceived, but there was nothing he could do about it now.

The emperor treasured the work. He copied it again and again and when he died, it was buried with him as his most precious sacrificial article. Later, his tomb was robbed and the original work was never recovered. Today, only copies exist.

Of all the copies, those made by Yu Shinan (558-638), Chu Suiliang, Ouyang Xun, and Feng Chengsu were considered the most important. But since Yu, Chu and Ouyang were all famous calligraphers themselves, their copies are influenced by their own styles. The "Copy of the Model of the Genuine 'Foreword to Lanting Pavilion' Calligraphy by Feng Chengsu of the Tang" is now kept in the Beijing Palace Museum.

The work was naturally written from beginning to end in running hand and regular script. The characters are arranged in vertical columns. The vertical columns are almost equal in length, but they are not always straight to the bottom and not all the characters are the same size. The form of characters varies with the strokes being naturally drawn. As a whole, the brushwork is exquisite with thick strokes being robust but not awkward, while narrow strokes are delicate but not weak. The calligraphy was completed in a rhyme with the proper use of force of the brush, light or heavy, fast or slow. Its strong and clear-cut lines and round and mellow forms present us with a fresh, clear, exquisite and closely linked work of art.

2. "Foreword to the Wild Goose Pagoda Sacred Teachings" by Chu Suiliang

Chu Suiliang (596-658 or 659) was an imperial minister and calligrapher of the Tang period. He died after he was demoted and banished from the court. He first studied the calligraphy of Shi Ling and Ouyang Xun, and later, Yu Shinan. Finally, he studied the two Wangs and evolved a style all his own. In the remaining years of his life, he created a flowing-style regular script which greatly influenced the calligraphy of later generations. Chu Suiliang, together with Ouyang Xun, Yu Shinan, and Xue Ji (649-713), became known as the four great calligraphers of the early Tang period. His most respected work is the "Foreword to the Wild Goose Pagoda Sacred Teachings."

The work was cut on two stone tablets inlaid in the brick shrines on either side of the south gate of the Greater Wild Goose Pagoda of the Ci'en Temple in Xi'an. It is said these tablets were laid by the master monk Xuan Zhuang in person. The tablets were written in the 10th and 12th months of the year 653 during the reign of Emperor Gaozong of the Tang Dynasty. Chu was then 58 years old. The tablets have been well protected, and are still in good condition.

Compared with his previous works, the brushwork here is improved from its simplicity and plainness toward richness and variety and the structure from simple regularity toward vividness and liveliness, without those inactive flavor prevalent in the making of tablets during the Six Dynasties period. These tablets are perfect and mature pieces produced during the last years of his life, with delicate and robust, pleasant and beautiful brushwork. The characters are written in small regular script, mixed with official script and running hand. The penmanship involves both round and square forms with good and natural execution of light and heavy, long and short, thick and thin, straight and curved, and upright and slant strokes of points and lines. Some traces of strokes can be found to link with the upper right corner of the following character, a technique belonging to running and cursive scripts, giving a flowing style of calligraphy. The structure of a character is always compact and intense with variations of strokes, spreading or unfolding, and upward or downward, all in distinct design and good execution without clumsiness. The written characters present an aesthetic feeling of thinness with strength and flowing without restraint. Once the tablets were erected, people flocked there to copy the rubbings from the stone inscriptions.

3. Yan Zhenqing: "The Yan Qinli Tablet"

Yan Zhenqing was a Tang minister and calligrapher, born into a prestigious family. He was killed by a treacherous minister of the court during the reign of Emperor Dezong.

He learned calligraphy from his family and Zhang Xu, a well-known calligrapher. He absorbed all the strengths of past masters and created his own style in both regular script and running hand. The Yan style, robust, solemn and elegant, reflects the prosperity and strength of the Tang Dynasty.

Although he was an amateur calligrapher, he was prolific. According to historical records, he produced 138 works, but only about 70 still exist.

The stone tablet was written and dedicated to Yan's great grandfather Yan Qinli. It is 268 cm high and 92 cm wide. The life-story on the tablet was written and cut in regular script. Today, it is kept in the Third Hall of the Forest of Steles Museum in Xi'an.

He produced this masterpiece at the age of 71, when he had firmly established his own style. His vigor can be seen clearly in this energetic, flowing and perfect work. The tablet was buried underground for many years, protecting it from damage, and the calligraphy is remarkably clear and fresh. It serves as a good model for beginners to copy.

The penmanship of the calligraphy on the tablet stresses the maneuverability of the middle edge of the brush, with the use of the brush tip at first in a pressed and backward way and then unfolding it to level to the end, to make the head of the strokes hidden and the tail protected. In this way, the edges of the brushwork cannot be seen and an effect of forceful penmanship is thus produced with characters smoothly and energetically written. Its typical strokes such as the long slanting lines and long vertical stems are unique. Its turns are mostly in the form of an inward square and an outward round. As a whole, the Yan style is solemn and great, elegant and robust, vigorous and primitive with an atmosphere of magnificence.

4. The "Xuanbi Pagada Tablet" by Liu Gongquan

Liu Gongquan was a calligrapher of the Tang period. He was famous for writing regular characters. He created his own Liu style by absorbing the compact structure of Ouyang Xun's style and the spreading brush movement of Yan Zhenqing. His calligraphy has a bony and energetic style with a firm and forceful framework of strokes, emphasizing a strong idea of buildup. His work is often referred to that of Yan Zhenqing. "Yan's veins and Liu's bones" mark the basic features of these two major types of Tang Dynasty regular script. Like Yan, Liu was also prolific.

His most famous work is the "Xuanbi Pagoda Tablet," which tells the story of the master monk Dada who was favorably treated by the emperors of the Tang Dynasty. The tablet was established in the 12th month of the year 841. The text on the tablet was written and cut in the regular script. Now it is preserved in the Second Hall of the Forest of Steles Museum in Xi'an. The stone tablet is cracked and some of its words are blurred, but generally, the writing is complete and clear and is considered to be a good model for beginners to copy.

The penmanship of the writing on the tablet is produced mostly with the use of the middle edge of the brush, square or round and raising and pressing. Long horizontal strokes are usually thin and short strokes are thick. Vertical stems include pendent-pin like ones and the dew-dropping ones. Its slanting lines are generally produced with a heavy force when moving toward the right and with a light touch when moving to the left. The structure is compact and stiff, intense inside and relaxed outside. As a whole, the style of the work is sharp with hard and bony strokes, and vigorous as if cut with a sword.

5. The "Su Ben Autobiography Scroll" by Huai Su

Huai Su was a monk and calligrapher, who had loved calligraphy from childhood and was famous for his cursive hand. He wrote so much that he wore out numerous brushes and ink-slabs, so he began to use the leaves of banana trees, which he grew himself, instead of paper. He called his studio the "House of Green Skies." At first he studied the calligraphy of Zhong You and the two Wangs. Later he learned the cursive script of Zhang Xu from Yan Zhenqing and created his own style of cursive hand, becoming a famous cursive-hand calligrapher like Zhang Xu, one known as "wild Zhang" and the other as "drunken Su." The wild cursive hand (*kuang cao*) is a style that is written completely freely. The producer expresses his feeling and will through the brushwork, which is extremely concise and often links several words in a single stroke. It is the most extreme form of the cursive hand. Huai Su's style has more variations than that of Zhang, without violating the traditional rules. It is also more recognizable and so had a greater influence than Zhang on the following generations. The "Su Ben Autobiography Scroll" is considered to be his best work.

The scroll had been written in several copies. And this one is generally regarded as the typical one. It is written in ink on paper. The original is now kept in the Taipei Palace Museum, Taiwan Province.

According to the author's note at the end of the scroll, it was produced when he was 41, in the prime of his life. The text describes his studies of calligraphy and experiences in creation. The latter part records praise for him by Yan Zhenqing and others.

His cursive hand is sometimes mixed with seal characters, and the brushwork is done mostly with the middle edge of the brush, round and turning inwardly, presenting a feeling of strength, flow and change. The spaces are well distributed and the size of the characters, large and small, spreading out and confined, seems to be produced at will freely but the space between them, the form, the size and the bulkiness and dryness of characters are well coordinated and laid out. A balanced beauty is thus achieved in the dynamic characters. This work is clearly modeled on Zhang Xu's style, but it is less wild than Zhang's works. Huai's style was greatly influenced by Wang Xianzhi.

"Lord Su praises himself in the autobiography," said Su Shi, "but no one criticizes him since his calligraphy is so good."

6. Su Shi's "Book of Handwritten Poems Written in April at Huangzhou"

Su Shi (1037-1101) was a writer, calligrapher and painter of the Northern Song Dynasty. Although he tried to pursue a career as an official, he was often frustrated and demoted. He was a man of many gifts in poetry, literature, and calligraphy, making a strong contribution to all these fields. He was well known for his running hand and regular script, following the styles of Li Yong (678-747), Xu Hao (703-782), Yan Zhenqing, and Yang Ningshi (873-954). He also established his own style, with a sense of fullness and charm, becoming the typical style of implied meaning during the Song and Yuan periods. Su Shi, Huang Tingjian, Mi Fei, and Cai Xiang (1012-1067) were known as the "four master calligraphers" of the time. The poems written in April at Huangzhou are his representative running hand works.

The work was written on paper, and consists of two of the writer's poems, each written with five characters per line. It is now kept in the Taipei Palace Museum.

When he was 42 years of age, Su Shi was the prefectural magistrate of Huzhou. Whenever he discovered some malpractice of the government and harm caused to ordinary people, he would write about it in his poems. Some imperial censors found about this, charged him with slandering the court, and had him sent to prison. On his release, he was given a post at Huangzhou (now Huanggang County, Hubei Province). Su often wandered along rivers and in the mountains with the local people. It was here that he wrote these two famous poems, in which he expressed his indignation and described his hard life and sorrows in the three years since he had arrived in Huangzhou. The drizzling weather before and during the Pure Brightness Festival (an occasion for mourning one's ancestors, usually falling in early April) made him particularly sad.

His poems and calligraphy complement each other, both strongly expressing his sorrows for his own life and his worries about the state. The work is his greatest achievement in the running hand script. The strokes are tough and full and the characters are written alternately in regular form and running hand. The words and the lines are well coordinated and executed as a whole. Each character, small or large, is laid freely at will with varied forms. The brushwork is, at times, heavy as a crouched bear, at others, as light as a flying swallow. Its composition includes a good use of space. Its rhythm is at a pace of the increased quickness of the brush, with the formation of small and large, thick and thin characters in strong and light ink. One can clearly see the writer's gloomy mood expressed in the flowing of his brush, like a torrent of water. It is a truly wonderful work. Su Shi said: "It becomes a good piece while you did not expect it."

7. Huang Tingjian's "Book of Calligraphic Poems Written at the Pavilion of the Wind Soughing in the Pines"

Huang Tingjian (1045-1105) was a poet and calligrapher of the Northern Song Dynasty, who became famous as one of the "four master calligraphers of the Song period." He created his own style of running hand and cursive script after studying the cursive script of Huai Su and the regular script of Yan Zhenqing.

His book of poems, written in running hand, is now in the Taipei Palace Museum.

Huang Tingjian's hardships and frustrations in life were like those of Su Shi. He, too, was frequently demoted. At the age of 57, he traveled to Mount Fanshan at Echeng in Hubei Province, where he found a pavilion called Pavilion of the Wind Soughing in the Pines standing amid the beautiful landscape. The sight moved him deeply and inspired his poems, in which he expressed the frustration of his dismissal and his yearning for freedom. He was determined, however, not to submit to the authorities. He missed his teachers and friends, and his warm and sincere feelings for them are vividly expressed in his poems.

8. Zhao Gou's "Luo Shen Fu in Running Hand"

Zhao Gou (1107-1187), Emperor Gaozong of the Southern Song, was on the throne from 1127-1162. Both he and his father were politically incompetent, but were gifted artistically. Zhao Gou's calligraphy surpassed that of his father, inheriting more from the past and displaying a more profound insight.

He first studied the calligraphy of Huang Tingjian, then Mi Fei, and later focused on the styles of Zhong Yao, a famous calligrapher of the Three Kingdoms Period, and Wang Xizhi. He worked very hard. "Over the past 50 years, I have never dropped my brush a single day if there were no more important things to be done," he said. "I have learned the styles of all the calligraphers since the Wei, Jin and the Six Dynasties." He wrote a book entitled *On Calligraphy*, a book full of insight.

"Luo Shen Fu (a descriptive prose interspersed with verse)" was copied in running hand style on a piece of satin. It was composed by Cao Zhi, a celebrated poet of the Three Kingdoms Period. With the threat of invasion from the north by Jin troops, who had already overrun half of the Song empire, Zhao abdicated at the age of 55 in favor of his son, hoping to live in peace in his remaining years. In copying the "Luo Shen Fu" he was expressing his desire for love, comfort and pleasure. His brushwork is a little bit thin, but in bold and vigorous strokes with a flavor of the implied meaning of the regular characters and running hand, and mostly in the styles of the "Two Wangs" (Wang Xizhi and Wang Xianzhi).

9. Zhao Mengfu's "Danba Stone Tablet"

Zhao Mengfu (1254-1322) was a calligrapher of the Yuan Dynasty. Like Su Shi, he was known for his versatility. He was well versed in poetry and literature, and had a good knowledge of Taoism and Buddhism. Skillful in painting, he was also good at calligraphy, particularly at regular script, running hand and small regular characters. He learned the style of Li Yong, based on the styles of the Two Wangs. He was said to be able to write ten thousand words in a day and his penmanship became known as the style of Zhao. Together with Yan Zhenqing, Liu Gongquan and Ouyang Xun, he was known as one of the "four master calligraphers in regular characters."

At the age of 63, Zhao was ordered by the emperor to write the Danba Stone Tablet, in regular script, which is now stored in the Palace Museum in Beijing.

The brushwork of the stone tablet is typical of the Zhao style. Its strokes are slender, mellow and beautiful, in rigid standard with vim and vigor. His penmanship is graceful but vigorous with bony strokes at the start and end of each movement.

Zhao Mengfu was a descendent of the Song imperial family, but served the conquering Yuan, so recalling his past filled him with sadness. By immersing himself in calligraphy, he sought to alleviate the pressure of his contradictory feelings.

Section 2 Chinese Painting and Traditional Culture

Chinese painting, also known as the traditional national painting, one of the traditional fine paintings with a long history, has its unique and independent system in the world's fine arts field. Using brushes, ink, and Chinese pigments, a painting is drawn on a special kind of paper (Xuan paper) or silk. The traditional subjects are figures, landscapes, flowers and birds. They are divided into two different styles: one is Gongbi, or meticulous painting, the traditional realistic style characterized by fine brushwork and close attention to detail, the other is Xieyi, or impressionist painting, the freehand brushwork style characterized by vivid expression and bold and vigorous outlines. The forms of painting include wall paintings, screens, scrolls, albums, and fan covers. There is also unique mounting and paper hanging skill for paintings.

In comparison with Western painting, Chinese painting has a distinguished national form and artistic characteristics. After a careful study of the object, a painter can discover the rules of its structure, and then produce it by the mind's eye. It is not merely a simple copy, but it combines the object with the artistic concept of the producer, turning a natural image into an "artistic image." The object can become endowed with feelings, and instilled with the artist's essence and personality to achieve the effect of "being alike not only in spirit, but also in appearance." Not all the objects are to be drawn on the paper, and much space is left for the imagination. Chinese painters tend to use "moving perspective" in their works. Modern artists call it a way of "scattering perspective," or "unfixed perspective." With towering mountains, murmuring waters, meandering hillside paths, dense forests, row upon row of houses, and the active people in one painting, a Chinese landscape artist can produce a full and imaginative view of a scene. The painting "Riverside Scene on the Pure Brightness Festival," presents a full scene of activities on and under a bridge, inside and outside a house. This is the "moving perspective," quite different from naturalism. The artist's eye makes use of and controls nature. The use of lines is important in Chinese painting. Clear, swift, sharp and changeable lines are combined with the push, point and press of the brush and ink to show the quality of the object and variations of tone. Ancient Chinese artists listed 18 different ways of drawing lines with the brush in figure painting. Different ways of creating lines are used when painting a landscape, flowers and birds, clouds, bamboos, chrysanthemums, plums and orchids.

Traditional Chinese painting and calligraphy are different branches of art stemming from the same origin. They use the same kind of tools and all the lines used in painting are variations of the points and lines of calligraphy. Though they are different artistic forms, they are closely linked in terms of their expression of thoughts and feelings. They influence each other to create another artistic feature.

The infancy of Chinese painting predated the appearance of written characters. The pre-historical culture and the whole Chinese cultural development had a close relation with it. The techniques used in figure painting had reached maturity during the periods from the later Zhou to the Han, Wei and the Six Dynasties. Landscape and flower-and-bird paintings had become an independent category in the Sui and Tang dynasties. There were many schools of wash and landscape painting artists in the Five Dynasties and the Northern and Southern Song and landscape painting became a major sector. Wenren Hua (scholar painting) appeared in the Tang period and further developed in the Song period. It became booming in the Yuan Dynasty, with a tendency of freehand brushwork style and vivid and bold expression. It further developed during the Ming and Qing dynasties, and the modern time, and a bold and free brushwork was further emphasized. From the period of Wei, Jin, and the Southern and Northern Dynasties, and Tang, Ming and Qing, traditional Chinese painting had been influenced by Buddhist painting art and the Western arts. The development of Chinese painting through the ages constitutes an important part of the history of Chinese culture. Without a knowledge of Chinese painting, one cannot have a complete knowledge of the fine traditional Chinese culture. Here we present a few of the artists and their works:

1. Yan Liben's "Emperor Taizong's Sedanchair"

Yan Liben (?-673) was a painter and an official of the early Tang Dynasty. His father and elder brother were highly versed in arts and crafts, architecture and painting. He inherited the skills of his family members and learned from Zhang Sengyou and Zheng

Fasi. He was versed in portrait painting and he could express the character and temperament of the object. He was the forefather of portrait painting of the Tang period.

The painting "Emperor Taizong's Sedanchair" is now kept in the Beijing Palace Museum. The painting tells the story of the marriage of Emperor Taizong's daughter Princess Wencheng with the Tubo (Tibet) King Songtsam Gambo in 641. It depicts the scene of the emperor receiving the envoy sent by the Tubo king to welcome the princess. On the upper part in the center of the painting, there are three characters "Bu Nian Tu" (Emperor's Sedanchair"), a dedication by Zhao Gou, Emperor Gaozong of the Song Dynasty, and a seal. To the right, Emperor Taizong is seated in the sedan, calm and composed with his legs crossed. Two court maidservants, one in front and the other behind, carry the sedan belts on their shoulders and hold the handles of the sedan, walking slowly forward. Four other maidservants are in attendance on each side of the sedan. Another three maidservants walk alongside and behind the sedan, holding fans and red canopies. To the left, a eunuch in white stands behind and a ritual guide official in red walks in front, holding a jade scepter. In the middle, stands the Tubo envoy, refined and courteous, a small cap on head, dressed in a long robe with narrow sleeves. His palms are held together, in a sincere and friendly mood to welcome the princess.

It is possible that Yan Liben attended the meeting ceremony. This picture is a vivid representation of the scene. The status, qualities and bearing of the figures and the relationships between them are all properly expressed. Simple and skillful lines are used to show the folds of their clothes with deep and plain colors. The work might have been first drawn with ink lines and then coated with colors. As a whole, the lines are smooth and flowing, and the colors are harmonious. It is an outstanding figure painting with fine brushwork and elaborate details.

2. Wu Daozi's "Birth of Sakyamuni"

Wu Daozi (c. 685-758) was a Tang Dynasty painter. He first studied calligraphy, but lack of success made him turn to painting.

He showed his gift in this field when he was barely 20. Later he was summoned to the imperial court of Tang where he was conferred the title " Erudite of the Palace." He was skilled in painting Taoist and Buddhist figures, as well as birds, animals and landscapes. He painted murals, each very different from the others, covering well over 300 bays in all in temples and monasteries in Chang'an and Luoyang. His paintings were always done at one stroke without rules and instruments. In his pictures, the folds of clothes were drawn smoothly and roundly, as if flowing in the wind. Wu Daozi is regarded as "the Saint of Paintings."

"The Birth of Sakyamuni," also known as "The Picture of the Son-bestowing King of Heaven," is drawn on paper without color. It was not signed by the artist. It is now kept in Osaka Museum in Japan.

In the picture, the newborn Sakyamuni is carried by his father Suddhodana to worship the heavenly God. There are two parts in the picture. The first shows that the King of Heaven summons the Son-bestowing God and the god together with his auspicious beast are on the way, and that the king is on the back of his own beast, composed and excited. And the attendants lead the beast to run on. The second part shows Suddhodana with the new-born baby in his arms, walking slowly toward the temple, while the gods of the temple kneel down to pay respect to him. From the images and actions of the figures, we can see that this is no ordinary child. The picture is full of figures and gods and monsters, all vividly portrayed. Its lines are vigorous with a sense of precise and lively rhythm. With their flowing sleeves and stripes, the figures are all animated.

3. Wang Wei's "Picture of Wangchuan"

Wang Wei (701-761) was a painter, poet and official of the Tang Dynasty. In his old age he led a life partly in the office and partly in his reclusive home in Wangchuan in present Shaanxi Province. His 400 poems have been handed down to the present time. He was highly skilled in ink and wash landscape painting. There is painting in his poems and poetry in his paintings, as connoisseurs say. He was the founder of the school of scholar paintings and wrote a book titled *The Formula of Landscape Painting*. He believed that ink painting is the best choice for a painter to show natural beauty and achieve wonders. He injected more water into black ink to express the beauty of landscapes, replacing the conventional use of green and heavy colors and contour of lines.

The "Picture of Wangchuan" is one of his famous works. It was painted on the wall of the Qingyuan Temple. This is a sketch painting of the landscape of the place, expressing the feelings of his peaceful and reclusive life. The style of the picture is unique with its unexpected motif and bizarre and vigorous brushwork.

4. Zhang Zeduan's "Riverside Scene on the Pure Brightness Festival"

Zhang Zeduan was a Northern Song Dynasty painter. The dates of his birth and death are unknown. During his early years, he studied in Bianjing (now Kaifeng in Henan Province), only later learning to paint. During the period of the reign of Emperor Huizong of the Song Dynasty (1100-1125), he worked at the Imperial Painting Academy, skillful in Jiehua painting (a technique of drawing lines with the aid of a ruler in painting palatial buildings). He liked to paint cities, palaces and other constructions, particularly ships, vehicles, marketplaces, streets, and bridges. His typical works include "Riverside Scene on the Pure Brightness Festival," a long scroll 24.5 cm in length. It is now stored in the Palace Museum in Beijing. The picture presents a scene of some of the streets of Bianjing, the capital city of Song, and a corner of its outskirts along the Bianhe River, during the Pure Brightness Festival in the 12th century. There are more than 500 people from all walks of life in the painting, and about 60 horses, donkeys, oxen, pigs, mules, and camels. There are also more than 20 carts and sedanchairs, over 20 ships and boats, and 30-odd pavilions, halls, cottages, and shops.

In the picture, all sorts of people are vividly shown, including shoppers, pedlers, wine drinkers, fortune-tellers, barbers, story-tellers, acrobats, people riding donkeys or in sedanchairs, buying medicinal herbs, chatting, dozing, pushing carts, visiting homes, or paying respect to tombs. The scene stretches away from the outskirts to the seething marketplace. Ponds, streams, small bridges, cottages, ancient willows and woods are shown in peace and tranquillity. Market goers with their loads on horse-drawn carts are trudging toward the streets. The Bianhe River runs through the city, with some ships moored at the river bank, and others sailing in the torrent. Further on is a ship with its mast lowered, preparing to pass under an arch-bridge. People standing on the bridge are leaning over the railings and cheering the boatmen on. A boatman standing on the roofing of the ship pilots the passing of the ship and two others under the roofing stretch their arms shouting. On the other side of the bridge is the downtown area, where shops, restaurants and officials' residences line both sides of the bustling streets.

Using scattered perspective, the artist presents a typical scene of Northern Song society. As historical material, it provides substantial images and pictures of the agriculture, handicraft trade, transportation, commerce, construction, daily life and cultural activities of the time. As a work of art, this wonderful and distinguished piece is the highest achievement of the Chinese genre painting with its spectacular design, rich content, and masterful technique.

5. Ma Yuan's "Four Farmers Singing Their Way Home"

Ma Yuan was a painter of the Southern Song Dynasty (1127-1279). The dates of his birth and death are unknown. He learned to paint from his grandfather and father. He was editorial assistant in the Painting Academy during the period of the reigns of Emperors Guangzong and Ningzong (1190-1224). He was skilled in painting landscapes, applying the ink with sweeping brushwork to form rocks and mountains. He was known in later years as one of the four master painters of the Southern Song, together with Xia Gui, Li Tang, and Liu Songnian.

The "Four Farmers Singing Their Way Home," painted at a time when the Song Dynasty was fighting its northern enemy, the Jin, reflects the healthy spirit and mood of farmers in a picturesque mountainous landscape. Four drunken, singing farmers are walking across a small bridge amid the field paths. The old man in front, holding a stick, turns his head over his shoulder and sings in an antiphonal style with the three others singing behind. The last of these, carrying a wine gourd, is extremely drunk. They beat time with their feet while they sing. Two children hiding behind a large rock peeping at them have burst into laughter. Not far away, there is a rock shaded by bamboo and willows. In the distance, the towering mountain peaks, with palaces and temples half hidden among them, cut into the sky. On the horizon is a rosy cloud. It gives a feeling of refreshing and joy. As well as the artist's signature, there is also a poem dedicated to the painting by Emperor Ningzong.

The painting is typical of Ma Yuan's landscape paintings. His brushwork technique was a new breakthrough. He seized an aspect of the natural scene from the most favorable angle and took a corner of the object as his close-up, making it natural and compact. Hence he was known as "Ma's corner." A good deal of space is left in the upper part of the painting for a broad and open sky and a clear distinction is made between close, middle and distant objects.

The joyful farmers are the descriptive theme, adding gay colors to a landscape painting and imbuing the natural scene with a human touch. The figures were drawn with a reducible brushwork, and the lines are vigorous, simple and clear. Various types of trees are being blown in the direction of the wind. He was skillful in drawing weeping willows and down-stretching twigs, hence his method is known as "Ma Yuan's dragging skills." His mountains and rocks are primitive and magnificent, while distant mountains are usually painted with light brushwork, amidst the mist of clouds.

The painting, done on silk, is now in the collection of the Palace Museum in Beijing.

6. Huang Gongwang's "Houses in the Fuchun Mountains"

Huang Gongwang (1269-1354) was a painter of the Yuan Dynasty, becoming a low-ranking official in middle age. He was involved in a case and sent into prison. After he was set free, he withdrew to a reclusive place and no longer served in the government. He became a devout believer of the Quanzhen (Complete Truth) Sect of Taoism and traveled around the country. At the age of about 50, he began to produce landscape paintings and in his later years he established his own style of painting. Most of his sketches were made while touring South China. In his ink and wash paintings, he employed the cursive and seal styles of calligraphy in his brushwork using a few strokes to give a feeling of remoteness and vastness. His paintings were described as "simple and vigorous mountain peaks and exuberant vegetation." He liked to use light red-brown, and invented his reddish landscape painting. Of the "Four Masters of the Yuan Dynasty" (the three others being Wu Zhen, Ni Zan, and Wang Meng) Huang Gongwang was considered the finest. He had a great influence on the landscape paintings of the Ming and Qing dynasties.

"Houses in the Fuchun Mountains" was his favorite work. At 79, he lived in the Fuchun Mountains to make this painting, which was completed in almost four years. Many painters of the Ming and Qing learned from this painting. It was passed down to Wu Hongyu in 1650 in the early Qing period. Wu cherished and valued it so much that he wanted to take it with him when he was about to die, and tried to burn it. The painting was snatched out of the fire by his nephew Wu Zhendu, but the painting was torn into two parts. One part was damaged and is now kept in the Zhejiang Provincial Museum. The second part is in the Palace Museum in Beijing.

The painting shows the landscape on both banks of the Fuchun River. Its composition uses "level, broad and high distant" perspective, making it replete with changeable scenes: waves upon waves of mountains, waterways and shallows, as well as landscape beyond distant mountains. The earth quality of the mountains, mainly covered with pine trees, is also shown. The slopes, pavilions, cottages, ships and bridges, and fishermen's homes are all vividly presented in the cool air of early autumn. Mountains and rocks are painted with the mid-part of the brush with light and half-dried ink to create their shaded and sunny sides. The woods are painted with horizontal points of brushwork.

7. Xu Wei's "Ink Grapes"

Xu Wei (1521-1593) was a writer, painter and calligrapher of the Ming Dynasty. In his childhood he proved himself to be very smart and at the age of 20 he passed the imperial examination at the county level. However, he failed in the later provincial examinations eight times, the last time when he was 41. He served as the private office assistant of Hu Zongxian, the viceroy of Zhejiang and Fujian provinces and joined the struggle against sea invaders in the southeastern coastal area. Later, Hu was dismissed, jailed and committed suicide. Xu Wei himself suffered from a mental disorder for some time and killed his wife. For this, he was imprisoned for seven years. During the remaining years of his life, he supported himself by selling his calligraphic works and paintings.

He produced a great number of literary works and traditional operas, including the *Collected Works of Xu Wenzhang*. In middle age, he began to learn painting. He pioneered a new path for the freehand ink and wash painting of the Ming and Qing periods. Zheng Banqiao (1693-1765), a writer, calligrapher and painter of the Qing period, cherished a profound esteem for him, calling himself "Green Vine's Running Dog," because Xu was named the Green Vine Taoist during his remaining years. Qi Baishi, famous modern painter, expressed regret that he had not been born three hundred years earlier to serve Xu as his studio assistant. His famous works include "Ink Grapes," "Lily Lotus and Crabs," "Chinese Parasol and Banana Trees," and "Peony, Banana and Rock."

"Ink Grapes" is now kept in the Palace Museum in Beijing. A bunch of grapes hangs from the upper right of the picture. The grapes and vines are produced by point and freehand brushwork with watery ink. The vivid grapes appear to dance in the wind. In representing an object, it is more important to grasp its spirit, or essence, rather than to copy its shape precisely. The grapes are a self-expression of the artist. The dedicated poem, which shows his mood of sorrows and dissatisfaction caused by frustration and depression, can be paraphrased as follows:

Being frustrated in the first half of my life,

Now I have become an old man.

Standing lonely in my studio, I cry loudly in the evening wind,

There's nowhere to sell the bright pearls from my brush,

I have to cast them, now and then, into the wild vine.

Xu Wei's ink and wash brushwork is unique. In this particular work, he used water to naturally dilute the thickly ink-colored grapes to voice his mind.

8. Zhu Da's "Lotus and Two Birds"

Zhu Da (c. 1626-c.1705) was a painter of the early Qing period, a descendent of the 16th son of Zhu Yuanzhang, the founding emperor of the Ming Dynasty. He was 19 years old when the Ming Dynasty was overthrown. Suffering the humiliation and agony of losing his country and home, he pretended to be a fool and lived as a recluse in the mountains. At the age of 23, he became a Buddhist monk, and then a Taoist. When he was about 60, he returned to the secular world. Zhu Da usually signed paintings and calligraphy as "Bada Shanren" (Eight-Mountain Hermit). He firmly opposed the high-handed ethnic policy adopted by the Qing government and often vented his discontent through his poems, writings, calligraphy and paintings. For instance, he often gave the eyes of his fish and birds an expression of hatred and resentment, symbolizing his own defiance of the Qing government.

Zhu Da's brushwork is simple and condensed, his images exaggerated. His landscape paintings, usually full of strange rocks and desolate hills, show a cold and voiceless world. His ink and wash technique produced a great impact on later freehand painting. In 1983, the People's Fine Arts Publishing House published a "Collection of the Calligraphy and Paintings of Bada Shanren" (Vols.1, 2, and 3).

"Lotus and Two Birds," now stored in the Palace Museum in Beijing, is one of his best pieces. In the painting, two stems of lotus wind upwards, fragmented and broken up, showing the high ideals but uneven course of the artist's life. The rock, larger at the top than at the bottom, is deformed and strange, challenging the world with a determined and defiant will. Two birds on the rock look at each other with the white of their eyes. Except for two seals, the whole painting is without color. The ease and verve of the brushwork shows that it was painted at one sitting, venting the producer's discontent. One might almost say that it is a self-portrait.

9. Yuan Ji's "The Resonant Waterfall"

Yuan Ji (1642-c. 1718) was a painter of the early Qing period. Originally, his name was Zhu Ruoji. After the fall of the Ming Dynasty, when he was five years old, his father was captured and killed. To escape from disaster, he became a Buddhist monk and took the name Yuan Ji. In his remaining years of life, he settled in Yangzhou, supporting himself by selling paintings.

He painted flowers, fruits and figures, and was particularly versed in landscape paintings, enjoying a very high reputation at the time. He learned well from his predecessors and he was also a very good observer of natural things. He held that "artists should be in tune with the time," and that a landscape painter should "originate in mountains and rivers," "search out and sketch all the strange peaks" and then "make his own rules." By doing this, an artist might succeed in breaking away from those before him and come to create his own style.

He tried to create his unique works with variable compositions. His brushwork is free at will and the design is vast and novel, differing greatly from the conventional practice of the time to mimic the style of the ancients. The Yangzhou school and modern Chinese painters have been greatly influenced by his works. He made a profound study of painting theory and wrote a book titled *Quotations from Balsam Pear Monk's Paintings* (Yuan Ji was also named Balsam Pear Monk).

Because his paintings have been held in such high esteem, there are many fakes on the market. Most, however, are so badly produced that they can easily be distinguished. Zhang Daqian, a famous modern artist who had studied the works of Yuan Ji, can produce works almost as good as the originals. But Zhang's brushwork is not as heavy as Yuan's and his lines are smoother. When carefully examined, they too can be distinguished from Yuan's original works.

"The Resonant Waterfall," a wash painting done on paper, is now kept in the Shanghai Museum. This painting best demonstrates the spectacular spirit of the artist, with its novel and unique composition and bizarre-shaped pines between rocks randomly scattered on the mountain, like flying dragons. A waterfall pours directly down through dense bamboo and the wooden pavilion, out of the deep mountain step by step. The resounding waterfall, the din of the forest, and the soughing of the pines in the wind, combine into an orchestral performance. Two scholars sitting in the pavilion listen to the grand and beautiful music and smile to each other in silence. Behind the front peak of the mountain, a dim forest can be seen. Above in the sky, dark heavy clouds threaten a sudden storm.

The brushwork in the painting is energetic and sharp but steady with free and bold use of ink. Mountains and rocks are lightly outlined and rubbed with heavy ink and a dry brush. The mosses in heavy ink and elaborately painted clumps of grass heighten the atmosphere of the impending storm. The use of ink is varied, creating many levels of colors. It can be regarded as a typical use of ink as the use of colors. Long lines are used for the contours of mountains, like fully strained bows to frame up the mountain bodies. In the lower part of the painting, slant lines denote the sweeping traces, which give the hint leading to the top of the mountain.

Chapter 8

Traditional Chinese Medicine and The Science of Health Preservation

Section 1 Theory and Classifications in Traditional Chinese Medicine and the Development of Traditional Chinese Pharmacology

Beginning from the Zhou Dynasty, traditional Chinese medicine (TCM) was divided into nutriology, internal medicine, surgery, and veterinary medicine. During the Tang period, further division appeared, such as internal medicine, surgery, pediatrics, ENT, external therapy, acupuncture, massage, witchcraft and incantation. More professional medical sciences appeared during the Song period. Apoplectic science, ophthalmology and gynecology were developed on the basis of Tang Dynasty classifications. In later dynasties, these classifications were preserved and further developed.

Fundamental TCM Theory

Legend has it that the ancient "Shen Nong tasted a hundred species of herbs and almost 70 species of poisonous plants a day." Some plants proved harmless and actually beneficial to man's health, capable of alleviating the seriousness of illness and restoring health. Repeated experience brought knowledge which was passed down through the ages. This simple accumulation of experiences brought about the birth of the earliest Chinese science of medicine and knowledge of health preservation. This is regarded as the stage of "cognition of medicine and food."

During the Xia Dynasty (c. 21st century to c. early 17th century BC), alcohol was produced and used to treat diseases. During the Shang Dynasty (c. early 17th century to c. 11th century BC) medicinal herb decoctions were being produced. During the Western Zhou period (c. 11th century to 771 BC), professional doctors appeared, dealing with nutriology, internal medicine, traumatology and veterinary medicine. *The Book of Rites* records five categories of medicine: herbs, wood, insects, stone and grains. *The Book of Songs* tells of more than 50 species of plant which can be made into medicines, while the *Classic of Mountains and Rivers* records 126 kinds of medicine.

During the Western Zhou period, a connection was found between some diseases and the change of seasons. People learned that the spread of disease could be increased by an abnormal climate and that epidemic diseases were infectious.

During the Spring and Autumn Period (770-476 BC), Yi He, a famous doctor of the State of Qin, created the theory of "six climatic conditions as the pathogenic factors of disease," believing that excess of any of the six climatic conditions (cloudy, sunny, windy, rainy, dark and bright) was the cause of disease. It was on this concept that the later theory of pathogenic wind, cold, dryness, humidity, fire and heat was based.

According to textual research, by the end of the period of primitive society, people already knew how to prevent or treat diseases by expelling pathogens and taking exercise. Historical documents refer to a kind of dance to treat diseases. This "dance" became a prototype of the later therapeutic methods for expelling pathogens, by which people could relax their muscles and tendons to promote blood circulation and improve breathing.

A jade pendant dating back to 380 BC is engraved with a description of the process and function of the promotion of Qi (vital energy, associated with breath): "The way to promote Qi is to take a deep breath and hold it. The retained breath can move, extending to the lower part of the body, where it can be settled and stabilized. As it is stabilized, it can develop and grow, and as it grows, all pathogenic evils will be expelled. The breath goes up and down naturally and smoothly to produce vitality. If one stops doing this, it will not work." Thus, methods of promoting and controlling Qi already existed in the early Warring States Period.

During the Spring and Autumn and the Warring States periods, the newly emerging relations of production under feudalism promoted the rapid development of the productive forces. It was under these conditions that TCM and health-preserving science formed their systematic theories.

The Yellow Emperor's Classic of Internal Medicine, China's first classic book of medicine, was published at this time, creating a comprehensive theoretical system of TCM and health-preserving science.

Before the publishing of the classic, TCM and health-preserving science were still being developed in practical experiments. *The Yellow Emperor's Classic of Internal Medicine*, despite its name, was actually the result of a joint effort by many physicians of the period. It is divided into two parts: "Plain Questions" and "Miraculous Pivot," involving a total of 168 essays in 18 volumes. "Plain Questions" mainly relates the basic theories of physiological, pathological and medicinal therapeutic science, while "Miraculous Pivot" deals mainly with the theory of acupuncture and moxibustion, channels, collaterals and anatomy.

The book's achievements are:

(1) Introducing the theory of Yin and Yang and the Five Elements (metal, wood, water, fire and earth) to establish an integral conception of TCM;

(2) Introducing the theory of vitality, essence and spirit, stressing them as the three vital and treasured constituents of the body;

(3) Presenting a study on the physiological phenomena of the human body and specifically identifying the different stages of its development as growth, maturity and ageing;

(4) Stressing preventive therapy; and

(5) Putting forward a health-preserving principle of the correspondence between man and Heaven and creating the theory of channels and collaterals, laying the theoretical foundation for TCM health preservation and Qigong (breathing exercise) health

preservation.

Another medical classic is *Emperor Shen Nong's Materia Medica*, which summed up the experiences of the ancients living before the Qin and Han dynasties in the use of herbal medicines. It is composed of three volumes, describing the use of 365 species of medicinal herbs, which are divided into three classes according to their toxic and curative effects. The first class, involving 120 species of non-poisonous herbs, may be used as tonic medicines. The second class of 120 varieties of poisonous or non-poisonous herbs may be used as medicines for treating diseases or as tonics, and the third class of 125 varieties of poisonous herbs as therapeutic medicines to relieve exterior pathogenic evils. These are the original classifications of medicines in ancient China. It also made a summary of the theory of medicinal formulae as "principals, associates, adjuvants and messagers" (the different roles played by different ingredients of a prescription) and the theory of "four natures of drugs" (cold, hot, mild and cool) and "five flavors of drugs" (pungent, sour, sweet, bitter and salty). Pathogenic cold should be relieved with heat-producing drugs, while pathogenic heat should be treated with cold-producing drugs. It closely relates the natures of different drugs to particular pathogenic factors, completing the therapeutic theory of TCM and laying a foundation of the development of Chinese herbal science.

Other medical classics, such as the *Treatise on Febrile and Miscellaneous Diseases*, performed the transition from theory to clinical practice.

The book was written by the celebrated physician Zhang Zhongjing at the end of the Eastern Han Dynasty (25-220), based on ancient medical instructions and a broad study of many others' medical formulas. Unfortunately, the original work, comprising 16 volumes, was lost in the turbulence of wars. What remained was later compiled, edited and revised into two books: *Treatise on Febrile Diseases* and *Synopsis of the Golden Chamber*. The former mainly relates the pathogenic factors and dialectical therapy of various kinds of acute febrile diseases, while the latter deals mainly with internal diseases as well as gynecological and pediatric diseases, surgery and ENT diseases. Its prescriptions are still used in clinical practice.

Zhang was the first person ever to propose the four methods of diagnosis: observation (of the patient's complexion, expression, movements, tongue, etc.) auscultation and olfaction, interrogation, and pulse feeling and palpation. He also introduced the diagnostic method based on the "eight principal syndromes" (Yin and Yang, exterior and interior, cold and heat, and deficient and excessive), on which much of TCM is based. This book integrated the basic theory of the *Classic of Internal Medicine* with clinical practice, becoming one of the most influential works of TCM.

Wang Shuhe, of the Western Jin (265-316), was not only versed in the medical classics but also in the ways of self-cultivation. One of his contributions was compiling and editing the *Treatise on Febrile and Miscellaneous Diseases*, which otherwise would not have been handed down to the present day. He also wrote and compiled the book *Pulse Classic*. This is the earliest treatise in China on the study of the pulse, giving a profound explanation of how various forms of pulse are related to different syndromes of diseases. Twenty-four variations of pulse conditions were classified, systemizing pulse diagnostic theory and therapy in a way that could be readily applied to clinical practice. The work has occupied a very important position in TCM diagnosis.

During the Sui Dynasty (581-618), Chao Yuanfang was commissioned by the imperial court to edit and compile the book, *Treatise on the Causes and Symptoms of Diseases*. This was the first treatise in China on the pathogenic causes and symptoms of disease. It analyzed the causes of various diseases and proposed a number of creative ideas, breaking away from some of the theories of his predecessors.

Wang Bing of the Tang Dynasty (618-907) proposed the doctrine of the motion of the Five Elements (metal, wood, water, fire and earth) and Six Natural Factors (wind, heat, mildness, fire, dryness and cold), describing how to detect the development and the degree of seriousness of a disease, its method being somewhat similar to Arabian astrology. This doctrine was further developed during the Song Dynasty (960-1279), combining the Heavenly Stems and Earthly Branches (a system of numbering years) with the motion of the Five Elements and Six Natural Factors. Using this system, one could detect and calculate a certain year that might be affected by a certain natural factor, during which people would be most liable to contract a certain disease. This was based on the theory that the causes of diseases and their treatment are closely linked to the environment, climate and seasons. From this, the principles and methods of therapy could be worked out.

Internal Medicine

During the Jin and Tang periods, although the terminology of internal medicine was unknown, some medical literature contained a number of descriptions about the understanding of internal diseases and their prevention and treatment. The books *Essential Prescriptions Worth a Thousand Pieces of Gold*, by Sun Simiao (581-682), and *Medical Secrets of an Official*, by Wang Tao (670-755), are two voluminous works of the Jin and Tang periods, giving many descriptions of internal diseases.

The books *Peaceful, Holy, Benevolent Prescriptions* and *General Collection for Holy Relief* are medical formularies compiled and edited by a staff of court physicians during the Song Dynasty. The categorization of diseases in these systematic and succinct books proved to be very valuable in clinical practice.

The book *Summary of Internal Diseases* by Xue Lizhai (1488-1558), a celebrated specialist in internal and miscellaneous diseases of the Ming Dynasty (1368-1644), was the first Chinese publication to use the term "internal disease" in its title. The book's descriptions of diseases are illustrated by cases from clinical practice, promoting the development of studies on internal and miscellaneous diseases.

The features of the studies on internal medicine during the Ming and Qing (1644-1911) dynasties include controversies among various academic schools of medical science focusing on theories, ancient medical doctrines and clinical practices and experiences.

Surgery and Osteology

Hua Tuo, the best-known medical specialist of the Eastern Han period, is honored as the founder of surgery in China. He is credited as the first to use the drug "Mafeisan" as an anaesthetic agent and is regarded as a pioneer in surgical treatment.

Liu Juanzi's *Remedies Left by Ghosts* was written during the Jin Dynasty and later revised and edited. It is the earliest treatise on surgery in China.

During the Song and Yuan (1271-1368) dynasties, a number of important works on surgery were published, such as the *Tested Formulae for Deep-Rooted Furuncles on the Back* by Li Xun, the *Essence of External Diseases* by Qi Dezhi, and the *Essence of Diagnosis and Treatment of External Diseases* by Chen Ziming.

The book *Effective Formulae Handed Down for Generations*, by Wei Jinglin, is the most detailed extant Chinese medical publication on osteology. It gives a detailed account of the fractures of the limbs and dislocation of joints, fractures of the spine, wounds and sprains, arrow wounds, and relocation and treatment. Many therapeutic methods and tools are described. The book gives the first description of treating a broken spine by hanging up the body. It also describes methods of anesthesia.

Wang Ji, of the Ming Dynasty, had presented many insights on medical theory, based on his studies. He summed up the results of his research on surgery in 1519 in the book *Theory and Case Reports on External Diseases*.

Other important works included the *Manual of External Diseases*, by Wang Kentang, and the *Orthodox Manual of External Diseases*, by Chen Shigong.

Obstetrics and Gynecology

Obstetrics and gynecology became an independent science in the Song Dynasty, a special department being created in the Bureau of Imperial Physicians.

Ten Problems in Obstetrics, by Yang Zijian, explains ten forms of normal and abnormal childbirth, based on clinical experience. In case of an abnormal childbirth, methods of diagnosis and treatment are given, including the turning of the infant in the womb.

Chen Ziming was not only a surgeon, but also a very good obstetrician-gynecologist. His book *Complete Effective Prescriptions for Women* gives a full account of the causes and symptoms of obstetric and gynecological diseases and their treatment.

Other works like the *Treatise on Obstetrics*, by Li Shisheng, the *Collection of Treasured Experiences in Obstetrics*, by Guo Jizhong, and the *Treasured Handbook for Household Hygienic Obstetrics*, by Zhu Ruizhang, all made important contributions to obstetrics and gynecology in China.

Pediatrics

Although there had been previous monographs on the subject, pediatrics reached a new high level in the Northern Song Dynasty with Qian Yi's *Key to Treatment of Children's Diseases*. This is the oldest surviving treatise on pediatrics in China.

The book was edited and compiled by Yan Xiaozhong, a student of Qian Yi, based on his teacher's theories and 40 years of clinical experience. It stresses the physiological and pathological differences between children and adults and describes dialectical methods of treatment based on the five key internal organs. It also presents a number of new prescriptions. Qian is honored as the founder of pediatrics in China.

Remedy Prescriptions for Children's Macula Disease written in the Northern Song Dynasty by Dong Ji was the first monograph in China on the disease.

Acupuncture and Moxibustion

In the voluminous *Classic of Acupuncture and Moxibustion*, the Western Jin physician Huangfu Mi systemized and substantiated the theory of acupuncture and moxibustion, laying the foundations for later development of the science.

During the Song Dynasty, Wang Weiyi created a bronze figure to demonstrate the acupuncture points and wrote the *Illustrated Manual of Acupoints*, greatly promoting the development of the science. Xu Feng, a famous specialist of acupuncture and moxibustion in the Ming Dynasty, wrote *A Complete Handbook on Acupuncture and Moxibustion*. Gao Wu's *Collection of Gems in Acupuncture and Moxibustion* reflects the comparatively high level of the science in the middle of the Ming period, making new contributions to the development of the science. *A Great Compendium of Acupuncture and Moxibustion*, written by Yang Jizhou of the Ming Dynasty, greatly influenced succeeding generations.

Pharmacology

Prior to the Qin Dynasty, the desire of rulers to achieve immortality led necromancers to produce so-called panaceas, based on metallurgical techniques. Thus, alchemy was born. The book *Kinship of the Three and the Book of Changes* written by Wei Boyang of the Eastern Han period is the earliest extant document of alchemy in the world. It is now universally accepted that China is the birthplace of alchemy, the forerunner of chemistry.

During the Jin Dynasty, alchemy was widespread. *The Works of Master Bao Pu*, by Ge Hong, contains some articles on the practice of alchemy, including the equipment needed and formulae.

Improvements were made during the Tang Dynasty. Alchemists at that time were producing calomel, Hongshendan and Baijiangdan for treating dermatosis; similar kinds of drug are still used today.

Medicinal Preparations

One of the key approaches of Chinese medicinal preparations is the roasting and boiling of medicinal herbs. Records of these methods can be found in the *Classic of Internal Medicine*. Formulae listed in such publications as the *Treatise on Febrile Diseases* and the *Synopsis of the Golden Chamber* recommended that ingredients be roasted and boiled. During the Song Dynasty (420-479) of the period of the Southern Dynasties, based on previous experience, Lei Xiao edited and compiled three volumes of *Lei's Treatise on the Preparation of Drugs*, the earliest monograph on the subject in China.

Lei was the founder of drug preparations. His book had a great influence on later generations and the 17 TCM roasting and boiling methods were developed on the basis of it.

Chinese Herbal Medicine

The development of materia medica constitutes an important part of Chinese medicine.

During the Southern and Northern Dynasties, on the basis of *Shen Nong's Materia Medica*, the famous medical and health-preservation expert Tao Hongjing edited and compiled three volumes of the *Collective Notes to the Materia Medica*, to which he added the "Records of Famous Physicians." It was on the basis of Tao's work that the Tang Dynasty *Newly Revised Materia Medica* was completed. It was the first pharmacopoeia to be published by a government in China and also the earliest state pharmacopoeia in the world.

Medicine was given a position of great importance by the emperors of the Northern Song Dynasty. From the sixth year of the Kaibao reign period (973), the imperial governments organized a series of revisions of publications on materia medica over a period of more than 140 years. These included the *Kaibao Materia Medica* and *Jia You's Supplementary Notes to Shen Nong's Materia Medica*.

The *Illustrated Canon of Materia Medica* was the first block-printed illustrated medicinal publication in China. It focuses on the discrimination of medicinal plants and each species in the book is illustrated and explained.

The great pharmacologist Li Shizhen of the Ming Dynasty developed the science of materia medica to a new height. In his book *Compendium of Materia Medica*, he gave a detailed account of the properties, flavor, origin, shape, way of collecting, process of preparation, pathological study and prescription of each species of herbal medicine. Li corrected many mistakes in the discrimination of drugs, which had appeared in past works. He classified herbal medicines into 16 groups according to their natural origin and properties. Within each of these groups are subdivided into 60 sub-groups, making a creative contribution to drug classification.

During the Qing Dynasty, Zhao Xuemin's *Supplement to the*

Compendium of Materia Medica was a further improvement on the *Compendium of Materia Medica*.

Section 2　The School of TCM and the Schools of the TCM Health-Preserving Science

Since the Northern Song Dynasty, a malpractice of determining diagnosis only according to symptoms, not seeking the causes of diseases, had been prevalent. So many insightful physicians began paying attention to theoretical study, advocating study and analysis of clinical pathological and pathogenic causes of diseases. As they had formed their different viewpoints due to living in different conditions, climate, time, and the differentiation of ethnic groups, ways of life, customs, occupations and experiences, various physicians in their medical practice created their different theories on medicine and health preservation and summed up their practical experiences and cases. As a result, a thriving academic atmosphere appeared in the medical circle at the time.

A commentary in the *Medical Specialists of the Complete Library of Qianlong* says: "Different schools of Confucianism came into being in the Song Dynasty; but different schools of medical science appeared in the Jin and Yuan dynasties." The "Four Large Schools of the Jin and Yuan" were those of Liu Wansu, Zhang Congzheng, Li Guo and Zhu Zhenheng.

Liu Wansu proposed the theory of "pathogenic fire," holding that the Six Natural Factors originated in an internal fire. He proposed the therapeutic principle of "relieving fire from the heart, and tonifying the kidneys." This later became known as "the school of coldness."

Zhang Congzheng proposed the principles of "preserving health by supplementing nutrition from food, and treating disease by taking medicines." He held that the causes of diseases, whether they came from inside or outside the body, were all evil Qi. The primary task of treatment, therefore, was to dispel these evil Qi. His method of treating diseases was an attack on them, so this became known as the "school of attack."

The "theory of internal injury" was proposed by Li Guo. He advocated that "the vital essence of man is formed by the Qi of the stomach. Various kinds of diseases are all caused by internal injury to the stomach and spleen." His methods of treatment included tonifying these organs and invigorating the vital energy, hence this was called the "school of replenishment."

Zhu Zhenheng proposed the "theory of ministerial fire," believing that the hyperactivity of ministerial fire was sure to consume a person's Yin substance. If one wants to prevent the hyperactivity of ministerial fire, he should clear away heart fire, desire nothing and control sexual passion to save and nourish the Yin blood. In clinical practice, he emphasized the therapeutic approach of tonifying Yin and relieving fire, hence he was called the "school of nourishing Yin."

These four schools generated a lively academic atmosphere at the time and had a great influence on the medical circles at home and abroad.

The School of Tonification with "Warm" Medicines

Liu Wansu's "theory of pathogenic fire" and Zhu Zhenheng's theory of "excessive Yang and deficient Yin" had a profound influence on physicians of the Ming Dynasty, and an excessive use of drugs of a cold nature by some physicians gradually surfaced. To stop the tendency, a school of tonification with "warm" medicines appeared in the second half of the dynasty. This school, which included Xue Lizhai, Zhang Jiebin and Zhao Xianke, was initiated by Xue Kai and his son Xue Lizhai. They held that most wind-syndromes and rheumatic and miscellaneous diseases were caused by deficiency of the spleen and kidneys. They should therefore be treated with tonics and drugs which were warm in nature.

Zhang Jiebin was the backbone of the school. He disagreed with Zhu Zhenheng and advocated the theory of "not excessive Yang but deficient Yin." Zhang developed the theory of tonification with medicines whose nature was warm.

Zhao Xianke, a contemporary of Zhang, who inherited Xue Lizhai's academic theory, made his particular contribution to the theory of the "gate of life." The school of tonification with "warm" medicines was an important remedy in curbing the prevalent mistakes of the time.

The School of Epidemic Febrile Disease

At the end of the Ming Dynasty, Wu Youxing was making keen observations of the nature of epidemic diseases based on his clinical experience. His studies and observations led him to write the book *Treatise on Pestilence*. The book dealt with epidemic diseases such as the plague, smallpox, and diphtheria and laid the foundations of the school of epidemic febrile disease.

The school reached maturity in the second half of the Qing Dynasty. Its adherents insisted that epidemic febrile disease was different from exogenous febrile disease. They produced books and established their theories, creating a complete system of differentiation and treatment of this class of disease. Ye Gui and Wu Tang were two representatives of the school.

Ye Gui was the founder of the school. His works include *Treatise on Epidemic Febrile Disease* and *A Guide to Clinical Practice with Medical Records*, based on extensive clinical experience.

Wu Tang proposed the theory of differentiation of syndromes according to the pathological changes of the Triple Energizer (the three visceral cavities housing the internal organs) and treatment. He wrote the *Treatise on Differentiation and Treatment of Epidemic Febrile Disease*, advocating the treatment principles of mild improvement, moderate nutrition and nourishing Yin.

The Health-Preservation School

In their clinical practice, Chinese physicians through the ages applied the useful health-preserving theories of Confucianism, Buddhism and Taoism to TCM and created the traditional science of health preservation on the basis of Chinese medicinal theories.

The development of this science can be divided into two stages. The first stage was from the Qin Dynasty to the Tang. During this stage, the main approaches were the use of elixir medicine, Daoyin method (of promoting health by regulated and controlled breathing) and sex guide. After the Song Dynasty, the application of drugs produced from animal and herbal extracts replaced the elixir medicines, and the health-preservation and medicare approaches for the elderly were established.

Having unified China under his rule, Emperor Qinshihuang wished to become immortal, and alchemists appeared to meet this demand. During the Han Dynasty, Emperor Wudi (r. 140-87 BC) issued an imperial edict to seek the elixir of life and recruited alchemists to produce such a drug. During the rule of Emperor Yuandi (r. 317-322 AD) of the Eastern Jin Dynasty, a Taoist and physician named Ge Hong studied alchemy for many years and wrote *The Works of Master Bao Pu*, persuading people to learn the skills of alchemy and eat "golden elixir." This influential book was responsible for an increase in the study of alchemy and eating golden elixir. During the Tang period, the practice gained in popularity. The Tang rulers regarded Li Er, the founder of Taoism, as their ancestor, and made great efforts to promote Taoism.

At the same time, mineral drugs were also popular. At first, this kind of drug was used to treat diseases, but their habitual use became very popular among the literati and officials. Since they also had harmful effects, they became gradually obsolete after the Tang.

The Daoyin method was also developed during this period. This method had already been practiced in society. During the Warring States Period, because of the rise of alchemists, the method was mixed with the Taoist thought of "discarding all desires and purifying the mind." By the Han Dynasty, the method's theory and practice had improved. The well-known physician Zhang Zhongjing explained the functions of the method in health preservation and disease prevention. Hua Tuo, the "master surgeon," further developed the Daoyin method with the Five-Animal Exercise, which was patterned upon the movements of the tiger, deer, bear, monkey and bird.

The theory, content and practice of the method further developed during the Wei, Jin and Southern and Northern Dynasties periods. Ge Hong emphasized in his theory the relations between man and Qi, pointing out that the function of Qigong was to "keep health inside and prevent evils from outside." He also advocated a combination of static and dynamic movements without a fixed form. Xu Xun, a Taoist of the Jin Dynasty, proposed a way to promote the smooth movement of tendons, bones and muscles, and blood circulation through Qigong exercise. This may be the first time that the term "Qigong" was used in a document. Tao Hongjing of the Southern and Northern Dynasties was the first to edit and compile Daoyin materials into a special collection that involves 12 kinds of regulated breathing, a six-character formula of breathing exercises and eight patterns of movements. They are still widely practiced today.

During the Sui and Tang dynasties, the imperial court officially recognized the Daoyin method as an approach to keep fit and treat diseases, and the method developed into its prime stage. The *Daoyin Method of Health Preservation* by Chao Yuanfang of the Sui, and the *Essential Prescriptions Worth a Thousand Pieces of Gold* and *Prescriptions for Health Preservation* by Sun Simiao of the Tang, record many Daoyin ways of health preservation. Sun himself was an active disseminator of the method. Based on the six-character formula, he described 12 practical ways of breathing regulation, and recommended that even people who were in good health should do them.

Early in the Spring and Autumn Period, the effects of sex on the body were noticed. The development of sex guide as a branch of learning was closely linked to the rise of Taoist doctrine, being a part of Taoist self-cultivation. They knew it would be beneficial to good conditions of one's mind and body if one controlled one's sex life.

During the Tang Dynasty, sex guide developed into its acme, because of the worship of Taoism by Tang rulers. Moreover, social stability appeared in the first half of the Tang, when emperors and princes, officials and wealthy people indulged in sensual pleasures. As a result, various kinds of diseases came close at heel. So correct sex knowledge was in demand objectively.

After the Song Dynasty, the emphasis on health preservation

and medical care began to change, with tonics and health-promoting food becoming the mainstream. By the Ming and Qing dynasties, a unique health-preservation system for the elderly had essentially taken shape.

Reference to the use of tonics can be found in documents as early as *The Book of Songs*. According to *Shen Nong's Canon of Materia Medica*, "The best-quality medicines are used to nourish life, the better ones to nourish nature and the good ones to cure diseases." It is a summary of health promotion by tonics practiced before the period of the Western Han. Alchemy and the use of elixirs to promote health was widespread during the Wei, Jin, Sui and Tang dynasties. This proved to be a mistaken approach and by the time of the Song Dynasty, herbal materials were being used instead. In his Ming Dynasty book *Compendium of Materia Medica*, Li Shizhen sharply criticized the use of elixirs, advocating the use of tonics produced from animals and herbs.

He also criticized previous malpractice in the use of herbal tonics. Such tonics, he said, should be non-toxic and fully edible, and a differentiation of syndromes was needed. This brought the practice of using tonics onto a healthy course and laid the foundations of its future development.

The *Classic of Internal Medicine* contains a discussion about the use of food for health preservation. Wang Chong, materialist philosopher of the Eastern Han Dynasty, wrote one of the earliest monographs in ancient China on health preservation, called *On Nature Cultivation*, involving 16 essays. In his book *Essential Prescriptions Worth a Thousand Pieces of Gold*, Sun Simiao of the Tang period devoted the 26th volume to nourishment and treatment with food. As the earliest monograph in this field, it records many principles and methods in food nourishment, laying the foundations of Chinese medicinal nourishment and therapy with food. Based on a wide collection of food prescriptions prevalent in society and on his own practice, Sun compiled and edited the book *Tonifying Prescriptions*, which was later revised by his disciples to become *Dietetic Prescriptions of Materia Medica*. The book gives a detailed description of ways of food processing, cooking, and the value of nutrition.

This was the first of its kind in the country.

In the Song Dynasty, special importance was attached to medical care. In the voluminous works *Peaceful, Holy and Benevolent Prescriptions* and *General Collection for Holy Relief*, a number of ways for food therapy are recorded. Chen Dasou wrote a book *Benxinzai Menu of Vegetables*, which relates the preparations for 20 courses of vegetables. In his work *Fresh Food of a Mountain Dweller*, Lin Hong lists 102 kinds of food. Based on the achievements made in health preservation for the elderly since the Tang and Song dynasties, Chen Zhi produced the book *Health Preservation for the Aged*. In its first volume, he gives a special scientific and practical discussion on food therapy, complete with a profound study of its mechanisms.

Principles of a Proper Diet by Hu Sihui, a Yuan Dynasty court physician responsible for diet, is a monograph of high academic value. It inherits the age-long tradition of combining food nourishing and food therapy, introducing the nutritive functions, therapeutic effect and methods of cooking of various varieties of food. The book also introduces the preventive food therapy for people in good health, breaking from past practices which concentrated on therapeutic methods.

The voluminous *Compendium of Materia Medica* of the Ming Dynasty also discusses food nourishing and provides a great deal of materials for its development. Many literati and scholars were also well versed in food nourishing approaches and wrote about their personal experiences.

Works on health preservation and medical care for the elderly did not appear until the publishing of Sun Simiao's *Essential Prescriptions Worth a Thousand Pieces of Gold*. Chen Zhi's *Health Preservation for the Aged* is the earliest Chinese work on medical care for the elderly. Zou Xuan of the Yuan Dynasty revised the book and compiled three more volumes to supplement it, renaming it *A New Book on Longevity and Health Preservation for the Aged*. The book became a household "necessity" in China and later spread to Korea and Japan.

Eight Discourses on Health Preservation by Tu Longwei of the

Ming period was a monograph on health care for the aged, based on the teachings of Taoism. It gives extensive and detailed discourses on factors that can influence health, such as changes of the seasons, diet, living conditions, drugs and tonics. It was very popular among the people.

During the Jiajing period of the Ming Dynasty (1522-1566), Xu Chuanfu wrote the two-volume *Attending the Aged*. The book linked health preservation with the ideas of loyalty and filial piety, promoting a further development of study on the subject. Gong Yanxian, imperial physician of the Ming period, in his book *Longevity and Health Preservation* introduces many principles and methods of health preservation and collects a great number of secret prescriptions for maintaining longevity. In another book *On Senility*, he discusses the causes of ageing in depth. Gong Juzhong, another imperial physician of the Ming, produced *A Guide to Five Blessings and Longevity* and *Snow Melted in a Hot Furnace*, in which he gives discourses on living environment, functional regulation, shape-keeping, control of desires, massage, exercise and drugs for the elderly. And a dozen of Daoyin approaches is also introduced.

During the reign of Emperor Qianlong of the Qing Dynasty (1736-1795), Cao Tingdong, a well-known health-preservation specialist, wrote *Common Sayings Serving the Aged*, in which he advocates health preservation through control of diet, regulation of spirit, taking care of one's daily life, and Daoyin exercises.

During the Ming and Qing dynasties, many non-medical publications also dealt with questions of health preservation and longevity for the aged, presenting a unique character in practices in this regard.

Section 3 Cultural Features of Chinese Medicine

Over the long course of their development, Chinese medicine and health-preserving science have evolved a whole body of unique principles that manifest the background and special features of traditional Chinese culture.

1. The spirit of healing the wounded and rescuing the dying. Sun Simiao summed up the morality required of physicians in his *Essential Prescriptions Worth a Thousand Pieces of Gold*: Physicians should never seek fame and personal gains. Any physician who merely pursued his profession in search of fine food and clothes would be humiliated and cursed by the people for neglecting the agonies of his patients. The primary duty of a physician should be protection and care of the health and life of his patients. He repeatedly stressed that a physician should "desire nothing" and be "devoted to the relief of patients," regardless of who they were. He should cherish a deep compassion for his patients, and be considerate of them. He should not be overcautious and indecisive in the treatment of his patients, merely worrying about personal gains and losses. He should overcome all obstacles and never recoil from those who were filthy and stinking. This humanitarianism embodies the sense of benevolence of Confucianism, the freedom from desire of Taoism, the love of the Mohists and the compassion of Buddhism.

2. Prevention before treatment, and health promotion before becoming old. *The Yellow Emperor's Classic of Internal Medicine* records the idea of preventing diseases before they appear. Prevention of disease should be started as early as the first day of birth. Man cannot become immortal or reverse the ageing process, but it is possible to prevent oneself becoming old before one's time, and to live a long life. Health care should be carried out throughout one's life, particularly during the crucial stage of one's life. Persistence in practice ensures the prevention of diseases. This accords with the traditional concept of "thinking of danger in times of peace."

3. The unity of Heaven and man, and of form and spirit. Chinese philosophy stresses that all things in nature are connected. Nothing under Heaven is independent; all things depend on each other and interact with each other. This principle also underlies the theories of Chinese medicine.

In Chinese medicine astrology, geography and human affairs are considered to be parts of a whole. Man lives in both natural and social circumstances. He cannot live independent of human society. Pathogenic factors come from either biological or social or psychological factors. TCM stresses the importance of natural circumstances and psychological factors in the understanding of human diseases, emphasizing the principle of "adapting to the change of seasons and climate."

At the same time, TCM holds that the human body is also an integral whole. It integrates the five internal organs of man with his five body constituents, nine orifices, five voices, five sounds, five emotions, five kinds of secretions, and five tastes to form the whole body and its five functional systems. On this basis, it also links the relationships between the internal organs and the channels and collaterals. Their operations in coordination make the vitality of life.

4. Equilibrium between Yin and Yang. TCM holds that Yin and Yang are two opposite aspects that constitute the human body as a whole. These two aspects are indispensable to man's growth. Under normal conditions, they maintain a state of balanced equilibrium. If one aspect becomes less than or more than the other, physiological disorders occur, resulting in disease. All activities in daily life, food, spiritual regulation, physical exercise and administration of drugs must have the purpose of balancing the two aspects. Ageing indicates a deficiency of Yin or Yang, or both. To prevent rapid ageing, it is advisable to regulate and control the balance of Yin and Yang. This manifests the idea of balance and symmetry in Chinese philosophy in traditional Chinese culture.

5. The idea of permanent dynamics based on the combination of static and dynamic states. Chinese philosophy learned the dialectical relationship between static and dynamic states early in ancient China. According to *The Book of Changes*, "the static and dynamic states of things are constant." *Lü's Spring and Autumn Annals* says that "Running water is never stale and a door-hinge never gets eaten by worms." Matter in nature is always in a state of motion and change. Motion means change and nothing in the world can be produced without motion. TCM holds that human life from its start to its end contains a series of motions of internal contradictions in the body, including rising and falling, entry and exit. The *Classic of Internal Medicine* says: "Change occurs between high and low, or is caused by rising and falling." Motion is a law of nature, and a cardinal factor of maintaining health. The law of life is the process of metabolism. If the process is blocked, it leads to disease. Therefore, the concept of motion and change is integral to Chinese medicine. Life relies on motion because motion is part of the nature of life. Every cell in the human body is always in motion. Physical exercise is essential to improvement of health and prevention of diseases.

Both the Buddhist and Taoist tenets contain the doctrine of "tranquillity." Meditation and Qigong have had a great influence on Chinese culture, also affecting TCM. Medical theories of nature cultivation and self-cultivation were developed and Taoist Qigong became medical Qigong.

Here, tranquility is not absolute, itself being another form of motion. Motion is absolute but tranquility is relative. Combination of static and dynamic states are needed to maintain health.

Section 4 The Health-Preservation Theory of Early Confucianism

Immortality believers, ancient physicians, and Taoists made great contributions to the formation and development of the science of health preservation. But the contributions made by early Confucians should not be ignored.

A famous saying of Confucius is that "longevity comes from benevolence." This is the earliest theory of health preservation in ancient China. According to him, one can live a long life only when one lives in peace and harmony. Here, he deals with both self-cultivation and health. The level of one's cultivation and mentality is the primary factor of health. This theory and his other discourses on self-cultivation of the mind and nature laid the first cornerstone of the Chinese theory of health preservation.

Following Confucius, Zeng Zi, Zi Si, Mencius, and Xun Zi all proposed important theories on health preservation. Mencius was one of the first two scholars to define the scope of health preservation (the other being Zhuang Zi). He held that health preservation means attending to one's parents and taking care of their health in their remaining years of life. Everyone has parents and everyone will become a parent. Mencius extended his health-preservation theory to involve the whole of society.

Early Confucian theory on health preservation involved nourishing the mind and nourishing the body. Nourishing the mind means the psychological buildup from which a positive effect may be produced to retard and delay ageing. Many things are required to nourish the mind, but some which are closely linked to nourishing the body are as follows:

First, to observe the principle of the Golden Mean to maintain a state of mind equilibrium. Confucius said: "The Golden Mean is a perfect virtue, meaning to maintain a way of 'correctness'; to do things 'excessively' and 'deficiently' are wrong." One who has virtue can deal with the relationship between Heaven and man as well as between man and man, in accordance with the law of nature and the accepted practice in society, neither excessively or deficiently. He will neither feel annoyance in dealing with all these things, nor will he fail in his career.

Zi Si further linked the principle of the Golden Mean with human emotions, saying that everyone has emotions of joy, anger, sorrow and happiness. Whether they are hidden deep in the heart, or are outwardly expressed, they should be put within appropriate bounds. This is the Golden Mean or harmony. Any one who can live in peace and harmony, will not be subject to changing moods, nor will he lose control of his temper. In this way, a harmonious atmosphere will be created in dealing with the relationship between man and man and the relationship between man and things. This equilibrium of the mind in a harmonious atmosphere is beneficial to health.

Second, bear no resentment against anything and foster a broad mind.

In *The Analects*, Confucius requires of people that they bear no resentment against their family, state, superiors and inferiors, parents and brothers, friends, people of the opposite sex or with different accomplishments. Everyone should be trained to become broad-minded. His disciple Zeng Zi gasped with admiration: "The way of Confucius is simply loyalty and forbearance." According to this thinking, he proposed the famous idea that "Good health lies in a broad mind." This is not only an ethical view, but also a way of promoting health. Health is linked to one's mood and one's mind.

Third, to observe the principle of the "three don'ts" to control abnormal desires. Confucius says: "There are three things which the superior man guards against. In his youth when the physical powers are not yet settled, he guards against lust. When he is strong and the physical powers are full of vigor, he guards against quarrelsomeness. When he is old, and the animal powers are decayed, he guards against covetousness." Here, according to the different stages of life and different physiological factors, Confucius summed up the experiences in controlling various desires. He takes lust, belligerence and greed as the three factors that can bring harm to a sound heart and mind. Early Confucianism did not aim to eliminate all desires. It was concerned with the question of how to satisfy people's desires and how to meet people's demands to an appropriate extent. It hoped to determine the boundary line between normal desire and abnormal desire. On this point, Confucius advised people to keep their desires within reasonable bounds. Greed was to be obsessed with a comfortable life, indulging in comforts and pleasures, and to gain what was not one's due. Greed, he said, leads people to destroy themselves. In *Zuo Qiuming's Chronicles*, a greedy man is described as being like a pig. The more it eats, the sooner it is sent to the slaughter-house.

All these discussions assert that greediness will harm one's health and even lead to one's total destruction. So says Mencius: "Mind nourishing means having less desires than is normal."

Nourishing the body means taking care of one's health while nourishing the mind. Early Confucianism proposed many creative suggestions for improving people's clothing, food, physical exercise, and medical care.

First, based on the experiences before and during the Spring and Autumn Period, it produced the earliest discourse on health preservation in *The Analects of Confucius*. Confucius stressed the importance of taking care of one's clothing and food. He held that people should be clothed according to the change of seasons and to the requirement on different occasions and colors.

Confucius also paid attention to food hygiene, describing eight situations in which one should not eat. For instance, one should not eat food when it is stale, unwholesome, or stinking, or rice which is underdone or overdone, nor should one eat when it is not the time for eating. He also advised that people should not eat and drink too much at one time. The advice is scientific.

Second, to do physical exercises to keep fit. Nobles and commoners alike began practicing physical exercise as early as the Shang and Zhou dynasties, but this was connected with hunting or military actions, and not with a direct aim of promoting health. During the Spring and Autumn and Warring States periods, early Confucians introduced physical exercise as a system, making it an important part of promoting the vitality of life. The approaches included a combination of physical exercise and school education, with a compulsory sports course. In the Western Zhou period, sports included the archery, chariot driving and dance of the six arts. With an educational system of officialdom, ordinary people had no right to education. After a private school system was introduced by Confucius, sports courses began to be offered in many schools. According to *The Book of Rites*, different sports courses and requirements were made for students of different ages. A 13-year-old child could learn civil dances and gentle exercises, while a 15-year-old child could learn military dances, and archery and chariot driving. In this way, teenagers were taught sports to keep fit. The other approach was the combination of sports and the ritual system. In various ritual ceremonies in government and public activities, many people were trained and practiced related sports courses. For example, archery usually took place in some ritual ceremonies. The archer was required to possess concentration, assuming a correct and straight posture so as to make good use of his strength to discharge his arrows. Driving a chariot, the learner was required to concentrate his mind, assume a correct pose, and not to look around or hasten to talk. All the standardized rules guaranteed the quality and safety of sports.

Through these systems, more and more people began to understand the positive role of sports to people's health. Chu Zhe, a director of studies of the State of Zhao in the Warring States Period, said he had lost his appetite remaining sedentary all day, but when he began to saunter or trot for two kilometers a day, his appetite returned and his health improved greatly. Xun Zi concluded that taking care of one's health properly along with physical exercise would enable one to maintain good health. Otherwise, he would contract disease. Health-preservation specialists at the time confirmed this.

Third, medical care. People do not usually think of *The Book of Rites* in connection with medical care.

The Book of Rites was compiled by early Confucians based on the political, economic and medical care systems of that time and the previous days. It was completed earlier than the *Classic of Internal Medicine*. The chapter on physicians in the book were the earliest works combining Confucianism and Chinese medicine, containing the fundamental ideas of early Confucians on medical care.

It first introduces a system for the division of medical science, such as internal medicine, surgery and nutrition according to the needs of medical care.

The Book of Rites also discusses pathogenic factors and preventive measures according to changes of the seasons and climate. Particular diseases were likely to occur at particular times of the year. In the spring, headaches and colds were often seen; in summer, skin diseases could occur; and malaria in the autumn and asthma in the winter were common.

It also gives suggestions on diet for the four different seasons. Rice should be eaten warm, soup should be hot, but juice and drinks should be cold. It is advisable to eat more sour food in spring, more bitter food in summer, more sweet food in autumn, and more salty food in winter. Beef is sweet and mild in nature, so it should be cooked together with light and bitter-tasting foods. Mutton is also sweet and hot in nature, and should also be prepared with light and bitter-flavored foods.

The book proposes regular preventive drives to eliminate rats, sweeping and cleaning houses, and draining out water from wells and channels. These are measures to be taken to maintain a sanitary environment and clear water sources to benefit health.

The health-preservation practice of early Confucians influenced Taoists and physicians in the pre-Qin period. Zhuang Zi's famous book on health preservation used the skillful dismembering of an ox by a butcher as one of his examples. Since the butcher understands the texture, bones and tendons of the ox, he is able to effortlessly dismember it. In the same way, those who wish to nourish life must first understand "nature." By adapting oneself to the way of nature, one can improve and prolong one's life.

Confucius' "longevity comes from benevolence" and Zhuang Zi's idea that "longevity comes from taking a natural course," though differing from each other, have a similar object and similar approaches in many respects. Both held that mental state was the basis of longevity and that health preservation consisted of nourishing both the mind and body. To some extent, Zhuang Zi's teachings in this connection were based on those of Confucius. The doctrines of Confucianism and Taoism complemented each other.

Chinese medicine began by being closely linked with witch doctors, then with Confucianism, but later moved on to develop into its own independent school. Early Confucians made an important contribution to its development. The health-preservation culture is an example of this, and discourses on this problem by early Confucians can be found in the *Classic of Internal Medicine*. A few examples are given as follows:

Health preservation depended on the unity of Heaven, Earth and Man. Man is a product of the "functional interactions of Heaven and Earth." Man is also a member of society. One must specify the position of man in the universe in order to deal with the relationship between man and nature, as well as between man and man. On this basis, one can live a long life, by adapting to the changes of seasons, balancing emotions, living in peace and calm, controlling the equilibrium of Yin and Yang, and complying with the natural course of hardness and softness.

The *Classic* also introduced the dialectical health-preserving way of "going too far is as bad as not going far enough" (the Golden Mean). The book contains the term "normal breathing" or "the way of normal breathing." It means that the normal state of the inter-promoting and inter-overcoming relations in the Five Elements. It is the dynamic balance of the functions of human internal organs. If imbalance occurs, "excess" or "deficiency" will occur and people will fall sick. Therefore, it is necessary to prevent the occurrence of dynamic balance, to limit "excess" or supplement "deficiency."

It also introduced the Confucian idea of nourishing the mind as the basis of nourishing life. Treatment of the mind should precede treatment of disease, and nourishing the mind should precede nourishing life. Only with this guiding thought, can one improve one's health and be free from disease. Therefore, nourishing life means to nourish both the body and mind. When a physician handles his patient, he has to know the psychological disorder of the patient first, then the physiological symptoms of disease, then he can match the medicine to the case. It can thus be seen that in the health-preserving culture, Confucianism and TCM complemented each other.

From the above analysis, two things can be concluded:

1. The early Confucian theory of health preservation and its practice are based on making groups of people of different ages as the object. Therefore they are part of the Confucian's doctrine of human studies.

2. Chinese health-preserving science is a comprehensive and multiple-discipline frontier science. Therefore, only by studying and analyzing the health-preserving cultures of various schools,. can people have a complete knowledge of it.

Chapter 9

The Culture of Chinese Food

Section 1 Features of the Culture of Chinese Food

Food and drink are physiological needs for both man and animals. But essentially they take their food in quite different ways. Through intelligence and skill, man has discovered and created numerous varieties of foods, thus making diet a cultural event. Dietary culture is an important part of traditional Chinese culture. It has rich connotations, including the resources of food, cooking skills, food production, dietotherapy, public dietary ways and customs, and dietary art.

Since ancient times, agriculture has been the foundation of China's economy. And it was the most typical Chinese material culture in ancient times. Dietary culture is closely linked with agriculture. Before agriculture, man depended on food in a way that was no different from animals, mainly including the flesh of beasts and roots of plants.

Since the introduction of agriculture, grains of cultivated crops have become the main source of man's staple food. Farming began to take up most of man's labor and time. Cultivation of crops was a process of man's work from sowing, applying fertilizer to harvest. It was the most important work in people's mind that could not be replaced by anything else. Growing crops was not the only way of obtaining food. The ancients began expanding their sources of food at a very early time, developing farming, forestry, animal husbandry, sidelines, and fishing in line with local conditions.

As early as the Xia (c.21st century to early 17th century BC), Shang (c.17th century to 11th century BC) and Zhou (c.11th century to 221 BC) dynasties, on the basis of well developed agriculture and the "nine squares" land system (one large square of land being divided into nine small ones like the Chinese character "井," the outer eight squares being allocated to eight households to till for themselves, while the central one was jointly cultivated by them for the state), animal husbandry and cultivation of crops were developed on scale.

During the Spring and Autumn and Warring States periods, iron tools and oxen were widely used for cultivation of land, and many water conservancy facilities were built up. This aided the development of food production and allowed small farming families to thrive. In the Warring States Period, crops and animal husbandry were equally important aspects of the agricultural structure. At that time, earnings from farming production and crop growing accounted for 60 percent of the total earnings of a household. Earnings from horticulture and animal husbandry each made up 20 percent, excluding fishery and sidelines production. This was a planning model of diversified operations centering around crop production.

Agriculture in the Han Dynasty (206 BC to 220 AD) was well developed. During the Western Han period (206 BC to 25 AD), because of wars against the Huns, the imperial court paid much attention to the development of animal husbandry, particularly to the breeding of fine strains of horses. The dynasty also introduced the state farm system, with both military and civil state farmland. Farmland was controlled by the government. Crop-growing and animal husbandry thrived and, in times of famine, the chamberlain for the national treasury could allocate stored grains and animals to disaster areas from state farmland areas.

After the Wei (220-265) and Jin (265-420) dynasties, the economic center of gravity gradually shifted from the north to the south where rice was widely grown. Cultivating techniques were greatly improved. Except for a few products such as sweet potato and tobacco, almost all products now grown in China were produced in the Tang period (618-907). Tea production, in particular, was booming at the time. Lu Yu was known as the "sage of tea" of the time. His *Classic of Tea* discusses the origin of tea, its growing, harvesting and processing, as well as the fine details of brewing and drinking tea. The cultivation of tea was very popular in the south. About 20 to 30 percent of the population of Jiangsu and Anhui provinces were involved in the tea trade. Because so many people were selling tea, a tea tax began to be levied during the mid-Tang period and a series of policies were instituted to control the transactions.

Fishery was also well developed in the period. Apart from the conventional methods of using nets and aquatic birds to catch fish, a number of new ways were also invented. Breeding fish in ponds was a common practice and people in the far south even bred fish in paddy fields.

Since the Ming (1368-1644) and Qing (1644-1911) dynasties, along with the development of a diversified agriculture, more and more approaches to expand the sources of food have developed. The Qing Dynasty book *An Outline of Agricultural Production* suggested: "It is advisable to build ponds to breed fish in areas with water and weeds, and to tend cattle and sheep in arid highlands. Geese and ducks are raised along waterways and chickens and doves in plains. In this way, the species will be developed and multiplied and profits will be doubled." The plan outlined in the book aimed at a comprehensive development of food supply, combining the cultivation of crops and animal husbandry for large-scale agricultural production. It advocated a highly efficient agricultural system for the recycling of materials and the multiple use of resources. A typical demonstration of this eco-agricultural system can be seen in the plain areas of Hangzhou, Jiaxing and Huzhou and the Pearl River Delta area.

In the area of Jiaxing and Huzhou, affluent sources of grains and animal husbandry were veritably realized. Crop production and cattle breeding promoted each other. Pigs were fed with agricultural sideline products, and their manure was used as fertilizer on the farmland. Silkworms were also produced in the area and the mulberry leaves that they fed on were fed to sheep in the winter and early spring. The sheep raised in the area reproduced quickly and the quality of their skin was famous. The mulberry trees themselves were fertilized with the droppings of silkworms and sheep. All this was a good and rational recycling of materials.

In the Pearl River Delta area, fishery was well known. Fish stocks in ponds were fed with mulberry leaves, sugarcane or fruit. After a long time of operation, the local farmers had accumulated their experience of breeding four species of domesticated fishes (black carp, grass carp, silver carp and flathead). They had known that grass carps could be fed with grass, but silver carps and flatheads could be fed only with planktons.

In a word, the development of agriculture in ancient times not only provided affluent sources of food for man, but also maintained an ecological system of recycling. This ecological agriculture is also known as complex agriculture. It is one of the important achievements in China's material cultural history.

China is the origin of a great variety of agricultural products, such as rice and soy beans. Through its long history, it has also cultivated many strains of crops and plants. At the same time, it has introduced a number of fine species of farm products from abroad. Of these products, some are staples and others are vegetables and fruits.

During the periods of the Han and Tang dynasties, a powerful China appeared with more agricultural exchanges conducted between the Central Plain and foreign countries. Emperor Wudi (r. 140-88 BC) of the Western Han Dynasty, relying on the powerful strength of the country, sent envoys to the Western Regions. Zhang Qian was sent to the region twice to open up a passage from the Central Plain: the world-famous "Silk Road." Zhang brought silk products from China to the region and brought fruits and seeds of various plants back home. Seeds and fruits were carried on the back of camels trudging across the vast desert to China. According to historical records, at the time, "rare commodities are imported from all directions." Zhang brought garlic back from Ferghana and coriander, linseed, walnut, pomegranate and lucerne from Bactria. Trials were undertaken, growing these seeds and plants in gardens and then they were disseminated.

During the Han period, a number of food materials were imported from the Western Regions such as grapes, pomegranate, lucerne, sesame, flax, walnut, garlic, garden pea, broad bean, water melon, musk melon, cucumber, spinach, lettuce, coriander, celery, carrot, lentil, onion, rose apple, castor oil plant, pepper, Persian date, fig, fennel, apricot, etc. All these were brought to China by envoys, monks and merchants, as well as Zhang Qian, enriching the varieties of food in the interior of the country.

Parallel to the "Silk Road" on land, there was also another "Silk Road" on the sea. Outbound from Guangzhou and across the South China Sea and the Indian Ocean, this sea course was also known as "Silk and Spices on the Sea" used mainly for transporting goods such as silk products and overseas spices. Imported products included jasmine, sea date, areca, and quinine.

During the Ming and Qing dynasties when China entered its later stage of feudal society, China's agriculture had attained a high level. However, its population also grew rapidly and the average arable land area per capita dropped drastically. In the year 1383 (or the 14th year of the reign of the first Ming emperor), the average arable land area per head was 14.56 *mu* (one *mu* =1/15 hectare). In 1834, the figure was 1.65 *mu*, or 88.7 percent less than that in 1383. During this period, communications between China and the West had become well developed. Many strains of high-yield crops were brought back by overseas Chinese and businessmen. This helped to alleviate the pressure of famine in various places and improve the country's supply of grain and vegetables.

Some of the crops introduced into China during the Ming and Qing dynasties are as follows:

Sweet potato: A plant native to America. After the discovery of the New World by Columbus, the sweet potato was soon introduced to Europe and many colonies in Southeast Asia. Its introduction to China was complicated. At the time, the Philippines was ruled by Spanish colonists, who prohibited the export of sweet potatoes. Chen Zhenlong, a Chinese national living there, learned that the sweet potato was a high-yield crop which could be stored up in case of famine. He became determined to introduce it to China. In 1593, he secretly carried it to Fujian Province by winding its stems around the ship's cables and coating them with mud. In this way, he avoided detection. Sweet potatoes were successfully transplanted in the province. Guangdong and Fujian provinces were often attacked by typhoons, resulting in successive years of famine. Sweet potatoes, therefore, became treasured as an insurance against natural disasters. During the 17th century, terrible floods occurred in south China, destroying farmland and crops and leaving great numbers of people homeless and starving. At that time, Xu Guangqi, a celebrated scientist, was experimenting with the cultivation of sweet potatoes in Shanghai. He succeeded, but his attempts to encourage others to grow the crop were met with skepticism. So he summed up the advantages of growing sweet potatoes and encouraged farmers to cultivate them.

Corn: Introduced into China some time around the 16th century. Foreign envoys presented corn as gifts to Chinese emperors. According to historical documents, it was believed that corn was first imported from abroad through the seaports along the southeast coast, or from the Western Regions. The question of how and when corn arrived in China needs further study.

These two crops are high-yield products, capable of resisting drought. Sweet potatoes are particularly delicious and nutritious and have a high rate of reproduction. The large and strong stems of corn are suitable for growing in hilly areas. They are conducive to alleviating the pressure from famine and the development of hilly areas.

Peanut: Originally produced in America. In the early 16th century, peanuts were imported to China from Southeast Asia. At first, they were grown only in coastal provinces. Later, they began to be grown along the Yangtze and Yellow rivers, becoming extremely popular among the Chinese people.

Potato: Another plant native to America. Potatoes were first introduced into China from Southeast Asia in the early Qing period. The *Chronicles of Songxi County*, written in the 39th year of the reign of Emperor Kangxi (1700), describes the potato as being "shaped like a jade, being small or large, black-colored and with a bitter sweet taste." Its use soon spread through north China and a part of south China.

During the Ming and Qing dynasties, many varieties of vegetable were also introduced from abroad.

Hot pepper: Introduced during the late 16th century. According to *Records of Herbs and Flowers*, "hot pepper grows thickly with white flowers. Its taste is hot, its color red and is a kind of ornamental plant. It has seeds."

Tomato: According to *The Book of Flowers and Plants* (1621), "the tomato is also known as June persimmon. Its stem grows more than one meter high. Its leaves look like Chinese mugwort and its flowers like pomegranate. One branch can bear about four fruits and one tree bears about 30 fruits. It is also a kind of ornamental herbal plant."

Other crops and plants were also introduced in the Qing Dynasty, such as kidney beans, wild cabbage, sunflowers (first introduced to the country from Southeast Asia around the late 17th century only for aesthetic value in gardens. Later, they were used to make medicines and produce oil and food) and cauliflower (first introduced in 1882 during the eighth year of the reign period of Emperor Guangxu from Europe, and grown experimentally in Pudong, Shanghai).

The introduction of foreign crops and plants enriched the material life and dietary culture of Chinese people, developing through cultural exchange between China and foreign countries.

Dietary Constituents and Ingredients

By dietary constituents and ingredients we mean the mixed preparation for a meal consisting of staple food, non-staple food and drink. Variations in these are closely linked with economic development, ethnic customs, and social changes. With the arrival of agricultural society, dietary structure was limited by the level of production and this structure changed through different historical periods. On the whole, however, a dietary mode developed using grains as the staple and meat, vegetables and fruits to supplement them and this continues to the present day. This dietary structure is quite different from the Western dietary mode, in which meat is taken as the main source of food with no clear distinction of staples and non-staples.

Food structure in ancient times seemed too complicated. Staples included various varieties of grain crops but non-staples were diverse, ranging from all kinds of delicacies to reptiles, wild herbs and vegetables. In the imperial court and the houses of bureaucrats, more superb and fancy non-staple foods might be supplied than staple food. For common citizens, the supplement food might consist of large quantities of chaffs and brans and vegetables. Both fancy foods and grains and vegetables had to be processed to make them edible and to improve their taste. The cooking methods of the gentry differed greatly from those of the common people. The former usually employed skilled chefs using the best materials and spices. Some of the most famous dishes in ancient times have been passed down to the present day.

Prior to the Qin Dynasty, meals mostly consisted of non-processed crops, such as beans, peas and wheat. During the Warring States Period and the Han Dynasty, the stone mill was invented to grind grains. Non-processed grains were thus replaced by flour meals which were easily digested and absorbed. After the Han Dynasty, flour products became common in north China which produced dry-farming crops. Various kinds of food could be made with flour according to different tastes and needs. Another processing method was fermentation, through which alcohol and soy sauce were produced for both feast and daily use. Sour fermented glutinous rice and cooked rice juice were used as fermenting agents to make *Mantou* (steamed bread) and *Baozi* (steamed stuffed buns). Foods made from fermented flour are fluffy, porous and soft. Yeast contains rich nutritive elements, while enzymes promote the nutritive effect of proteins, starch, fat and vitamins in flour, allowing them to be easily absorbed by the body.

The significance of food processing in ancient times should

not be underestimated. Before the Qin and Han dynasties, soya beans were used as a staple food, but without grinding, the body was unable to absorb much of their nutritive content. After the invention of the stone mill, people began to produce bean milk. While experimenting with alchemy, Liu An of the Han Dynasty invented beancurd, a great invention in the development of food processing, making the vegetable protein much easier to absorb. One study suggests that about 65 percent of the protein of un-processed beans are absorbed by the body, compared with 92–96 percent for beancurd. A series of derivative products followed, becoming widely popular and solving the problem of protein deficiency.

Section 2 Preservation and Development of Dietary Culture

Works on dietary culture were included in various historical documents, with monographs on diet appearing very early. The *Chronicles of the Han Dynasty* recorded pre-Qin cuisine. Scores of works on diet and cuisine were produced in the Wei, Jin, and Southern and Northern Dynasties periods and before. One of these is the voluminous *Food Book of Prince Huainan* involving 130 essays. The experiences collected in these works now can be found in many other books, though most originals were missing.

Apart from the above works, many articles and essays on diet can be obtained from the works of various schools of thought in the period from the Qin to the Han Dynasty and other works which need to be further screened and edited. Of these, the *Monthly Ordinances for the Four Classes of People* and *Important Arts for People's Welfare* devote most space to the cuisine of north China.

Important Arts for People's Welfare is an encyclopedia on the whole process of food production, cooking and preservation, involving the growing of grain crops, fruits and melons and vegetables, and the raising of poultry, animal husbandry, and fishery. It includes the cooking skills of minority ethnic groups in the north. It collects many works on diet that had been missing. The collection introduces materials from various schools of thought and about 140 ancient classics and documents as well as 30 or more ballads and folk songs. Many scattered or missing works were thus discovered and passed down to posterity.

Before the book's publication, many of the works on diet had been produced only with the nobility in mind. *Important Arts* takes note of the daily needs of ordinary people, containing average and lower-quality food as well as delicacies such as barbecued suckling pig. The book also provides many methods of preserving food such as underground storage, sealing, drying and the use of salt.

After the Tang and Song dynasties, the south became developed and agricultural exchange between north and south increased. Traditional northern cooking techniques were transferred to the south, but adapted to local conditions, creating various new styles. As a result, more and more works on southern styles of food appeared. *A Collection of Southern Styles* written by Liu Xun of the Tang Dynasty recorded the products, dietary customs and lifestyles in the south. The book followed the example of *Important Arts for People's Welfare*, covering various aspects of food materials, the making of special food, tableware, dietary customs, as well as food processing, cooking skills, and how to eat the food in the south.

Fresh Food of Mountain Dwellers written by Lin Hong of the Southern Song Dynasty records food materials and processing methods prevailing in mountain areas. It particularly discusses vegetables and cooking methods, introducing more than 40 ways of cooking in addition to the cooking ways for other eatables and wild herbs and animals found in the mountains. Instant boiled-rabbit meat, a course of food, was first introduced in the book. Later, instant-boiled mutton was also introduced.

A Book of Bamboo Shoots by Zan Ning, an eminent monk of the Northern Song Dynasty, is a monograph on the gathering and ways of cooking bamboo shoots. It first gives an introduction to the use of bamboo for medicinal purposes, and then the cooking method, stressing the necessity of boiling bamboo shoot without taking off its shells so as to have its "original flavor." He also introduces how to preserve bamboo shoots.

The Dietary System of the Hall of Yun Lin by Ni Zan, a rich recluse of the late Yuan and early Ming period, introduces the dietary customs and ways of Wuxi, his hometown and the birthplace of Jiangsu-style cooking. These works of mountain dwellers and recluses provide many valuable materials and documents on vegetarian diet and dietotherapy.

In the Ming and Qing dynasties, land annexation became a serious problem. Natural disasters occurred frequently, causing famine and homelessness. In order to solve the problem of starvation, a number of intellectuals produced works on disaster relief, discussing a number of ways of gathering and cooking edible wild herbs and materials. The most famous of these is *Herbs for Famine Relief* by Zhu Su, a member of the Ming ruling house. To help people in their selection of wild herbs to avoid being poisoned, Zhu collects in his book several hundred herbs and plants with illustrations. He even showed the edible parts of the plants and how to use them. Li Shizhen in his *Compendium of Materia Medica* also gives explanations of how to distinguish many harmful herbs from safe ones. All these works are valuable references for us to develop wild plant resources.

The dishes described in *The Book of Songs*, the earliest collection of poetry in China, and the *Elegies of Chu*, are worthy of a grand feast. Many folk songs and ballads in *The Book of Songs* directly reflect the sources of food and the dietary customs of ordinary people at the time, while the *Elegies of Chu* reflects the dietary customs of the people in the State of Chu. Flowers were first introduced as food in ancient times, as reflected in some lines in *Li Sao* (*The Lament*), a long poem of patriotism by the great poet Qu Yuan of the Warring States Period.

Many men of letters in the Han Dynasty showed an interest in food and drink in their poems and essays. In his *Ode to the Capital of Shu*, Yang Xiong lists various varieties of food and cooking ways common in the Sichuan Basin. Mei Cheng in his writings also recorded the quantity of food being supplied to the imperial court of the Han Dynasty. One of the three menus handed down from the Han period can be seen in Mei's *Qi Fa* (*Seven Matters of Universal Concern*).

From the Tang Dynasty down to the Qing, many men of letters were versed in the art of cooking. They were not only gourmets, but also produced delicacies themselves, leaving many menus and cookbooks.

The Song Dynasty writer Su Dongpo happily admitted that he was a gourmand, referring to himself as an "old glutton" who hoped to eat delicacies prepared by the most famous cooks. He had risen and fallen in officialdom and suffered much frustration. He traveled to almost every corner of the country, enjoying the different flavors of each. Wherever he went, he paid close attention to the cooking methods of the local famous cooks. This formed the basis of his culinary books such as *Classic of Wine, Cold Dishes of Huangzhou,* and *Prose Poems of the Old Glutton.* He became a skillful cook himself and created many delicious dishes, the most famous being stewed pork. It was usual in the Song Dynasty to undercook pork, but Su found that overcooked pork not only tasted good but also was easy to digest. He advised that "simmering the meat with less water would make it taste good so long as it is done to a turn." He often entertained his guests and friends with this course, hence the name of "Dongpo Pork." The dish is still famous in Guangdong and Zhejiang provinces today.

Lu You, a Song Dynasty poet, was the opposite of Su, being a great lover of vegetarian food. He hardly had meat during his last years and scores of his poems praised vegetarian food. His staple materials were grains of various kinds and he was particularly fond of porridge. In ancient times, there were various kinds of highly nutritious and flavorsome porridge.

Li Yu, a playwright of the late Ming and early Qing period, made a theoretical study of food in general. He emphasized "freshness" so as not to lose any of the flavor of the food. According to him, the most delicious food should be cooked without adding any other materials. Bamboo shoots, for example, when cooked with other ingredients and spices, might taste good, but their original natural flavor would be lost. This he considered to be a great mistake. Fish should be cooked while still fresh and boiled simply in pure water or used to make soup. Grass carp, however, could be cooked with other ingredients. Li had a deep abhorrence of eating rare and treasured birds and animals.

Yuan Mei, a man of letters of the Qing period, also studied cooking. His *Menu from the Garden of Leisure* is divided into 14 parts including "directives for food," "prohibited food," "fresh sea-food," "fresh river food," "special animal food," "miscellaneous animal food," "poultry," "aquatic and scaled food," "vegetarian food," "side dishes," "pastries," and "rice and porridges."

Chinese culinary culture regards cooking as an elegant art, seeking for a perfect unity of color, smell, taste and appearance. Food is considered to be a work of art, and the artistic scheme and design of painting, sculpture, music and dance, even poetry and prose are applied to the making of food. The aim is to produce delicious food with a beautiful pattern, bright color, and fantastic design, even an enchanting name.

From the above discussion, we may see that dietary culture as a part of traditional Chinese culture includes the following features:

First, it is the product of the development of agriculture in China. It not only requires nutritive food to support man's livelihood, but also to guarantee man's health with easily digestive and absorbable food. Therefore, it is scientific.

Second, two tendencies have always existed in Chinese dietary culture. One is the delicacies much sought after by nobility and the rich, the other is the everyday food of ordinary people. Since ancient times, people of insight have advocated that suitability and frugality are the two most important principles in cooking, and this is the mainstream of Chinese dietary culture.

Finally, Chinese dietary culture can communicate with other forms of art, thus making it a genuine art winning a high reputation at home and abroad. With its diverse flavors, its complicated and magical techniques, and the combination of appearance and taste, Chinese food culture has become a colorful art form, redolent with a strong sense of aesthetics and artistic appreciation.

Chapter 10

Ancient Chinese Architecture and Traditional Chinese Culture

Section 1 Traditional Culture As Manifested in Ancient Chinese Architecture

China's traditional architecture is an important part of traditional Chinese culture, reflecting an aspect of the features of the culture.

Traditional architecture evolved and changed along with the development of traditional culture. During the early Paleolithic Period about 500,000 years ago, primitive men made use of natural caves as their habitats. They knew nothing about architecture at that time. During the Neolithic Age, tribes of clans in the middle reaches at the Yellow River built their simple houses in the caves or half caved-in houses with wooden frames and mud and grass. Later, houses were built on the ground. Along the reaches of the Yangtze River, buildings supported by stiles high above the ground appeared. During the Xia Dynasty dating from the 21st century BC, buildings constructed with rammed earth appeared, like palaces built on high and large rammed-earth terraces. More important was that constructions began embodying the relationships between men and the introduction of a hierarchy. According to the hierarchy, "the Son of Heaven may have a nine-*chi* (foot) sized residence, and princes a seven-*chi* sized house, minister a five-*chi* sized house and literati a three-*chi* sized house. At the same time, special officials in charge of building called *Si Kong* (minister of works) appeared. From the Spring and Autumn Period (770-476 BC) to the period of the Qin (221-206 BC) and Han (206 BC-220 AD) dynasties, as architecture further developed and varied types of buildings were introduced, a complete construction system was gradually built up to create the simple and open style of the early stage.

From the period of the Wei (220-265) and Jin (265-420) to the period of the Southern and Northern Dynasties (420-581), the social turbulence caused the split of the state. Under the conditions, Buddhism was widely popularized. Influenced by the Buddhist culture, Buddhist constructions such as temples, pagodas and grottoes mushroomed. Buddhist art introduced from India and the Western Regions began to blend with traditional Chinese art. This cultural communication and mixing-up further expanded in dimensions and deepened in content in the period of the Tang (618-907), resulting in the formation of an elegant and poised style of the prosperous Tang Dynasty.

Since the Song Dynasty (960-1279), urban economy had developed and great change had taken place in the cultural field. The function of construction was more stressed to suit the demand of cultural life and its shape and appearance tended to smoothness and beauty. By the period of the Yuan (1271-1368), Ming (1368-1644) and Qing (1644-1911) dynasties, the architectural style of the late stage represented by the constructions of the Qing period was formed on the basis of further blending of cultures of different ethnic groups and regions and the growing influence of foreign cultures. By now, the form of building had tended to stylization with dexterity and perfection in workmanship.

From the history of traditional architecture, one can find that architecture has developed alongside the development of the material and spiritual cultures of society and reflected the changes of traditional culture.

First, it embodied the traditional ethical idea. The construction of houses of ordinary people or palaces of emperors, and the planning of a courtyard or the layout of a city, all reflected the relationships between people in social life and the political and ethical standards to be observed by them through the stiff pattern and strict order symbolized by constructions. Take the planning of a capital, according to *The Book of Rites* published in the Warring States Period, "The capital to be built by workers has a size of nine square *li* [0.5 km], and has three wall gates on its three sides. Within the city, it has nine roads going through from north to south, and nine roads from west to east. On the left, a temple of ancestors is located, and on the right, lies the sacrificial altar of the state. The buildings of imperial court were set in the front, and the marketplace at the back. In the center is the group houses of the palace." This style of layout emphasized order and the ritual system, expressive of the ethical conception of feudal society.

The layout of the Forbidden City (Imperial Palace) in Beijing was also designed in line with the traditional system with its grand halls in front and living quarters behind, all built along the central axis from north to south. Those grand halls, a symbol of center, were the places for the emperor to issue his edicts, known as the Outer Palace. Located at the back along the central axis were the residences of the emperor and his consorts, known as the Inner Palace. But the residences of the emperor's father, empress dowager, great consort and heir-apparent should be built on both sides of the former. The layout remarkably stressed the importance of hierarchy in traditional culture, giving prominence to the supreme authorities of a ruler of feudal society.

In another example, the traditional courtyard buildings in Beijing are also built along a distinct central axis with houses in individual and separated courtyards. The few houses in the front courtyard are for guests. The main buildings are located behind this courtyard. The main chambers are all built facing south along the north-south axis, with other rooms built on either side. The main chambers are for senior generations of the family and other rooms are for younger generations. This arrangement shows the order of superiority and inferiority in a family and the ethical relationships between people in daily life.

Second, China's traditional architecture attached great importance to the idea of "unity of Heaven and man," emphasizing the unity of nature and man, the organic combination of buildings and nature and the injection of human feelings and spirit into the natural environment.

"Imitating nature" is the fundamental rule of China's art of horticulture. Whether in the magnificent imperial gardens, or in private gardens, much attention is paid to the re-creation of a natural environment in the garden. In the design of a small garden, the aim is to make a small space suggest an effect of more space. The settings in the garden should be disposed in such a way as to give a continuation of appeal. The design of a large garden should make good use of the hills and water in the natural environment to form a main scene, complemented by a number of subordinate ones. Particularly in a small private garden, every possible way is tried to condense a landscape scene to reproduce a picturesque miniature. In the harmonious relationship between man and nature, all things in nature are personified.

The idea of unity of nature and man was expressed both in palaces and common buildings. Discussing the layout of a city, *The Book of Guan Zi* stressed natural factors, saying that "it must be built either beneath a high mountain or by a broad river. It should not reach so high into uplands that it lacks sources of water, nor so low into marshland as to have to build a dam."

Ancient planners paid attention to the combination of palace construction and city layout with natural scenes. For example, the Forbidden City, located on the central axis of the city from north to south, harmoniously combines its regular rectangular pattern design with the landscape of Jingshan Hill, making the magnificent palace constructions shaded by the majestic natural scenery.

Natural factors were also used in constructions for ritual ceremonies, to increase their beauty. The Temple of Heaven in Beijing was built against a backdrop of a forest of cypresses. Contrasting with the shape of cypresses and their grave hue, the limited group constructions achieve a great artistic appeal.

Traditional civil buildings have developed into various styles. In the north, common buildings are usually designed in a regular and closed pattern with simple colors. Their shape is steady and solemn. In the south, the houses are freely designed and have bright and simple colors. Their shape suggests a sense of vividness. Houses in mountainous areas are built along the topographic curve of mountains. Those by the water are usually built together with bridges and piers to link buildings with water as a whole.

Third, the principle of integration of variety is another feature of traditional architecture. Importance is given to group composition and design in line with the order of sequence in space. It is skillful to unite individual multifunctional constructions of different styles with each other according to actual need to achieve a harmonious and unified artistic effect.

In the composition, various ways and means are used to combine large buildings with small ones, complicated structures with simple ones, and to regard the hollow as solid and the solid as hollow, and to complement each other. For example, the entrance of the Zhuo Zheng Yuan (Humble Administrator's Garden) in Suzhou leads to a circular gate through a meandering narrow lane between houses. A rockery stands in front of the gate as a screen to prevent one from getting a full view of the garden. Walking along the corridor and around the hills, one finally arrives at the Hall of Remote Fragrance, suddenly seeing an open and bright area with clear water in a pond, rocks upon rocks, and dense trees amid which are scattered buildings and pavilions.

This scheme of scenery, providing a changing view of space, can often be found in the layout of gardens, particularly in ancient private gardens.

In the layout of the Imperial Palace (Forbidden City) in Beijing, for example, in front of the magnificent Hall of Supreme Harmony (Taihedian), the spacious courtyard is flanked by many *chao fang* (chambers where courtiers met before court was held). Between each is a two-storied pavilion. The varied appearance and simpler structure of the comparatively smaller pavilions stand in contrast to the larger and more elaborate Hall of Supreme Harmony, thus making the latter stand out, but not alone.

The order and sequence in the layout is important in China's traditional architecture, producing an effect of smooth flow and contrast which stresses the relationships between individual buildings and reflects social rank and order. This can be seen in the group constructions of the Forbidden City. From the Daqing (Great Purity) Gate to the Hall of Supreme Harmony, the Palace group of constructions stretches through a series of five gates and six courtyards. In the course of 1,700-meters, there are three climaxes: the Gate of Heavenly Peace (Tiananmen), the Meridian Gate (Wumen) and the Hall of Supreme Harmony. The order in which these climaxes occur emphasizes the progressive increase in importance, until one reaches the strict order and ultimate superiority of the Hall of Supreme Harmony.

Fourth, China's traditional architecture also embodies communication and blending of traditional culture with other cultures. This ethos of communication expressed in ancient constructions lies in the exchanges of architectural skills and art between different regions and different ethnic groups and the blending and assimilation of outstanding foreign cultures. Traditional architecture stresses the learning from history and new creations, showing the broadmindedness of the Chinese nation and its cultural maturity and richness. It is not simple absorption and copying, but a culture of creativity in which foreign culture which has been assimilated bears a distinct national stamp. Cultures of different regions and ethnic groups have been blended with each other and developed as architecture has advanced. Religious constructions, especially, absorbed foreign culture in the process of their development. Their forms, in the initial stage of development, changed along with the introduction of foreign religious cultures, such as the introduction of Buddhism during the Western Han period, Islam during the Tang period, and Christianity during the Ming and Qing periods. When new forms of religious constructions were introduced, they combined with traditional Chinese culture and developed to become part of a Chinese national style.

A typical example of this is the pagoda, which has various forms and appearances as a result of absorption from other cultures. The pagoda has a mainly spiritual function. It originated from the Indian stupa in which the Buddhist sarira and relics were preserved. Stupas, after being introduced into China, developed into various types of pagodas. Pavilion-style pagodas were modeled on traditional multilevel wood-framed constructions. They were the earliest and chief form of Chinese religious towers and were widely built across the country. Apart from storing Buddhist sarira, relics, scriptures and images, a pavilion-style pagoda can be ascended to provide a distant view from its height.

After the Tang period, wood-framed pagodas were replaced by brick towers. Most close-eaved towers were built with bricks and stones, could not be ascended and had a different purpose from pavilion-style pagodas. During the Yuan period, Tibetan Buddhism was widely popularized. Accordingly, bottle-shaped Lamaist dagobas were built everywhere. Built in the Yuan Dynasty, the white dagoba in the Temple of Divine Response (Miaoyingsi) in Beijing is the largest of its kind in the country. It is a memorial construction built by both Chinese and Nepalese workers for friendly and cultural exchange between the two countries. The Mian-style tower built by the Dai and Va minority ethnic groups in Yunnan Province is similar to the Myanmese-type pagodas, a different style which also originated from the stupa. The Vajrasana pagodas, built in the Ming and Qing periods, are symbols of Mount Sumeru in the Buddhist sutras, and are composed of five pagodas built on a high terrace.

Section 2 The Four Major Types of Traditional Architecture and Their Cultural Connotations

The palace and the pattern of city construction is one of the important types of traditional design.

The earliest palace to have been discovered so far is the remains of a palace of the early Shang Dynasty discovered at Erlitou in Yanshi City, Henan Province. A rammed foundation was found, on which constructions were built, surrounded by corridors and with a wide courtyard.

Comparatively complete remains of a palace, built in the capital of the Shang Dynasty, have also been found in Xiaotun Village, two kilometers northwest of Anyang, Henan Province. These are now known as the Yin ruins (Yin being another name for the Shang Dynasty). Excavation of the site has revealed group constructions laid out in three sections along a north-south axis, involving functions such as sacrificial ritual, administration and residence. This basic pattern of layout was followed in the building of all imperial palaces through the ages.

Early capital constructions were extended on the basis of palaces. The capital of the Western Zhou at Fenggao (west of present-day Xi'an City) and the Eastern Capital Luoyi (now Luoyang of Henan Province) were constructed in line with ritual requirements. This pattern had also produced some impact on the constructions of capitals of later dynasties.

When China was unified by Emperor Qinshihuang, he built up the city of Xianyang (now Xianyang City in Shaanxi Province), and the gigantic Epang Palace. On the basis of the Xingle Palace built at Xianyang in the Qin period, the Han Dynasty built its capital in Chang'an, involving the Changle, Weiyang and Jianzhang palaces. At the same time, the Northern and Southern palaces were also built at Luoyang. All these constructions composed the huge and extensive imperial palace constructions. Chang'an, now Xi'an, the capital of the Sui and Tang dynasties, was the largest city in the world at that time. The Palace of Benevolence and Longevity (Renshougong) of the Sui period, and the Palace of Great Brightness (Damingong) and the Palace of Prosperity and Celebration (Xingqinggong) of the Tang period are all magnificent constructions. The Song Dynasty built its capital at Bianjing (now Kaifeng in Henan) and an imperial residence. The Yuan Dynasty built its capital in reference to the requirements of the rites of Zhou at Beijing with more beautiful and magnificent palaces. In the changes of dynasties, the palaces built up by the previous dynasty were usually destroyed by fire or demolished for reconstruction. Today, the existing palace relics without serious damage in the country are the Imperial Palace built during the period of the Ming and Qing and the Imperial Palace of the Qing at Shenyang.

The Beijing City of the Ming period was rebuilt and expanded on the basis of the capital of the Yuan. It was divided into three sections: the Palace City (Forbidden City), the Imperial City and the Great City (or Inner City). For the purpose of strengthening the defense of the capital, it had planned to construct an outer city to encircle the whole capital. But for lack of money, only outside walls were built to the south of the capital. They were 7,950 meters long from west to east, with one gate on each side and 3,100 meters long from north to south with three gates on both sides respectively. The three gates (Xuanwumen, Zhengyangmen and Chongwenmen) on the north led to the Inner City. The two gates on the east and west were called Dongbianmen and Xibianmen. Within the Outer City, there were handicraft industry and business centers and the Temple of Heaven and the Altar of the God of Agriculture. In the north of the Outer City is situated the Great City, 6,650 meters long from west to east, and 5,350 meters long from north to south. Its south wall had three gates, that is, the three gates on the north of the Outer City. There were two gates each on its east, north and west walls. The Imperial City was situated in the south to the center of the inner city, 2,500 meters long from west to east, and 2,750 meters long from north to south. The Imperial City was constructed in an irregular square form with gates on its four side walls. The Gate of Heavenly Peace (Tiananmen) was on its south wall. Within the Imperial City were located the Palace City (Forbidden City), temples, administrative offices and granaries. The Forbidden City is 960 meters long from north to south, and 760 meters wide from west to east and there are one gate on each of the four sides.

There was an axial alignment from north to south measuring about 7.5 kilometers long, along which the whole city of Beijing was located. Parallel to the alignment were two thoroughfares from north to south on both sides, which linked up numerous lanes to form a network with a number of streets stretching from west to east, thus forming the square-pattern style of the Inner City.

The Palace City, or the Forbidden City, of the Ming Dynasty was built during the 14 years starting from 1406. During the Qing period, its pattern was essentially kept intact. It is a city of a rectangular design, generally divided into two sections, court halls in the front section (Outer Palace) in the south, occupying the greater part of the city, and residences in the back section (Inner Palace) in the north. On the whole, group buildings form individual courtyards of different grades and positions, disposed along the north-to-south axial alignment. The alignment of the Forbidden City is the same alignment as the Beijing City. Along the alignment, in the front section there sit the Hall of Supreme Harmony (Taihedian), the Hall of Central Harmony (Zhonghedian) and the Hall of Preserving Harmony (Baohedian). And in the back section, there sit the Hall of Heavenly Purity (Qianqinggong), the Hall of Earthly Tranquility (Kunninggong), and the Hall of Union and Peace (Jiaotaidian) as the residences of the emperor and empress. On the western side of the residence, there is the Hall of Peace and Longevity (Ningshougong), the residence of the emperor's father. On the eastern side is the Hall for the Consolation of Mothers, (Cininggong), the residences of the empress dowager and concubines of the deceased emperor. Parallel to the central axial alignment, are two axial sub-lines, along which there are two more groups of constructions. These two sub-lines are intercrossed with a horizontal line extending from west to east. The Gate of Supreme Harmony (Taihemen) on the central axial alignment serves as the joint point to link the horizontal line. Between the sub-lines and the central line, sit the Hall of Abstinence (Zhaigong) and the Hall of Mental Cultivation (Yangxindian). Behind them are buildings for imperial concubines. And many other halls and auxiliary buildings are also scattered between the lines. This design of disposition of buildings mainly along an axial line from north to south is intended for the standing out of the three halls, the Hall of Supreme Harmony, the Hall of Central Harmony and the Hall of Preserving Harmony, which reflect the traditional idea of "the center position means the superlative." In this design, the gigantic and magnificent Forbidden City was spread out in a planned way to meet the demands of both the functions of administration and residence.

The superlative authorities of the emperor was fully demonstrated by the design of the disposition of constructions in the Forbidden City as well as in the detailed decorative treatment of constructions, inspiring his subjects to subordinate themselves to him. Now, let's go around the Forbidden City and see and experience its cultural aspects. From the southern Gate of Everlasting Stability (Yongdingmen) on the central line, the wide and straight thoroughfare leads us to the Gate of Heavenly Peace (Tiananmen). In front of the gate, the opening extends eastward and westward. Under the azure skies, the gate wall painted with a dark red color suggests a mysterious world behind it. High up on the wall is the tower of the gate. Its solid and powerful configuration and the strong hue are in high contrast to the backdrop of the low and gray houses around it. Before the gate, there is the outer Golden Water River running across, over which five marble bridges are set. A pair of ornamental columns and a pair of stone lions stand on both sides before it. Behind them is the deep and reclusive passage through the gate.

Through the gate, the Imperial Street flanked by well-laid and low houses quietly extends forward to the Gate of Correct Demeanor (Duanmen). Passing the gate, a long and narrow path leads to a huge and complicated construction. It is the front gate of the Forbidden City, known as the Meridian Gate. The plan of the platform on top of the gate looks like an inverted "U." The courtyard behind the gate used to be a place for lashing those officials who had offended the emperor during the Ming period. But in the Qing Dynasty, it was a place for offering war prisoners to the imperial court and a venue for the announcement of emperor's edicts and gathering of officials who were going to attend court discussion.

Through the Meridian Gate, a wide-open ground appears, across it there runs the Inner Golden Water River from the west to the southeast, over which there are five stone bridges. Across the bridges, there is the Gate of Supreme Harmony.

Passing the Gate of Supreme Harmony, a more spacious ground comes in sight. A magnificent hall sits high on the marble stone base. The base is a platform composed of three tiers with railings on each tier. The white stone railings with fine decorative patterns serve as a foil to the hall, making the latter seemingly taller and more grandiose. This is the Hall of Supreme Harmony where an emperor was enthroned, his birthday was celebrated, his wedding ceremony held, and his empress crowned. It is 63.9 meters wide and 37.7 meters long. Outside the hall, a pair of bronze turtles, bronze cranes, a solar corona, and a standard measurement container are on display to symbolize the everlasting sovereign of the state and the unification of the nation. Whenever a grand ceremony was to be held, rosin, agalloch eaglewood and boughs of pine were burned in the cavity of the turtles and cranes from which fragrant smokes would diffuse.

Behind the Gate of Supreme Harmony, on the same base there lies the Hall of Central Harmony and the Hall of Preserving Harmony. The former was the room where the emperor took a rest before his attending any grand ceremony. The latter was the place where the emperor feasted princes and ministers and hosted the imperial court examinations.

In the names of the three halls, a character "he," meaning harmony, is each used. This is the fundamental idea of value of traditional Chinese culture. Early in the pre-Qin times, Chinese culture had advocated the idea of harmony without identity, favoring a harmonious development and opposing monopoly and blind obedience. This idea has been cherished as a treasure over the past 2,000 years. When it is applied to social, political and life problems, rich cultural connotations will be produced. The meaning of these names bears the social and political ideals of pursuing peace, prosperity and everlasting sovereignty and order of the state.

Beyond the three halls, there lies the Inner Palace. Its front gate is called the Gate of Heavenly Purity. Through the gate, a passageway in the courtyard leads to the Hall of Heavenly Purity, where was the residence of the emperors during the Ming Dynasty. During the Qing period, Emperor Yongzheng used it as the hall to receive visiting foreign envoys. The Hall of Earthly Tranquility behind it used to be the residence of the empress. Later, it was used as a place for holding Shamanist sacrificial ceremonies, and the nuptial chamber of the emperor. In between these two halls is the Hall of Union and Peace. These three halls were built on the same one-tier platform. They are laid out similarly to the hall in the Outer Palace, though not as large and imposing as the latter.

At the back of the Hall of Earthly Tranquility is the Imperial Garden. In the garden, there are halls, pavilions, man-made hills, and a pond. They are all balanced in disposition. Though the place abounds in natural scenes, the settings still well match the whole style of the Inner Palace.

The climax on the central line is the Prospect Hill (Jingshan), situated to the north of the Forbidden City. Looking out from within the Imperial Garden, or from the space between buildings, one can get a glimpse of the hill against the blue sky. The hill is the commanding point of the city. Ascending it, looking over the capital, one can see the crowded constructions in the various courtyards of the Forbidden City, their roofs covered with yellowish glazed tiles just looking like golden waves shimmering under the brilliant sunshine.

Of all the ancient city constructions, the Imperial Ancestral Temple, the Altar of Land and Grain and the Temple of Heaven have their respective particularities. The Altar of Land and Grain where the emperor usually hosted the sacrificial ceremonies in person was built on the west side of the Imperial City in front of the Forbidden City in accordance with the rites of the Zhou Dynasty, opposite to the Imperial Ancestral Temple on the east side. Within the dimensions of the altar, there are three front gates on the north and then the Big Halberd Gate and the Hall of Worship on the south. Finally, the square altar surrounded by low walls.

The altar is a three-layer square platform, the top layer covered with five-color earth. According to the doctrines of the heavenly stems and earthly branches and the Yin and Yang and Five Elements, green earth is laid in the east, red in the south, white in the west, black in the north and yellow in the center, symbolizing the territory of the entire country. The color on the four inner sides of the wall surrounding the alter is identical to that of the earth in the four directions. The wall is coated with colored glazed tiles. Its external sides are coated with yellow glazed tiles. In the center of each outer side of the walls, there stands a white marble stone gate. Outside the gates, verdant cypresses grow in profusion.

The Temple of Heaven was the place where emperors of the Ming and Qing dynasties prayed for a good harvest in the year. It was built on the outskirts of the capital city in accordance with the ancient system on the east side of the South-Facing Gate, covering an area four times the size of the Forbidden City. To worship Heaven had been an important political event of every dynasty through the ages. When the parents of emperors passed away, memorial ceremonies might be suspended for a time, but offering sacrifices to Heaven could never be stopped. The Temple of Heaven is more important than the Imperial Ancestral Temple. Therefore, the Temple of Heaven became the superlative ritual construction.

The temple was first built in the early Ming period. After repeated renovations it has formed the style as it is now. In the general design, breaking off from the traditional way of building up multiple gates and courtyards along the central alignment, it adopted the way of "replacing more by less" to dispose the flat Altar of Heaven, the delicate Imperial Vault of Heaven with single cornices and a spiral top, and the Hall of Prayer for Good Harvest with upward three-tiered eaves and a spiral piercing top amidst the vast woods of cypress along the north-to-south alignment. The alignment is a high and wide causeway running through the woods, called Red Stairway Bridge. Since the Temple of Heaven is situated on the east side of the central axis of Beijing, its main entrance is on the west from where a straight coach way leads to link the bridge.

The atmosphere is solemn and quiet when walking along the coach way amid the dense woods. Ascending the bridge, one can look over the cypress woods that are roaring and surging in the wind just like the rolling sea. But the sky seems becoming more open and wider and deeper. It gives people a special feeling that the mysterious Heaven is so close to them while the earth on which numerous living beings and creatures are loaded has withdrawn afar.

At the south end, the Altar of Heaven is a white-stone two-level circular terrace, surrounded by two rounds of low walls. The inner wall is in the shape of a circle, and the outer wall is a square symbolizing the old Chinese idea about Heaven being round and Earth being square. On the center of the four sides of both walls there are white stone doors. On the Winter Solstice Day every year, emperors would come to the Altar to hold a sacrificial ceremony for gods in Heaven.

At the north end, on the broad three-layer foundation, there stands the round Hall of Prayer for Good Harvest. Its three-tier vaults covered with blue glazed tiles tower high up to the sky. Looking back to the south, one seems to find the Altar of Heaven and the Imperial Vault of Heaven and the Hall of Prayer for Good Harvest are set aloof from the world and to have experienced the boundlessness of Heaven and the sacredness of the God.

Garden or park is another important part of Chinese architecture. China has a long tradition of upholding its culture after nature. Under the influence, gardens built with natural scenes have developed. The garden art that stresses an artistic and poetic effect has made its brilliant achievements.

In the pre-Han period, gardens were the hunting ground for emperors and nobles without any artificial cultivation. Later, a few establishments were introduced into gardens such as the Gusu Stage built by King Helu of the State of Wu during the late Spring and Autumn Period.

Emperor Wudi (r. 140-88 BC) of the Han Dynasty built the Imperial Forest Park, which involved facilities for residence, entertainment and rest. Particularly, a pond was built in the park, with an isle in the center of the pond, on which a pavilion was erected. This design is a duplicate of the fairyland of "one pond and three mountains" which is imbued with man's spiritual demands.

The unique private landscape garden originated in the Wei, Jin and Southern and Northern Dynasties periods. Starting from this time, Chinese garden developed toward two orientations, imperial garden and private garden. As the landlords of private gardens were mostly literati and officials who represented the highest level of feudal culture, private gardens are usually regarded as the epitome of the culture of ancient times.

During the Wei and Jin periods, because of political turbulence and rivalries among rulers, the literati class, complaining of the vicissitudes of life and fame, used to lead a reclusive life in natural landscapes. At this time, garden building tended to the model of nature and endowed nature with a perfect personality. As a result, garden became a genuine art of architecture. As the theme of a private garden, man-made rock hills began to represent a scene of a forest. The firm and unbending pine, the bold and proud plum and the pure and sticky bamboo were the favorites of people in their gardens.

During the Tang Dynasty, garden building entered its prime stage as the country was strong enough to develop its economy and liberate the mind. Gardens mushroomed, most of them being concentrated in Chang'an and Luoyang. The tendency was to build small gardens suitable for the functions of daily life. Bai Juyi, a famous poet of the period, built his garden house at Luoyang, which was typical of the landscape gardens at the time. It covered an area of just over one hectare, one-third of which was for houses, one-fifth for water space, and one-ninth for bamboo grove. The garden was constructed centering round a pond, in which there were three isles. On these isles, there were pavilions and a bridge linked the bank and isles. In the pond, there were white lilies, and purple water chestnuts. The meandering bank was shaded by a thick bamboo forest. On the west bank, there were a pavilion, buildings and a veranda for feasting visitors, enjoying the moonlight, and listening to the murmur of a spring. On the north bank, stood the library for pupils to study. On the east bank was the granary. The residence was located on the south bank. In the garden, famous stones from Lake Taihu and other places were disposed for admiration. Black stone slabs were placed for sitting and lying on. Even there were a couple of cranes to match the atmosphere of a music performance. The elaborated scheme and the gallant style of the garden was unique.

Garden building in the Song period was very popular among the rich literati and people of other walks of life in various cities. Such gardens were more suitable for daily life and had a delicate and exquisite style. At the same time, more public parks developed rapidly in the outskirts of cities. Private gardens were also regularly open to the public.

Garden building during the the Ming and Qing dynasties was concentrated in north China around the area of Beijing and in the south around the area of Suzhou. During this period, the theory and practice of garden building gradually became mature and professional garden builders appeared such as Tai Jicheng and Li Yu. Monographs on garden building such as *How to Build a Garden*, were also available. Contrast and unity were one of the principles often used in construction, emphasizing the principles of "more in less," "much in little," "the subordinate supplementing the principal" and "substantiality shaded by un-substantiality." By using these skills, an artistic effect of a continuation of different scenes arising before one's eyes could be achieved. It embodied an aesthetic pursuit of "originating from nature but on a higher plane than nature."

Private gardens built in this way in Suzhou are the best examples.

The Liuyuan (Lingering Garden) in Suzhou covers an area of more than three hectares of land. It has four sections. The middle section, built in the Ming period, is the most splendid of these. The east, north and west sections were built in the years from 1875 to 1908 (the reign period of Emperor Guangxu of the Qing Dynasty). Located in the northwest of the residence, the garden can be entered through the front part of the residence. Other passages also lead to the garden without going through the residence. Entering the garden gate, one can see a meandering path leading to a small pavilion through two small courtyards. Looking through the windows of the pavilion, one can see hills, a pond, and pavilions dimly in the shade. Looking westward, one has a view of wave upon wave of foliage and buildings stretching into the distance, imbued in an atmosphere of tranquility and elegance.

Leaving the pavilion and entering the middle part of the garden, one finds a clear pond before him. The middle part can be divided into two sections. Hills and the pond lie in the northwest, while in the southeast there is a courtyard and buildings. The Keting Pavilion is in the center of the north hill, and a small room with windows is built in the center of the west hill. The two buildings are all located on the rocks of the hills, shaded by trees. Tall cypresses and poplars grow in the garden. Together with towering rocks, they give a feeling of being deep in a forest. A bay huddles in the southeast side of the pond, and on the bank stands a small hut hidden in the green foliage, called "Green Shaded Room." On the east of the pond there is an island and a bridge and on the bank, a pavilion and a hall, which constitute another scenic spot.

Going eastward from the Quxi Tower, one can see buildings in deep courtyards. The key hall, called Wufeng Xianguan (Celestial Hall of Five Peaks), with the beams and pillars built of *nanmu* wood, is also known as the Nanmu Hall. It is spacious and exquisite. Selected lake stones are on display, firm and vigorous, in strong contrast to the two small and quiet courtyards east of the hall. There is a veranda around the courtyard. The veranda and walls sometimes meet and sometimes part, seeming to form multiple courtyards. In these small courtyards, so small that they cannot even hold one person, rocks, stone bamboo shoots, bamboos, and palms are on display.

Going eastward from Jifeng Peak, one finds a group of buildings around a delicate and slim stone in a lake, named "the Cloud-capped Peak." A tower, called the Cloud-capped Tower, stands to its north as a screen. Ascending it, one can get a distant view of Huqiu (Tiger Hill) outside the city.

To the north of the west section, there is a small hill, the highest point in the garden, from where one can have a distant view of the city outskirts.

The layout design of the garden is full of changes in the use of space and light. From a narrow and twisted stretch of courtyards to an open ground with antique trees and then to the pavilion one is guided with one's view obscured until coming to a sudden bright and wide open space where the Green Shaded Room stands.

This is an approach often used to execute the rule of "first restrain, then relax." The small courtyards beside the veranda of the Celestial Hall of Five Peaks communicate and intermix with the large courtyards to make the latter appear as if they were much larger than they really are — an approach based on comparison.

Another type of construction is that of religious structures. Various schools of religion have appeared in Chinese history. The most influential of these include Buddhism, Taoism and Islam. Buddhism has produced a profound impact on the development of traditional Chinese culture. From the evolution and development of Buddhist temples, one can easily find the spirit of communication by which traditional Chinese culture adopted and assimilated foreign cultures.

The earliest Buddhist temple recorded in historical documents is the White Horse Temple built outside Luoyang during the reign of Emperor Mingdi (r. 58-75) of the Eastern Han Dynasty. It was rebuilt on the basis of an imperial office.

Buddhism was not widespread until the Jin and Southern and Northern Dynasties periods, when many monks came to China to preach their religious teachings. At that time, the types and styles of Buddhist temples were introduced from India and other countries. During this period, Buddhist temples and pagodas in China were modeled on Indian temples. The typical design of temple construction was a tower around which monk's rooms were built to form a single courtyard. This courtyard type of temple construction design is centripetal, with the central tower standing out, forming a characteristic architectural style.

The blend of Chinese and Indian designs of temples became very popular in the Wei and Jin dynasties. Though the pagoda was still the major construction, additional great halls appeared, either in front of or behind it. The Temple of Eternal Tranquility (Yongningsi) at Luoyang, built in the Northern Wei period, is composed of a pagoda, a hall and a courtyard. The key construction is a nine-storied square pagoda on a three-level base. To its north is a Buddhist Hall, surrounded by walls to form a rectangular courtyard. Sarira was preserved in the pagoda, which was worshipped by Buddhists, so it was built in the center of the temple premises, becoming the key construction. The image of Buddha was set in the hall and worshipped, so a Buddhist hall is next only to a pagoda in importance.

There were other types of temples that were rebuilt from residences donated by nobles and officials. They usually took the form of a hall in front and a preaching room at the back. With the introduction of this style into temple building, temples with a number of houses with flowers and trees appeared and the traditional Chinese architectural style was preserved, showing more vestiges of Chinese culture.

At the same time, construction of grotto temples was also prevalent. Grottoes were originally a form of Buddhist temple, where monks could practice their self-cultivation in peace. Since the Wei and Jin dynasties, when they introduced into China, they quickly became blended with traditional Chinese constructions, quite different from their original style. Generally, in these grottoes, only images of the Buddha and murals were presented for worship. Other constructions were built in front of or beside the grottoes for monks to live and to chant scriptures in. China's grotto temples are depositaries of treasured sculptures, murals and other relics. Well-known grottoes in China include the Dunhuang Mogao Caves in Gansu, the Maijishan Caves at Tianshui in Gansu, the Yungang Grottoes at Datong in Shanxi, and the Longmen Grottoes at Luoyang in Henan.

From the Sui, Tang and Five Dynasties periods to the Song Dynasty, Buddhism developed into its prime stage. Buddhist temples had also formed their own Chinese style. The most important feature is that the design of temples was gradually transforming to adopt the pattern of imperial constructions. The conventional idea of constructions being built along a central axis was introduced into the building of temples. The central pagoda was now replaced by a Buddhist hall as the principal construction and the centripetal layout was replaced by one running along an axial line. On either side of the main hall, there was a supporting hall and a courtyard with buildings on three or four sides. The pagoda was moved to the back or to one side of the hall to form a new courtyard. Sometimes, two pagodas might be built in front of the main hall or the main entrance. Typical of this pattern is the Temple of Prosperity (Longxingsi) in Zhengding County, Hebei. At the time, murals were also very common in temples. With the appearance of many large statues of the Buddha, multiple-storied buildings were also built. Wooden towers or pagodas were replaced by brick and stone ones. Several types of these more stylistic main towers or pagodas appeared. A complete Chinese style of Buddhist construction had been created on the basis of the intimate combination of traditional Chinese culture and foreign Buddhist culture.

During the Yuan, Ming and Qing dynasties, the unique form of lamaist dagoba, shaped like a bottle, of Tibetan Buddhism became widespread across the country. During the Qing Dynasty, the Vajrasana type of pagoda appeared. The form of this pagoda originated in India but it changed a great deal after its introduction into China. Most temples of the Tibetan sect of Buddhism were built amid mountains. Large and magnificent temples were built along the slopes and curves of mountains, changing the design of conventional temples. With their high terraces and red and white outer walls, gilded tiled roofs and trapezoid windows, these temples contrasted strongly with conventional temples. Their spacious but dim halls added a mysterious atmosphere to temples, quite different from the traditional temple art that is full of worldly appeal.

Taoism is a native religion originating in China. Its temple constructions are *gong* or *guan*. This sort of building originally was used to make a watch-out because it is said immortals are fond of living in buildings of floors. Thus, storied buildings or pavilions have become the features of Taoist temples. In the Tang Dynasty, many emperors were believers in Taoism and called Taoist temples *gong* (palace) out of their respect for the faith. Taoist temples were wooden-framed constructions. Their design, like other traditional Chinese constructions, follows the pattern of a central axial line with symmetrical buildings on both sides. The decoration of buildings includes the symbol of the eight-trigrams and supreme being (the Yin-Yang symbol), and the images of the Eight Immortals, in addition to many other creatures and plants symbolizing longevity, such as red-crowned cranes, deer, turtles, glossy ganoderma and hairvein agrimony. Taoist temples were usually built on mountains or beside rivers, in pursuit of a natural environment and a peaceful unworldly atmosphere. The existing famous Taoist temples include the Temple of Mystery (Xuanmiaoguan) and Triple Purity Hall (Sanqingdian) in Suzhou, Jiangsu Province and the White Cloud Temple (Baiyunguan) in Beijing.

Islam was introduced into China during the Tang period. The form and style of its constructions are different from those of Buddhist and Taoist temples. An Islamic mosque has a minaret or steeple, from which Moslems are called to prayer, and an ablution room for worshippers to bathe in. In the hall, there are no idols, but an empty shrine pointing in the direction of Mecca. Decorations on mosques are simply the text of the Koran, patterns of plants or geometric figures.

The mosques built during the Tang, Song and Yuan dynasties retained more vestiges of foreign influence. They had towering minarets and semi-circular domes. By the Yuan period, the Chinese wood framework had been adopted in Islamic constructions and the plan layout was also used. But most of the Arabian style was still preserved. During the Ming and Qing dynasties, Islamic constructions, apart from shrine and decorations, all used a wooden framework to form a Chinese Islamic style. A typical example is the mosque at Huajue Lane in Xi'an City. The Huajue Mosque is 246 meters long, extending through five courtyards. Each courtyard is separated from the others by walls, and each has a different style. In the first courtyard, there is a wooden archway, in the second a stone gateway, in the third a tower, in the fourth a pavilion, and in the fifth the main hall, which is also the main construction of the mosque. Combining the variations into a unified whole, the mosque was built along a central axial line. The constructions in the first four courtyards are comparatively smaller in scale than the main hall in the fifth courtyard to emphasize the grandeur of the latter. Its design and layout is identical to that of a

Chinese palace construction. In some minority ethnic group areas, such as the Xinjiang Uygur Autonomous Region, however, the original style, structure and materials used in mosques remain intact. Apart from the Huajue Mosque, other famous mosques include the mosque in Ox Street in Beijing and the Aitigar Mosque in Kashi, Xinjiang.

Another type of traditional Chinese architecture is houses of common people. The settlement areas of different ethnic groups in various places differ from each other in natural conditions, customs and ways of life and cultural traditions. Civilian houses bear most of the differences.

The Shui, Dong, Dai, Va and Jingpo minorities live in the damp tropical forests in Yunnan Province. Their houses are built above the ground, supported by pillars and columns. The space beneath the house is used to raise poultry and domesticated animals and as storeroom. This type of house helps protect against harm from water, worms and snakes.

In north China, living on the prairie, the Mongolian, Kazakh and Tajik peoples often live in yurts. The yurt is a domed tent, supported by a frame structure bonded with leather bandages and covered with sheepskin or felt. It is erected on a grassless and leveled ground covered with sand, leather pads and felt. The yurt is portable and suitable for nomadic life.

The thick-walled terraced flat-roof house built by Tibetans in Tibet, southern Sichuan, Qinghai and southern Gansu is mainly a stone construction. Generally it is a three-storied house. The first floor is used to raise animals and as a warehouse, the second floor for living, including bedrooms, a kitchen and a storeroom, and the third floor has a prayer hall, balcony and toilet. Tibetan houses are constructed with materials of original colors such as yellowish earth, black slabs and red timbers. Today, a number of such houses with their special characteristics remain in the Aba Autonomous Prefecture in Sichuan Province.

The Uygurs are chiefly settled in the vast area south and north of the Tianshan Mountains. Their flat-roofed houses with arched verandas are of their own specialties. They are in favor of using a fireplace, or warm-wall or a fire Kang bunker in the house to get warmth. Windows are designed on top of the house or toward a courtyard. They pay much attention to internal decorations, everything is tidy and clean and tapestries with bright colors are used for decorative purposes, an impressive presentation of the joyful, amiable and broad-minded character of the Uygur.

The cave dwellings scattered along the middle reaches of the Yellow River are classified into three types: the dwellings built into a hillside, houses built in pits, and brick or stone cave-in buildings. These dwellings, with thick walls and high raised ceilings, are warm in winter and cool in summer. Constructed with simple and economical materials, the readily made dwellings are full of a sense of intimacy and harmony between man and nature.

The Hakka clay houses scattered across Longyan area in the southern part of Fujian Province are castle-type constructions built for defense by the Hakka people when they migrated from the north and settled in the area. This type of castle, with its special earth-ramming skill and a romantic history, is often admired by strangers. It is in the form of a circle or a square, supported by heavily rammed earth walls, which are five-storied high and one meter thick. The diameter of the circle is about 70 meters at most. Inside the enclosure, there are three rings and about 300 rooms, making a residential community, colossal and steady.

Common timber houses built by the Han people vary in form in line with diverse topography and climate from north to south. Generally, houses in the north are built with thick walls and roofs, together with a spacious courtyard. In the south, houses are built with long-protruding eaves and a small courtyard, only for good ventilation and shield from sunlight. And their appearance is delicate and good-looking. However, in the southwest region, the first choice in a construction design is the liable orientation of seasonal winds, rather than sunshine from outside.

The compound with houses around a courtyard (*siheyuan*, or quadrangle, or courtyard house) in Beijing is typical of the traditional dwelling in north China. The type of dwelling features its strict seclusion from outside, and emphasizing the disposition of chambers in the order of superior and inferior standings of occupants and the symmetry of buildings. It is simply a secluded compound, something to bear the last vestiges of the feudal patriarchal system in China.

The entrance of the compound houses is usually open toward the east or south. This design is said to be affected by the belief of geomantic omen based on the doctrine of Yin and Yang and the Five Elements.

Through the entrance and turning to the west, the front courtyard can be seen. It is short in length. In the courtyard, there sit the janitor's room, guest rooms, and a parlor. Visitors are received here. Passing the courtyard, and entering a gate leading to the internal courtyard, one can see the main chambers, and other rooms on both sides of the main rooms. The main chambers are for senior members of the family and others for junior and younger generations. In some cases, to the north of the main chambers, there is another small courtyard, where a kitchen, a toilet, storerooms, and rooms for housemaids and servants are disposed.

A large compound can be extended to have more courtyards along a central axis. Passage halls can link the courtyards. The main chambers in each courtyard are located along the central axial line. More houses in a larger compound can be expanded horizontally further to both sides from the central axis, which are linked by passages through the side rooms. Houses in a compound are surrounded by walls to form a secluded enclosure, in which flowers and trees are planted. The courtyard is usually spacious and all the rooms have good ventilation and abundant sunshine, isolated from wind and sandstorm, noise and disturbance.

Common houses in the vast areas such as Jiangsu, Zhejiang and the western part of Hunan Province are characteristic of their combination with natural environment. The idea of dwelling is no longer confined in a man-made construction enclosed on six sides with walls, but extended into natural environment.

Villages and towns in Jiangsu and Zhejiang provinces are situated mostly along waterways. On both banks of a river, buildings are usually located. Piers are built to link with various places along the river. A river is the lifeline of the small towns. The river is flanked on both sides by long and meandering streets, which are the center of the town, where there are ancestral temples, work-shops, shops, wine-houses and tea houses. All the shops are facing the street with the river at the back. Commodities are carried in through the water transportation. The narrow and twisted streets just like paths in a garden make one feel pleasant and convenient when going shopping in it. Amid the seething town, people can enjoy the buoyancy of the marketplace. The streets serve not only as traffic, but also a venue for public activities, where a busy and interwoven social relationship and a simple and comfortable cul-tural life are undergoing day after day.

Bridges in various forms are placed across the river rhythmi-cally. Sailing in a boat along the river, one can see the streets bus-tling with activities, men carrying water from the river, women doing laundry at banks, children playing under the shade of trees, making up a lively and beautiful scene.

Landing on the bank, one can see many lanes between high walls extending out from the river at a right angle. High above the lanes are black-roofed houses in rows leaving a narrow sight of the sky. Opening the door, one can see a small courtyard enclosed by thick walls, in which a path leads to the depth of the compound. A wisp of white cloud in the blue sky above, the courtyard is beamed with warm sunshine and full of the beauty of spring.

Chapter 11

Traditional Chinese Culture Faces Challenges

Section 1 Western Culture: Its Spread and Influence

The First Opium War (1840-1842) broke out at a crucial time when China was at a transition point of development. The isolated China was invaded by Western colonialism and, from this point, China entered a period of suffering and hardships. Western aggressors forced open the door of China with gunboats to dump opium and other commodities and this was followed by a deluge of Western culture.

The declining imperial government of the Qing Dynasty was unable to defend itself from the attack or to deter the dumping of foreign goods. Repeatedly losing wars against such aggression, China was relegated to a semi-colony and thrown into the bondage of a series of humiliating treaties. Meanwhile, the traditional Chinese culture that had always been dominant and never been shaken in the country began to face challenges from the West that China had previously never met. Two societies and two cultures collided.

At this time, a number of progressive and sober-minded scholars began to examine the traditional culture, trying to find a new way out for it in face of the Western challenge. These enlightened Chinese intellectuals and the cultural community launched a fervent discussion about where traditional culture should go.

From the mid-19th century, China faced what could be regarded as either a cultural crisis or a new opportunity for development. Confronting the flood of Western culture, some scholars were awakened from their dreams of blind self-complacence and pride. Facing reality, they acknowledged that China, in some areas, was not as good as its Western counterparts. By this, they meant that Western countries had better and more gunboats and better-trained armed forces than those of other countries. This became the consensus of many people at that time.

Many believed that the cause of victories in the wars of aggression against China was good gunboats and well-trained armed forces. In his book *Illustrated Record of Maritime Nations*, the famous scholar Wei Yuan (1794-1857) proposed that China should "defeat the enemy by learning his strengths." The government attempted to follow this advice by first purchasing warships and armaments from abroad and then copying them. Soon, it became clear that this was not enough; well-trained soldiers, equipped with technical and operational skills, were essential.

Many of the warships and cannons imported from abroad at that time were worn-out products and proved useless. To make matters worse, the quality of domestically produced warships was very low, and soldiers were short of the necessary skills to operate them. As a result, accidents involving cannon explosions occurred frequently. These failures emphasized the need for education in science and technology.

From the 1870s, China began to import natural science and technology instead of weapons and ships. Eager for quick success and benefits, those who introduced Western culture at that time neglected the translation of works in the humanities, looking only to industrial and mechanical manufacturing and other practical sciences. However, many scientific disciplines were thus introduced into China, such as mathematics, physics, chemistry, astronomy, mineralogy, paleogeology, and medical science.

Books on science were chiefly translated and printed by the translation bureau subordinate to the head-office of the Kiangnan Machine Building Works. Over a period of some 20 years, the bureau translated a total of 163 titles of books on science. These, from today's viewpoint, were often no more than popular readers but, having such a different cultural background from the West, most Chinese intellectuals still had difficulties in reading them.

Ancient China had made many brilliant scientific and technological achievements, but modern science and technology was only introduced after the two Opium Wars. At first, when they first came in touch with modern Western mathematics, a number of conservative scholars arrogantly believed that China's achievements in the subject were greater than those of the West. They therefore refused to introduce and assimilate modern mathematics and its theories. Moreover, many scholars, who knew nothing about natural sciences, refused to learn from Western sciences.

However, a number of successful Chinese scientists also emerged during this period. Scholars, such as Li Shanlan (1811-1882), Xu Shou (1818-1884), and Hua Hengfang (1833-1902), made great contributions to the popularization and study of natural sciences. They differed from both natural scientists in ancient times and from scholars of their own time who refused to adapt. Being equipped with a substantial traditional cultural knowledge, including natural sciences, and conscientiously assimilating and studying modern Western science and theory, they adopted an experimental scientific method using logic, inference and deduction in their studies.

As they were well informed, it was possible for them to achieve results in their research. The chemists Xu and Hua wrote monographs on natural sciences. Li studied the "derivative of the circumference" independently, acquiring the fundamental idea of calculus. Li also translated analytic geometry and calculus and popularized the Copernican theory, giving Chinese people their first understanding of modern astronomy.

Another form of introduction was through the establishment of modern industrial enterprises and schools in the country, spreading modern science and knowledge over a wider area. Through this contact with new science, ideas and knowledge, the Chinese began to abandon outdated ideas and ponder over the value of science and technology. In 1862, the Institute of Diplomatic Relations was set up in Beijing, in which English, French and Russian language studies were conducted. In 1867, the Institute of Astronomy and Mathematics was established which caused a sensation in society at the time. By the time the imperial civil examination system was abolished in 1905, Chinese people had gone through a long and hard period of learning natural sciences. During this time, China began to join the outside world in the field of science and technology.

In order to inspire more Chinese people to learn and appreciate natural sciences and to instill modern science and knowledge into the minds of Chinese intellectuals, the scientists Xu Shou, Hua Hengfang and the missionary John Fryer (1839-1928) founded the Academy of Natural Sciences in Shanghai, giving lectures, exhibiting various kinds of scientific apparatus, conducting scientific experiments in the classroom and studying the history of natural sciences. This pioneering work proved a success. Many intellectuals also did mathematical exercises and physical and chemical experiments in addition to their studies of the "Four Books" and "Five Classics." Gradually, they became interested in natural sciences, thereby starting the history of modern natural sciences in China.

Because of the need for China to modernize and assert its independence, science and new knowledge introduced into China through translations produced a great influence on Chinese intellectuals. The introduction of Western culture became inevitable in modern China. Along with the growth of the patriotic movement for national salvation and rejuvenation, a modern new cultural movement also began to rise and develop. Modern scientific findings were often reflected in philosophical theories and ideological concepts, and new knowledge and new doctrines became the theoretical bases for political reform.

A series of calls for national salvation through science, literature and education caused repercussions in society. Ever-increasing importance was given to the position and role of culture. Until the eve of the May 4th New Cultural Movement in 1919, people had always regarded culture as the primary approach to solve the problems of China. No doubt, this had actively promoted the cultural development in China.

After the introduction of Western scientific knowledge, many scholars became interested in speaking out their opinions on life, society and political issues by way of propagating scientific knowledge. In his work *On Benevolence* (completed in 1897) Tan Sitong (1865-1898) discoursed on mathematics, physics, chemistry, astronomy, and geology. He discussed the origin of the planet, its evolution, the relationship between the orbit of the earth and universal gravitation, and calculation of the earth's volume and mass. Kang Youwei (1858-1927) was deeply fascinated by physics, astronomy and paleogeology, attentively studying Copernican heliocentric theory, and Isaac Newton's celestial mechanics. In his book *On Celestial Bodies* (finished in 1885), he explained the origin of the solar system, the relationship between the planets and the sun, eclipses, comets, meteors and sunspots, striving to integrate scientific knowledge with ideological reforms.

Some scholars began to teach that the earth is a sphere, using scientific evidence to end arrogant, ridiculous and outdated ideas that the heavenly imperial court was the center of the universe. They inspired the enthusiasm and patriotism of their compatriots with knowledge of electricity and heat, encouraging them to actively join in the movement for national salvation. One example is Yan Fu's translation of H.E. Huxley's *Evolution and Ethics* (first edition published in 1895), which he hoped would shake the mind and soul of the Chinese people with the laws of nature. While the subject of the book was biological evolution, both the translator and his readers were far more interested in its social implications.

By the end of the 19th century, modern Western natural sciences had become an important part of the thinking of many Chinese intellectuals. At the same time, Western philosophy and social sciences were also exerting a strong appeal. Li Shanlan, Xu Shou and Hua Hengfang were succeeded by a new group of modern scholars represented by Yan Fu, Liang Qichao (1873-1929), and Wang Guowei (1877-1927). The introduction and promotion of

Western natural sciences reached new heights. The intelligentsia was eager for further knowledge from Western culture; as well as natural sciences, they also wanted to understand Western political theories. "These are the years of academic poverty," said Liang Qichao.

To meet the needs of the intelligentsia, Yan Fu and other scholars continued to introduce the chief academic schools of thought and their representative works, as well as biographies of some celebrated scholars and their main viewpoints. Later, the famous American scholar John Dewey and others went to China to give lectures. Western pragmatism and new realism attracted a number of Chinese supporters. Henri Bergson's life philosophy and Friedrich Nietzsche's superman philosophy also appealed to many scholars. Immanuel Kant's critical philosophy and the idealism and dialectics of G.W. Hegel all had an extensive impact on the academic community in China.

In social sciences, a number of works were published, introducing Western humanity science, its schools, and theories. Yan Fu translated many famous works on humanity science adding up to well over several million Chinese characters, including Adam Smith's *The Wealth of Nations*, Charles Louis de Secondat Montesquieu's *The Spirit of the Laws*, J.S. Mill's *On Liberty*, and H. Spencer's *The Principles of Sociology*. In the *Xinmin Miscellany*, Liang Qichao also introduced biographical and academic materials on Benedict de Spinoza, F. Bacon, I. Kant, Jean-Jacques Rousseau, Montesquieu and C. Darwin. This produced a great impact on the academic community at the time. The pessimistic philosophy of Arthur Schopenhauer, advocating voluntarism, had a profound influence on Wang Guowei.

In 1919, around the time of the May 4th Movement, although Chinese scholars had achieved some success in the introduction of various schools of Western philosophy and culture, some problems still remained. Western culture covered a broad spectrum, including theories of democracy, progressive realistic social science works, advanced scientific thought, Darwinism, Christian theology, and some of the works imported were badly written.

Generally speaking, the import of Western thought was unsystematic, superficial and heterogeneous.

Another problem was that different scholars had very different understandings of Western ideas. For example, Sun Yat-sen (1866-1925), Liang Qichao and Yan Fu each had their own interpretation of the concepts of freedom and democracy. Their tendencies differed in their assimilation of Western ideas and, to varying degrees, mixed these ideas with traditional Chinese culture. These differences influenced further theoretical explorations.

The introduction of Western natural sciences by the Chinese intelligentsia proved to be very difficult. The introduction of Western humanities took an even longer time. It was only a hard struggle that minds could be changed. Despite this, many scholars eventually discovered the truth of Western democracy and science. Using ideological weapons such as "The theory of the inalienable rights of man," they sharply criticized the monarchical power and the feudal ethical code and cried out for democracy, equality and freedom for all. The spread of such thinking subdued and weakened the dominance of feudal ethics and laid the foundations for the 1911 Revolution, led by the revolutionary pioneer Sun Yat-sen, which overthrew the feudal Qing government. After the revolution, such advanced thoughts exerted an increasingly profound influence on the development of the nation.

Section 2 A Review and Critical Examination of Traditional Chinese Culture

China had experienced the biggest historical change ever in modern times. At this crucial point of time, the inheritance and development of traditional culture aroused great attention among the general public, particularly the intelligentsia.

Over the past 150 years, the nation, especially its intellectuals, has been troubled by the problem of how to adapt traditional culture to the world, the future and modernization. To solve this problem, it is imperative to first make a critical examination of traditional culture, analyzing its advantages and disadvantages in comparison with Western culture.

In the second half of the 19th century, a number of far-sighted intellectuals and people of other walks of life advocated opening China to the outside world and implementing reform. They believed that traditional culture was by no means perfect and that some of the culture, if not changed and improved, could not adapt to modern society. They were correct, but their vision was far from profound. For instance, they held that the essence of traditional Chinese culture was the way of the sages, while that of Western culture was material products and technology. The central defect they saw in traditional culture was the extent to which China lagged behind the West in scientific development; more specifically, China's lack of gunboats and weak armed forces.

They proposed that China should retain its traditional political system and ideology, while making use of Western science and technology, warships and armaments. This proposal was summed up as "Chinese learning as the base and Western learning for application." It became the cardinal principle to deal with the Chinese and foreign cultures.

Both the East and West have made their contributions to world civilization as a whole. Traditional Chinese culture and modern Western culture were originally independent from each other. Both had rich but diverse connotations in lifestyles and cultures. When the two clashed, the question was whether or not the cardinal principle it to be applied in such a way as to make use of the strengths and eliminate the weaknesses of one or the other.

In the Sino-Japanese War of 1894-1895, the Qing government was defeated by Japan. The tide of the times violently shook the thinking of the Chinese people of the time.

Those who worried about the destiny of the country and were determined to pursue reform felt that the cardinal principle needed to be improved. Many of them intensified their studies of Western learning and critical examinations of traditional culture. By the turn of the 20th century, these intellectuals formed a new generation of cultural scholars.

This generation of scholars were critical of the principle. Zhang Zhidong's 1898 essay, "Encouraging Learning," which was supportive of the principle, was strongly criticized by Liang Qichao. It would become absolutely useless, he said, within ten years. Others said that without the establishment of a modern social and political system, China would never have modern science and technology; and without modern ideology, China would never achieve modernization. An ox cannot do the work of a horse, said Yan Fu, and a horse cannot do the work of an ox either.

In the Reform Movement of 1898, led by Kang Youwei and supported by Emperor Guangxu, the reformists attempted to carry out bourgeois political reform, which aimed to learn from the West, promote science and culture, reform the political and educational systems, and develop agriculture, industry and commerce. The movement lasted only 103 days before it was crushed. From this time through the Revolution of 1911 and the eve of the May 4th Movement in 1919, a number of scholars proposed that studies of traditional Chinese culture should be guided by the principles of science and democracy.

Some, critical of feudal ethics, held that Confucianism was the primary content of traditional culture and should be eliminated. Others wanted to preserve the essence of traditional culture. Anyhow, they were trying to solve the inheritance and development of traditional culture.

Debate on the problem became acute, involving cultural, political, economic, military and diplomatic issues. These problems inevitably triggered further examination of both the traditional and Western cultures. Divisions and differences on the subject grew.

Many learned scholars believed that the immediate problem was the independence of the state and the nation. Unless this was addressed, the nation would fall. Only when this problem was resolved, could China afford the luxury of debating ancient classics, historical documents and traditional culture. This argument convinced many young people.

In fact, this attitude and approach was consistent with traditional Confucian thought. Confucianism advocates "cultivating yourself, putting your family in order, running the government well and bringing peace to the entire country"; that "Every man has a duty toward his country"; and "Be the first to endure hardships and the last to enjoy comforts." Many patriotic scholars believed that by reforming traditional Chinese culture, it could be adapted to the modern age.

In this sense, traditional Chinese culture has not lost its value and appeal in modern times. Its essences should be preserved. Apart from the aforesaid patriotism, these essences include indomitability, peace loving, defying intimidation, constantly striving to make oneself stronger, and pursuit for a target with unremitting efforts. All these will promote people's conviction.

In the retrospective examination of traditional culture, far-sighted scholars' standpoint and purpose were doubtlessly correct. Chinese culture embracing its extracts and dross would by no means be easily defeated by foreign culture. Therefore, neither the preservation of the national cultural essence nor the realization of a total Westernized culture should be held as a correct approach. They could not solve the problem of whither the traditional culture would go. A number of modern scholars had sought a way out for the culture between these two extremes.

For instance, Kang Youwei was clearly influenced by the modern concepts of freedom, mutual equality, universal fraternity and man's inalienable rights, and also by Confucian culture. Sun Yat-sen also absorbed much of Western democratic thought, but elements of the traditional concepts of the great harmony, equilibrium and Confucian orthodoxy can still be seen in his theoretical system.

Scholars who were successful in modern times had all closely studied traditional culture. And almost none of them took a nihilist attitude or a completely assertive attitude toward the national culture. Toward both traditional and Western cultures, they took an analytical, selective and screening attitude. At the time, ideology and culture, both past and present, Chinese and foreign, influenced, contradicted, infiltrated and assimilated each other to form a complicated and interwoven colorful scene. This was inevitably reflected in the thinking of far-sighted scholars. The developing and changing times forced people in China to study afresh, though it would cost very much.

During the May 4th Movement, progressive scholars held high the two banners of democracy and science. Their ideas differed from both the advocates of the cardinal principle of "Chinese learning as the base and Western learning for application," and from Yan Fu and those like him. These scholars reached new heights of achievement in the comparative study of Chinese and Western cultures, surpassing their predecessors and leaving a valuable legacy for following generations.

However, there is a question here to be carefully analyzed. During the period of the May 4th Movement, a number of scholars were severely critical of the traditional culture with Confucianism at the core. Why?

Chen Duxiu (1880-1942) believed that these scholars were so indignant at the feudal ethical code that their radical expressions of resentment were more extreme than their true attitudes to traditional culture. Complete negation of traditional culture was not the mainstream of the cultural movement.

The idea of total Westernization could be rooted neither in the soil of China nor on any other lands. If any nation wants to realize modernization at the expense of first giving up its own traditional national culture, then introducing everything from the West, it would prove an impasse theoretically and practically.

For this reason, the idea was criticized. When Hu Shi (1891-1962) who had been in favor of the idea, was criticized, he argued in his article "Total Westernization and Complete Globalization" that total Westernization meant complete globalization of the culture, that is, to know and improve traditional Chinese culture in accordance with the principles of democracy and science. He added that this did not mean that everything should be Westernized. He doubted, for example, if the Chinese would be willing to abandon chopsticks in favor of knives and forks.

However, they forgot a fundamental truth that there will be no globalization without nationalization. The more nationalization is developed, the more chances there will be for cultural exchange in the world. This is the basic law of cultural development.

Section 3 Achievements and Value of Traditional Chinese Culture in Modern Times

There were several occasions when foreign culture was introduced into China on a large scale, such as the introduction of Buddhism during the Han Dynasty. However, the introduction of foreign culture never changed the system and structure of traditional Chinese culture, which, based in Confucianism, remained dominant in Chinese social life. Western culture arrived in China through colonial invasion. From the time of its arrival, traditional Chinese thought and culture underwent a transitional change, exercising a far-reaching and profound influence on the modernization of Chinese society.

In the face of the challenge of Western culture, insightful scholars still furthered their studies of traditional culture. Through hard work, they scored many achievements in various sciences of modern culture. The growth of new ideas and new culture and the formation of new methods of study began operating in the study of traditional culture. Under these circumstances, scholars pioneered a number of new frontiers, setting up many new disciplines. On the basis of carrying forward the merits of traditional culture, they also made new creations, thus further enriching the culture of antiquity. This is really an ideological and cultural advancement.

For example, in historiographic research, scholars making use of modern Western theory and methodology, broke away from the confinement of conventional study on history, opening new vistas for research. Modern historians sought out traditional ideas beneficial to the new epoch from inherent cultural thought evolving the historiographic theories and methods that combined the Western theory of evolution and the Confucian classics. With these theories and methods, they made a creative study of Chinese history, producing a spate of prestigious monographs on ancient Chinese history, the Chinese cultural history, and the general history of China. The most influential of these included Liang Qichao's "A Commentary on Chinese History" (1901) and "A New Science of History" (1902). In these two essays, Liang applied the theory of evolution for the first time to a theoretical and systematic criticism of feudal China's historiographic theories and concepts. Traditional methods, he said, should be abandoned and history should no longer be merely a record of the family history of feudal emperors. He also put forward the watchword of the revolution of history science that was of great significance in the emancipation of the mind. It showed that modern scholars had begun creating a new theoretical system of history and philosophy.

Since then, a profound change has taken place in the study of history. The first book of Chinese history compiled and edited with the new historical viewpoints was the *New Teaching Book of Chinese History for Middle Schools* written by Xia Zengyou (1863-1924) and published in 1904. Later, it was renamed *History of Ancient China*. At the same time, Zhang Taiyan (1869-1936) published the second edition of his book *Qiu Shu Remonstration* (in 1904), Liu Shipei (1884-1920) published *A Teaching Book of Chinese History* (1905-1906) and Wang Guowei *A Study of Ancient History*. All these works were edited with the viewpoints of modern history science in terms of their division of history into periods, basic contents and style of edition, and proved valuable for medieval history study.

Many scholars took a skeptical attitude toward ancient Chinese classics and traditional accounts of ancient civilization, negating a number of hitherto unquestioned assertions. The seven-volume *Discrimination of Ancient History* compiled the findings of a number of scholars who had re-examined ancient history, seeking to distinguish between what was true and what was false. With new methodology and new findings these scholars eliminated superstitions and blind faith in ancient books. They also contributed to textual criticism, discrimination of true materials from false ones, and correction of mistakes in ancient documents.

But the school of skeptics was also limited by the times. Sometimes, they went so far that they even doubted the truth.

The theory of evolution not only presented a severe challenge to traditional culture, but also provided a good opportunity for it to develop. Academics introduced the philosophies of Friedrich Nietzsche, Arthur Schopenhauer, Immanuel Kant and others, and all these helped to improve the exploration of the history of Chinese philosophy and the history of thought. The traditional concept of change was adapted to the Western theory of evolution, analyzing and explaining the historical change of Chinese philosophic thinking with the theory of evolution, while also beginning to introduce and systematically study the history of Western philosophy.

An Introduction to Philosophy, compiled by Hou Sheng at this time, appears superficial and contains many mistakes. Nevertheless, it was significant in the enlightenment of modern thinking in China.

The influence of Western philosophy changed the direction of development of traditional Chinese philosophy, both in modes of thought and in academic style. Much of ancient Chinese philosophy grew in a context of political struggle, and stressed the importance of social and political ethics. Modern philosophy added to this the study of the universe and nature and the outlook on nature.

Since ancient times, the Chinese had adopted, altered and assimilated foreign doctrines of thought according to their own logical structure and cultural psychology. This now included the introduction of the theory of evolution and mechanical materialism. Chinese thinkers made a new theoretical summary and recreation of the theory of evolution to form their own unique philosophic theoretical system on the basis of modern conditions, while inheriting the best achievements of traditional philosophy.

When H.E. Huxley's *Evolution and Ethics* was translated and introduced to China, by Yan Fu, Chinese readers paid more attention to the translator's preface and notes than to the original text itself. The principles of evolution in Chinese philosophy, while containing a lot of evolutionist terminology, concepts and categories, differed from Western evolutionism. But sometimes a proper understanding of these principles was lacking because of the different backgrounds of Chinese and Western cultures as well as many alterations of Western philosophy made by Chinese scholars, adding new applications to the principles. This is the new achievement made in the philosophic field of the traditional culture in the face of the challenge of Western culture.

Under the influence of modern Western concepts of democracy and equality, remarkable achievements were also made in the introduction and study of modern Western science of law during the late Qing period and the early period of the Republic of China.

The Aid-in-Governance Council (similar in form to a parliament in Western countries) and the Advisory Bureau (on the order of a local council) were set up toward the end of the Qing Dynasty. In the early stage of the Republic of China, the first session of the First National Assembly was convened and a cabinet was created, attempting to introduce a party-led political and electoral system. All these needed to be built on the basis of law. Meanwhile, turbulent modern society also needed legal regulation and control. An extensive study of the subject was conducted, involving the definition of law, its origins, the five major legal systems of the world, international law, criminal law, civil law and administrative law. These laws, however, could not be applied to the semi-colonial and semi-feudal society that existed at that time in China.

With this background, the famous scholar Shen Jiaben (1840-1913) of the late Qing period, who was versed in ancient Chinese legislation, tried to reform it with elements of Western law. It was Shen who first introduced modern Chinese legislation. At the same time, many researchers were studying and debating a series of important modern Western legal and political issues such as man's inalienable rights, the concept of the state, nationalism, government system, constitutionalism, and local self-government. For example, in 1906, the Commercial Press published the *Teaching Script of Politics* by Yan Fu, the first modern Chinese work of political science. After the Wuchang Uprising of 1911, the Hubei revolutionaries drafted and published the "Provisional Constitution of Hubei." Later, Sun Yat-sen, representing the provisional government, published the "Outline of the Provisional Organizational Law of the Republic of China" and the "Provisional Constitution." Both these laws were based on the American system of congress and the cabinet-presidential system.

Progress was also made in linguistics and literature, applying Western linguistics and literary theories to the classical Chinese language, literature and art.

After the two Opium Wars, an increasing number of new words, including loan words, appeared, changing the structure of the Chinese language. *Ma's Book of Grammar* by Ma Jianzhong (1845-1900) was the first work applying foreign grammatical principles to the Chinese language laying the preliminary foundation for the study of Chinese grammar.

Many others continued what Ma had begun, making further and deeper studies of Chinese grammar. Reform programs of the Chinese language and a phonetic system for transcribing Chinese characters (Pinyin) were also proposed. Most scholars agreed to reform Chinese characters on the basis of Pinyin, thus solving the most urgent problem in the reform.

The highly stylized nature of classical literature had put it beyond the reach and comprehension of ordinary people. Scholars now proposed to reform literature through a drive to promote the vernacular, holding that literature should not be restricted to being only a means of expressing the author's feelings; it needed to allow ordinary people to express their joy, anger, sorrows and happiness. Some writers proposed that authors should avoid affected pose, cliché, literary antithesis and quotations in their works, but not the use of slangs and colloquialisms. In 1904, the famous scholar Chen Duxiu set up *Anhui Vernacular News* to publicize new thoughts and ideas in popular forms and plain and simple language. It was widely welcomed by the public. The promotion of the vernacular was not limited to literature; it was significant in the history of culture and promoted a transformation of the mode of thinking of the intelligentsia in China.

Theories of literature and art were greatly influenced by the West. Scholars discoursed on many important theories, their social functions, and the method of writing. For instance, Lu Xun (1881-1936), a modern writer and thinker, made perceptive commentaries on both foreign literature and Chinese literary classics. His important writings included *A Brief History of Chinese Fiction*. Wang Guowei (1877-1927), also a modern scholar, studied traditional Chinese literature with the viewpoints of Western philosophy, aesthetics and literary and art theories. His pioneering work on novels, dramas, and poetry included a study of the classic novel *A Dream of Red Mansions*.

There were also new variations of literary and art works on the basis of traditional culture and many new literary and art frontiers were also opened. The translation of foreign novels by people such as Lin Shu rapidly developed, providing new references for modern Chinese writers.

The Chinese word for "tradition" has the connotation of inheritance. The relationship between a modern society and its traditional culture should be first of all the relationship of inheritance. This does not mean that everything should be retained; rather, it is a process of selection and creation. Therefore, traditional culture embraces both a culture of antiquity and a culture of the modern times.

This process is both a right and an obligation of every generation. The unique traditional Chinese culture, formed over several thousand years, has a strong ability to renew itself. It has been able to regulate itself, both with the spirit of the nation and the ethos of the times, capable of adapting itself to domestic changes and assimilating and matching its foreign counterparts. The reason for the longevity of traditional Chinese culture is its ability to renew and regulate itself.

More examples could be given of the accomplishments of traditional culture in modern times. But we only mean that China belongs to the world. In the modern opening world, mutual influence, mutual penetration, even mutual assimilation of different cultures are inevitable and necessary. So long as we adopt a correct attitude toward foreign cultures which have been introduced and deal with them properly, Chinese culture will be sure to develop without interference, with further opportunities for growth and vitality.

Over the past one hundred years or more, whenever China came to a crossroads of development, Chinese intellectuals would review and discuss traditional culture and the direction of its development.

In spite of the challenges from the West, the fruit of Chinese culture in modern times was still plentiful. However, in general, the attempt to reform and renew it had not yet been fully realized. After World War I, social turbulence and the chaotic state of thought in the West made Chinese thinkers more skeptical and disillusioned with Western civilization. Many scholars began to further consider the advantages and disadvantages of both Chinese and Western cultures in a bid to find out a new way for modernizing traditional culture.

Throughout the history of civilization, all cultures have had their essence and dross, and there can be no such thing as a pure and perfect culture. Therefore, the research method of dividing traditional culture into that which is essential and that which should be discarded is not the same as a mere compromise between total preservation of Chinese culture and total Westernization. Neither of these two extremes can achieve a modernization of Chinese culture.

Both traditional Chinese and Western cultures should be dealt with according to the principle of using the essence and leaving out the dross. Some people might disagree, holding that nothing in the culture could be seen as essence and dross. But in fact, only this principle can survive in the traditional culture study and help to produce research findings favored by most people. Of course, careful analysis must be made of what is essence and what is dross.

Only by inspiring the national spirit, can we carry out the modernization of our nation and state. The great cohesiveness of a nation originates in its history and cultural creations. If everything of the nation is negated as a burden, the nation itself is negated, resulting in its disintegration and collapse. So, only by recognizing and confirming the essence of traditional culture, can we assume a scientific attitude to get rid of the dross.

The questions we have discussed here cover only the period from the First Opium War of 1840 to the May 4th Movement in 1919.

In most recent years, there have been two major views in the discussion on national culture problems in the world community: "global consciousness" and "roots-finding consciousness." The two are contradictory. Exponents of the former hold that the trend of cultural development should be viewed in the global light. The IT age has brought about rapid exchange and influence between various new thoughts, theories and cultures. Contact between regions or countries has become considerably easier. Therefore, the trend of cultural development is comprehensive. The cultural development of any country or region must inevitably consider the major issues of the whole world.

"Root-finding consciousness," or "national consciousness," has aroused increasing attention among people with each passing day. After World War II, national awakening and national independence have become an irresistible trend, along with recognition of the need to discover its own cultural tradition for the development of a nation.

Both views are reasonable, but biased. Stressing root-finding consciousness to the neglect of global consciousness would make it impossible to consider national culture in relation to the rest of the world, or to correctly reflect the requirements of the times; while emphasizing global consciousness to the neglect of root-finding consciousness would make it impossible to create a new culture with distinctive national characteristics.

For this reason, to develop culture in modern times, especially to develop a culture of such a great country as China with its long traditional culture, the fine aspects of the nation's traditional culture should be esteemed, while absorbing and assimilating fine cultural products from the rest of the world. A careful analysis of traditional culture is necessary and casualness should be avoided.

There has been a strong element of non-utilitarianism in traditional Chinese culture, which can be seen clearly in foreign relations. The geographic discoveries by Christopher Columbus and Ferdinand Magellan were motivated by the desire to gain wealth, an economic impetus and cultural utilitarianism. In contrast, the Ming Dynasty voyages to the Western Seas by Zheng He and his huge entourage had no economic purpose, being merely a demonstration of the power and prestige of the imperial court.

Westerners' pragmatic attitude contrasts with that of Chinese emperors and their subjects who were willing to harm their real interests rather than lose face. When George Macartney arrived in China to trade, he was received as an envoy coming to pay tribute to the Qing imperial court. Whether or not to meet a foreign envoy and whether the envoy was required to kowtow to the emperor was a problem that began in the reign of Emperor Xianfeng (1851-1861) and was not resolved until the 18th year (1892) of the reign of Emperor Guangxu. This sort of non-utilitarianist culture had its limitations.

However, there are many fine aspects in traditional Chinese culture. For example, it stresses honor over gain, and emotion or credibility over gain. In old China, private banks operated by reliance on honor and credibility. A merchant's reputation and personality was considered more important than wealth. Business was done on the basis of honor or credibility, not by a written agreement or contract, the parties being bound by a moral sense. Today, many financial institutions in cities and towns across China are still called "credit cooperatives." Many foreigners were astonished when they first arrived in China and saw such things.

It could be argued that honoring credit rather than contracts reflects Chinese people's low sense of the legal system. Agreements and contracts are based on law, and both the society under natural economy and the society under commodity economy need control with the enforcement of law. Moral prohibition, however, is also necessary. The healthy development of society depends on both a sound legal system and social morality.

The purpose of studying traditional culture is to try to preserve it, but not simply as an ancient treasure. Through inheritance, reform and development, it must serve the needs of today and used to help solve the problems we now face.

Conclusion: The 21st Century and Traditional Chinese Culture

1. Prospects for World Culture

With the advent of the 21st century, scholars and others have pondered what impact culture will have on the world in the coming years. One view is that during the 21st century, clashes among cultures will affect world politics. People with this view hold that interactions between some seven or eight basic cultures will dominate the world. The clashes that will occur among these cultures — Western, Eastern-Confucian, Muslim, Indian, Slavic-Eastern Orthodox, Latin American and African — are sure to influence world economy and politics.

This view is flawed as an attempt to explain cultural trends of the 21st century because it over-stresses conflicts between different civilizations without regard for the mutual influences and attractions between them. Clashes as well as a blending together are quite natural between two cultures. One aspect can't exist without the other. Moreover, the view has not been able to explain how these cultural clashes will influence the development of world economy and politics. Therefore, it is not so convincing.

Another view is that Eastern (Chinese, strictly speaking) Confucianism will have a great impact on the world. Western scholars with this view have offered detailed evidence. They say that Asia and Africa won their independence at almost the same time but so far Asia is better off than Africa in terms of its economic and political development. Why is this? They argue that many Asian countries turned to their traditional cultures as a base for their development without blindly copying the Western model. Most leaders in these countries have been inculcated with Confucianism. Confucian values have greater influences on the countries of the entire Southeast Asian region. Confucianism advocates establishment of a well-disciplined, stable, multi-level society with high moral values. So this helped enable these countries to undergo economic and cultural development in a planned way. These countries have achieved, and are achieving, good results.

This view does reflect some aspects of the realities of the 20th century, but it has yet to explain what influences the fine tradition of Chinese culture will have on the world in the 21st century.

There is still another view that it will be Taoist thought from traditional Chinese culture that will have more and more influence on the world, particularly on those economically well-developed Western countries. People who hold this view cite that *The Book of Lao Zi* has been translated into about 30 different languages. Many great Eastern and Western scientists have enriched their thinking through their reading of the book, exploring the mysteries of nature and the universe according to the model of Lao Zi. The "Way," or the "Tao," set forth in the book has appealed to a number of natural scientists. For example, the British scientist Dr. Joseph Needham focused in *Science and Civilization in China* on the great impact Taoism had on the development of science and technology in ancient China. Other prominent natural scientists from Western countries hold that although the West has made great progress in science and technology, it has neglected the development of the humanities. If the humanities are neglected, a society will become an abnormal and deformed one in which individuals become subordinated to materialism and machines. In ancient China, in *The book of Lao Zi* the thought of combining "science" and "humanities" had its genesis. This is exactly what will guide the development of science in the 21st century. That is to say, in the coming century, "science" and "humanity" will march hand in hand to get rid of all evils and defects in the world to create a happy and joyful life for all people.

The above views based on the experiences of scientists in the West are profound and visionary. However, they do not fully explore the relationship between the 21st century and traditional Chinese culture. Obviously, it is a complicated and difficult subject that needs further public discussion. First, a matter-of-fact analysis of traditional Chinese culture is needed. Only on this basis, can its future role in the world be determined. In the foregoing chapters, traditional Chinese culture was introduced. Here, a further analysis will be made of the moral values of Confucianism and the natural philosophy of Taoism.

2. The Value of Confucian Principles on Life

Confucius, the great thinker and teacher of the late Spring and Autumn Period, proposed a system of moral principles. He absorbed the moral and cultural inheritance of the earlier Shang and Zhou period, and then created his own ideas in light of the needs of the times in which he lived. His theories include the following:

1) Differentiation between what is civilized and what is barbarous. The theory was developed long ago of differentiating between the civilized and the barbarous, opposing barbarism and upholding civilization. To enable a civilized life, Confucius introduced moral codes for people to observe. He believed that after learning them, people could become refined with a high level of morality.

2) Gentility. This is an important part of Confucian thought, advocating the perfect integration of the soul and actions of a person, or of the inner quality and outward appearance of a person. To be a person of morality requires not only good deeds, but also a noble soul and heart. Confucius believed that a person would be tough and wild so long as his basic, unsophisticated nature held sway over his better, cultivated nature. But when cultivation in a person overshadows his basic nature, this leads to immodesty and conceit. Only by balancing the two, the form and the content, can a perfect and morally well-cultivated person of

refinement be produced.

3) The way of the golden mean. Confucius proposed the highest standard of morality, holding that morality should be an integral part of every action. To handle any problem, do it properly — not overdoing it but doing it in a timely and judicious manner. This is the ultimate requirement of morality. The way of the golden mean is a way of understanding. It can help give an all-round perspective on things. As a moral educational theory, it encourages a person to pursue a personality of individual perfection and to become a noble person of good morality.

4) Harmonious but diverse. A person of morality is broad-minded, able to tolerate dissenting views and to learn from the merits of others. Confucius said that a person of morality takes "harmony" as his criterion, but he doesn't follow others blindly and can speak out what he thinks right. Indecent people are liable to follow others blindly without independent views of their own.

5) Entertainment within education. Teaching of ethics is not a dreary preaching. For best results, it should be vivid and lively, combined with the teaching of rites and music.

The above is the theoretical basis of Confucian moral education. Confucius lived in times that date back 2,500 years. That he proposed these principles so long ago is surely a great accomplishment in the history of China's ethical thought. These theoretic principles will continue to be enriched and developed along with the advancement of human history and society.

Following Confucius, Mencius and Xun Zi also made creative contributions to ethical and moral theories. Mencius, especially, made the most significant contributions. Inheriting the spirit of humanism from Confucianism, he proposed profound views on moral psychology in ancient China.

The early Confucian science of morality holds that lofty morality is ordained neither by Heaven nor by external force. Anyone who wants to become a perfect gentleman needs only to decide and work hard. Confucius said: "I want to be benevolent, and then benevolence is at hand." Mencius developed the theory further by saying that everyone can become a perfect person of refinement if he exerts himself to that end. Everyone has the psychological ability to become a saint like Yao and Shun. Early Confucian scholars believed that a person had the ability to regulate the differences between self and environment. As Confucius said, Yan Hui led a hard life in a simple house, eating coarse food. But he had a strong desire to learn and an earnest wish to be a perfect gentleman of moral virtue. So his spiritual life was not limited by his environment. He was confident in his pursuit of truth. This sort of firm and unremitting spirit was developed as a "noble spirit" by Mencius. He said, a true man or woman will not give up a lofty goal whether living in comfort and affluence, under hardships and destitution, or under threat by violence and power. In other words, with the right convictions, people can exert the force of persistence and patience to overcome difficulties, thereby guarding the nobility of their personalities. This may be taken as a treasure in the history of ethical and moral theory in China.

These Confucian moral teachings produced an inestimable impact on the cultivation of people with ability in the following ages. For example, Dr. Yang Chen Ning (Frank C.N. Yang), a Nobel Prize laureate, mentioned Mencius when he recalled his life, saying, "I had a good command of mathematics and natural science when I studied in primary school. When I entered a middle school, my father, a university professor, did not support my study of infinitesimal calculus, but rather invited a teacher of Chinese classics to teach me *The Book of Mencius* through the whole summer vacation. I really found this benefited me throughout my whole life." Of course, not only Yang, but also many other successful people have been taught how to be a person by the early Confucian ethical and moral thinking.

During the period of the Qin and Han dynasties, along with the establishment of a unified feudal state, China's ethical theories made new progress. Sima Qian was not only a celebrated great historian, but also a great scholar of moral theory. He proposed a view on life and death, saying: "A death may be weightier than Mount Taishan and a life may be lighter than a feather," presenting a lofty idea of value. He also put forward "state comes first" as a morality standard and a view of life, that is, "Be calm and composed before honor or dishonor. And, righteousness alone goes before anything else." He advised that people should take a correct attitude toward either good fortune or adversity, and never give up moral principles at any time. He also proposed that morality is not a patented product owned exclusively by scholars and gentlemen. Noble deeds of moral virtue can also be found in peasants, rich merchants and ordinary people in the lower class.

The value of a human being lies not in power and officialdom or in high position and great wealth, but in thinking and action. The feudal ethical code is different from the traditional Chinese fine virtues. The feudal ethical code has in general the following features:

First, the establishment of the relationship in which one person is an appendage to the other, basic to the feudalistic social system, as an ethical principle and a religion. The core of the ethical code including the "three cardinal guides" (ruler guides subject, father guides son, and husband guides wife) is a concise description of the relationship. That the feudalistic social system is characterized by one person as an appendage to the other, as pointed out by Marx, is a scientific view. The French thinker of the Enlightenment, Charles Louis de Secondat Montesquieu, in his work *The Spirit of the Laws* said that the dependent relationship between people became the big enemy of law. The difference between a modern society and a society of dictatorship lies in the former having broken off from the dependent relationship to hold high the banner of everyone being equal before law.

The feudal ethical code was made a religion by some people, who said the emperor was god and the history of emperors was a history of emperors transformed from the god. But the ethical code never became a true religion in China because of the dominating spirit of humanism of the early Confucianism and other reasons.

Secondly, the feudal ethical code only dealt with such problems as the obligations of various ranks in society to society and the emperor in an ethical view. It did not involve the problem of human rights. It also stressed the rule by human volition, not by law. In retrospect, one will find when making a review of the history that it was only empty talk that punishment was meted out to princes who violated law in the same way as it was with ordinary people. That was only propaganda of the Legalists. Real examples were few. In feudal society, lack of the idea of human rights and inadequate rule by law had a close relation to the feudal ethical code.

Thirdly, the feudal ethical code had not yet deterred the development of China's humanism. But the humanism of feudal society was different from that of the Spring and Autumn and Warring States periods. During the period of the Warring States, the humanism advocated by Mencius contained the simple idea of equality of everybody in society. For example, someone had asked him: "Could a tyrant be executed?" Replied Mencius: "Yes. The tyrant is no longer a ruler." In the Qin and Han periods, this view had almost become obsolete. During these periods, humanism was recognized only under the premise of the rule of emperors, different from that of Mencius without any premises. It was because such humanism could not escape the influence of the feudal ethical code.

Therefore, it is necessary to differentiate the traditional virtues from the feudal ethical code. The Confucian ethical value of humanism is full of vitality and will not fade away. When it is applied in practice, it should be modified under the requirements dictated by the present and future. It should not be copied mechanically. As to the feudal ethical code, it has long since lost its life. It must be totally eradicated.

3. The Taoist Philosophy of Nature and the World

Some historians in the West have said that Chinese culture is based chiefly on political ethics without the philosophy of nature. The assertion, in fact, is incomplete. Chinese culture is teeming with the philosophy of nature. But it does not talk about nature without involving human problems. It talks about nature beginning with the problem of human life. And its theory in turn is used to guide human life. So the formula is: Human life — nature — human life.

Two major lines go through Chinese culture: One is Confucianism, the other Taoism. Taoist thought more distinctly expresses the character of the above formula.

Lao Zi, the founder of Taoism, studied nature and created his philosophical theory through sayings about many problems relating to human life. Some of them follow:

Lao Zi says:

Under the sun, nothing is weaker than water.

Water can pass through mountain valleys, and across plains.

Water can overcome the hardest things when it passes.

These observations illuminated his view of human life in the philosophical sense:

People should be as weak as water.

Keep in mind: The most treasured things are teachings "without words" and the benefits of "non-action."

Lao Zi says:

The rivers and oceans can hold water coming from a hundred streams because they lie in the lowest position. Hence the theory: A sage who wants to be really trusted by common people should be kind and treat his people with humility.

Lao Zi says:

Anything that is strong will die.

Anything weak and gentle in nature can live forever.

Therefore, resorting to arms is doomed to failure. The toughest bough will break one day. So anything that has strength and power is temporal and will be gone in a flash. But weakness and gentleness will exist forever.

Lao Zi then applied his philosophy of nature to the philosophy of life. He held that whatever a person does during a lifetime should be done in a manner as weak as water, with modesty and little said, "saying nothing" and "doing nothing." "Doing nothing" does not mean one should not do anything, but rather that one should not do things against the law of nature or the nature of things; should not do things while showing off one's ability, and should not do things while making trouble for others. By so acting, anything can be done. As Lao Zi said, "doing nothing" is in a bid to "do anything."

Lao Zi was a keen observer of nature, with brilliant wisdom. In this respect, he resembles the Greek philosopher, Heracleitus. But they also had a distinct difference. Heracleitus stressed "struggle" when he observed human life from nature. But Lao Zi believed that the miraculous cure for maintaining youthful vigor is "harmony" and "going back to nature." This reflects the different historical backgrounds of Chinese and Western cultures. The Taoist classics are filled with profound discourses based on keen observations about nature and human life. Some intelligent discourses on life experience and social activities are regarded as contributions particularly to the practice of nourishing life and fostering longevity. It seems no accident that the international academic community today attaches great importance to *The Book of Lao Zi*.

Lao Zi lived in the late Spring and Autumn Period. Zhuang Zi, another important representative of Taoist thought, lived in the Warring States Period. Zhuang Zi was more philosophical in his observation on nature. In *The Book of Zhuang Zi*, he described natural phenomena and told fables, trying to lead people to think about the mystery of nature as a way of determining what they could do to deal with nature and society.

For instance:

"The ruler of the Southern Sea is called Shu; the ruler of the Northern Sea is called Hu, and the ruler of the Center is called Hun Dun. Shu and Hu often met in the territory of Hun Dun, and being always well treated by him, determined to repay his kindness. They said: 'All people have seven holes for seeing, hearing, eating, and breathing. Hun Dun alone has none of these. Let us try to bore some for him.' So every day they bored one hole; but on the seventh day Hun Dun died."

In Zhuang Zi's view, nature is a whole. It cannot be broken.

Taoists declared that nature should be protected, that it should not be destroyed. It is interesting that the famous Japanese scientist Yugawa Hideki — after studying elementary particles of about 30 varieties for a long time and exploring the fundamental material behind those particles, finally was enlightened by the above fable. He concluded that the fundamental matter was most likely similar to Hun Dun. He wrote the following line after he had succeeded in his study: "The Chinese were, among all human beings in the world, the earliest to enter a stage of spiritual maturity .... And it seems that Taoists with their insights were able to achieve a thorough understanding of the destiny of individual human beings and of the whole humankind.

Taoism also appealed to, and still appeals to, the scientists of the world. *Kinship of the Three and the Book of Changes*, by Wei Boyang of the Eastern Han period, was translated into English in the 1930s. So far, many monographs and commentaries on the book have been published abroad.

If we may say that the European thinkers of the Enlightenment during the 18th century attached great importance to China's Confucianism, then European and American scholars during the 20th century and forward have paid more attention to the study of China's Taoism.

4. Traditional Culture and Its Future

Chinese culture is not an isolated, closed culture. The reason it has a long history lies in its attribute of openness. This openness early on spurred mutual learning among all the ethnic groups of the country, resulting in common inventions. Early in the Spring and Autumn Period, way back about 2,000 years ago, thinkers and statesmen were not restricted to preaching their philosophies in the places of their birth in various states in the Central Plain area. They settled down anywhere they could fully exercise their talents. Confucius traveled around all the states, but he found his ideal could not be realized in any of them and returned to his native home, the State of Lu, where he became a teacher.

A brilliant ancient culture was created during the period of the Tang. During that time, the Han people learned from all other minority peoples, and vice versa. The Tang culture was composed of the cultures introduced either from the minorities or other countries in Asia. During the Han Dynasty and the period of the Tang, there was a street called "Foreigner's Street" in Chang'an, the capital city, where all the foreigners lived. In restaurants, there were also foreign waitresses. At the time, in the city, it was the prevailing fashion to wear foreign dresses and imitate foreign dances.

Secondly, the openness feature also included China's knowing how to learn from foreign countries. Indian Buddhism, first introduced into China in the late Western Han Dynasty, entered its primary stage in the period of the Tang through the Wei and Jin and the Southern and Northern Dynasties periods. But Chinese believers did not mechanically copy it. The Buddhism introduced from India was adopted, assimilated and modified into Chinese Buddhism. Tiantai, Huayan and Chan were all sects of Buddhism in the Tang period. During the Song Dynasty, some Chinese Buddhism was absorbed by Confucianism to create a blend in the ideological and theoretical system of Neo-Confucianism (a Confucian school of idealist philosophy).

During the period from the 16th century to the 18th century, many European Christian missionaries came to China where they learned the Chinese language, got to know the local customs and way of life and made many friends among Chinese intellectuals and officials. Intellectuals and officials also learned Western natural sciences from foreign missionaries and promoted their scientific research. As a result, such great scholars as Xu Guangqi (1562-1633) and Fang Yizhi (1611-1671) appeared. Emperor Kangxi of the Qing Dynasty (r. 1662-1722) also learned geometry and land surveying from foreign missionaries.

In modern China, a number of personalities of broad vision went abroad to study to find ways of making China strong and prosperous. When they returned to China, they introduced Western culture and science. For example, Yan Fu introduced the biological evolutionism of C. Darwin and H. E. Huxley, which produced a great impact on China's intellectual community.

The facts mentioned above show that the richness of Chinese culture needs a mix with foreign cultures. But history is complicated. In the feudal society of China, particularly in the declining stage of many of its dynasties, imperial rulers became conservative and followed a closed-door policy, thinking they would rule forever. But that was only a daydream. The policy not only held back the advancement of history, but also brought a negative impact on cultural development.

In the 21st century, such problems as over-population, environmental pollution, and modern diseases cannot be treated by one kind of approach and one kind of medicine. They need a comprehensive treatment by the whole world. When industrial civilization brings both happiness and misfortune to the world, human beings need a healthier spiritual civilization. In this sense, some values of Chinese culture may become accepted by more people in the world as those values are transformed and adapted by them during the 21st century.

For example, the idea of attaching importance to family values may help deal with such social phenomena as loneliness among the elderly in economically developed countries, family education of children, and even the control and prevention of the AIDS virus.

Another example: Chinese culture holds in high regard the ideas of ideological self-cultivation, the effect of spiritual functions, the philosophy of nature and the idea of "going back to nature." These ideas may be applied to the treatment of the physical and mental problems, and to the promotion of the development of science.

Other values in Chinese culture such as respect for the spirit of humanity, emphasis on team play, and belief in the doctrine of the mean may lead people to take a more pragmatic attitude as they observe the world in the 21st century.

Some scientists have pointed out that in the 21st century, people may discover the influence of some aspects of Eastern culture on the world. This prediction, we believe, will be probably realized.

However, we don't think any one culture will come to dominate the world. It is impossible. Any country, no matter how many years it takes in the development, will surely have its own national culture as the dominant culture. Even if a foreign culture is introduced to it, that foreign culture must be combined with its national culture. So far, nobody knows of any pure foreign culture that has become exclusively and fully realized in a country after being introduced into that country. Therefore, the rise and success of Chinese culture in the 21st century only means that its merits and strong points will be adopted and absorbed by the world. As for China, in the new century, it has to carry out modernization. So the country must concentrate more on the absorption of the merits of foreign cultures to enrich and develop the traditional Chinese culture.

A Brief Chinese Chronology

Xia Dynasty	(c.21st century-c. early 17th century BC)
Shang Dynasty	(c. early 17th century-c. 11th century BC)
Zhou Dynasty	(c.11th century-256 BC)
Western Zhou	(c.11th century-771 BC)
Eastern Zhou	(770-256 BC)
Qin Dynasty	(221-206 BC)
Han Dynasty	(206 BC-220 AD)
Western Han	(206 BC-25 AD)
Eastern Han	(25-220)
Three Kingdoms	(220-280)
Jin Dynasty	(265-420)
Western Jin	(265-317)
Eastern Jin	(317-420)
Southern and Northern Dynasties	(420-589)
Sui Dynasty	(581-618)
Tang Dynasty	(618-907)
Five Dynasties	(907-960)
Song Dynasty	(960-1279)
Northern Song	(960-1127)
Southern Song	(1127-1279)
Yuan Dynasty	(1279-1368)
Ming Dynasty	(1368-1644)
Qing Dynasty	(1644-1911)
Republic of China	(1912-1949)
People's Republic of China	Founded on October 1, 1949

INDEX

322

327

图书在版编目（CIP）数据

中国传统文化：英文 / 张岂之主编.
— 北京：外文出版社，1999
ISBN 978-7-119-02033-4
I. 中... II.张... III. 传统文化—研究—中国—英文
IV. G04
中国版本图书馆 CIP 数据核字（1999）第 03597 号

外文出版社网址：
　http://www.flp.com.cn
外文出版社电子信箱
　Info@flp.com.cn
　sales@flp.com.cn

责任编辑：杨春燕
英文编辑：梁良兴
封面设计：蔡　荣

中国传统文化
张岂之　主编
*
© 外文出版社
外文出版社出版
（中国北京百万庄大街 24 号）
邮政编码　100037
北京外文印刷厂印刷
中国国际图书贸易总公司发行
（中国北京车公庄西路 35 号）
北京邮政信箱第 399 号　邮政编码　100044
2008 年第 1 版（28 开）第 4 次印刷
（英）
ISBN 978-7-119-02033-4
5800
7-E-3180 P